Oz before the Rainbow

THE JOHNS HOPKINS UNIVERSITY PRESS *Baltimore and London*

Mark Evan Swartz

OZ

BEFORE THE RAINBOW

L. Frank Baum's
The Wonderful Wizard of Oz
on Stage and Screen to 1939

9 8 7 6 5 4 3 2 1

The Johns Hopkins University Press
2715 North Charles Street
Baltimore, Maryland 21218-4363
www.press.jhu.edu

Library of Congress Cataloging-in-Publication
Data will be found at the end of this book.

A catalog record for this book is available from
the British Library.

ISBN 0-8018-6477-1

Illustration credits may be found on page 293.

Untitled poem attributed to Virginia Foltz, who played Sir Dashemoff Daily, the Poet Laureate, in the stage musical *The Wizard of Oz* during the 1905–6 season

Savants there be, who sagely go
  For erudition to the play,
And seek epigrammatic glow—
  The pedantry of matter gray.
Others there be who wildly pay
  What price the managers request
To hear R. Mansfield rant away—
  I like "The Wizard of Oz" the best.

What though there be a few who throw
  At opera stars the fair bouquet?
Some love to list to Romeo,
  Say things that sound to me passé.
Tho' Ibsen may be here to stay,
  Tho' Bernard Shaw has been suppressed,
I want no morals far astray—
  I like "The Wizard of Oz" the best.

I like the tinsel and the show,
  The Scarecrow and Tin Woodman gay,
Nor ask, seeking surcease from woe,
  "Where are the gods of yesterday?"
I like the music light and gay,
  The poppies, cyclone, all the rest
Of things too numerous to say—
  I like "The Wizard of Oz" the best.

    L'ENVOI
Oh, girls of 'Oz,' be yours the bay!
  The heart that beats beneath this vest
Can only this refrain convey—
  I like "The Wizard of Oz" the best.

Table of Contents

Preface & Acknowledgments

LIKE MANY OF MY GENERATION, I grew up with the movie version of *The Wizard of Oz*. Of course, I had an edition of L. Frank Baum's original 1900 book, *The Wonderful Wizard of Oz*, but I am sure I am not alone when I say that it was the 1939 MGM motion picture that defined Oz for me. I remember watching, as a small child, the annual television airings of the film with a mixture of awe and anxiety—Margaret Hamilton's Wicked Witch of the West is, after all, a fearful thing to behold.

My first viewings of the film were on a black-and-white television, making the world over the rainbow as colorless as Dorothy's Kansas. But my father, a television repairman, soon bought a large color television console for the family, at a time when such appliances were still considered a luxury for the lucky few. We had the new television just in time to watch one of the annual broadcasts of *The Wizard of Oz*, and as my parents tried to prepare me for what I would see, I was full of eager anticipation. Now when Dorothy opened her door onto Munchkinland, the screen burst forth with color.

Then, as a young adult in college, I came across some photographs of a 1902 stage show, *The Wizard of Oz*. I was surprised to learn of such an early production. The strange and comical costumes and sets left a strong impression on me. Years later I began to wonder about other productions, and in researching the topic I uncovered a vast number of stage and screen productions based on Baum's narrative. But what intrigued me most was the significant body of work that preceded the 1939 film, a collection of stage performances and films that, though largely forgotten today, led directly to the influential MGM motion picture and laid the iconographic groundwork for later depictions of Dorothy and her world in various media. The desire to expose these early works to scrutiny and to show that the infiltration of the Wizard of Oz story into our cultural bloodstream was not an overnight process resulted in the present book.

Much research went into this study, but among the primary sources I consulted, the Townsend Walsh Collection of the New York Public Library deserves special mention. Walsh was the business manager and press representative for the 1902 stage musical of *The Wizard of Oz* and for the show's subsequent tours. Fortunately, he saved a treasure trove of material relating to the play. His business correspondence can be found in the Manuscript and Special Collections Division, while his scrapbooks and ephemera are housed in the Billy Rose Theatre Collection.

Aside from the New York Public Library and its staff (especially Jeremy Megraw and Brian O'Connell), many other institutions and people were indispensable to the preparation of this book. I list here those that were especially helpful, and I apologize for any major omissions: Academy of Motion Picture Arts and Sciences, Academy Foundation, Margaret Herrick Library, Beverly Hills (particularly Kristine Krueger, National Film Information Service); American Museum of the Moving Image, New York (Richard Koszarski, Collections and Exhibitions); Baylor University, Moody Memorial Library, Waco, Texas (Gregg S. Geary); Boston Public Library (Diane O. Ota, Music Department); British Library (C. M. Hall, Department of Manuscripts); Brown University, John Hay Library (Rosemary L. Cullen, Harris Collection); Chicago Historical Society (Emily Clark, Library, and Larry Viskochil, Prints and Photographs Department); Chicago Public Library (Lauren Bufferd, Special Collections); Dallas Public Library (Robert C. Eason Jr.); Elgin and Winter Garden Theatre Centre, Toronto (John Wimbs); Free Library of Philadelphia; Harvard University Libraries (Joseph Keller and Jeanne T. Newlin, Harvard Theatre Collection); Huntington Library, San Marino, California (Susan Naulty, Rare Book Department); Indiana University, Lilly Library, Bloomington (Sue Presnell); International Museum of Photography and Film at George Eastman House, Rochester, New York (Paulo Cherchi Usai, Film Department); Johns Hopkins University, Milton S. Eisenhower Library (Joan Grattan, Special Collections); Library of Congress; Los Angeles Public Library; Missouri Historical Society, St. Louis (Duane R. Sneddeker and Ellen Thomasson, Photographs and Prints Department, Jill E. Sherman, Pictorial History Collections, and Jean D. Streeter); Municipal Theatre Association of St. Louis (Connie Lewis); Museum of Modern Art, New York (Mary Griskin, Film Stills Archive, and Jennifer Tobias, Library); Museum of the City of New York (Peter Simmons, Byron Collection, and Kathryn Mets, Theatre Collection); New York University, Elmer Holmes Bobst Library (Thomas McNulty, Humanities

Reference); Newberry Library, Chicago (Cynthia Wall, Special Collections); Royal Shakespeare Company, London (Cameron A. Duncan, Press Office); St. Louis Post-Dispatch, Library (Mike Marler); St. Louis Public Library (Suzy E. Frechette); San Francisco Performing Arts Library and Museum (Kirsten Tanaka); Seattle Public Library (Marlene Jameson); Shakespeare Birthplace Trust, Library, Stratford-upon-Avon (Marian J. Pringle); Syracuse University Library, Department of Special Collections, Syracuse, New York (Carolyn A. Davis); University of California, Los Angeles, University Library (Victor Cardell, Archive of Popular American Music, and Brigitte J. Kueppers, Theatre Arts Library); University of Illinois, Music Library, Urbana-Champaign (Leslie Troutman); University of Minnesota, Twin Cities, Music Library (Laura K. Probst); University of Oregon Library, Eugene (Leslie Bennett); University of Texas, Austin, Harry Ransom Humanities Research Center (Melissa Miller-Quinlan, Theatre Collection); University of Wisconsin, Madison, Mills Music Library (Geraldine Laudati); University of Wisconsin, Madison, Wisconsin Center for Film, Television and Theatre Research (Gina Grumke, Film and Photo Archive); Washington University, Gaylord Music Library, St. Louis (Nathan W. Eakin); and Yale University, Beinecke Rare Book and Manuscript Library (Ngadi W. Kponou, Public Services).

The members of the International Wizard of Oz Club, Inc., have been supportive and encouraging. Through their admirable periodical the *Baum Bugle* they have made significant contributions to scholarship in the study of Baum and his work. Club member Michael Patrick Hearn must be singled out not only for his help in shaping my study in its early stages but for being extremely forthcoming with his time and with information and items from his personal collection. A scholar in the field of children's literature, Hearn is generally acknowledged to be the leading expert on Baum; he is currently working on a biography. John Fricke, a longtime editor of the *Bugle* and a club officer, as well as an author in his own right, gave me invaluable assistance and liberally shared with me his collection of Oz materials. Joe Yranski was more than generous with his time and with his own wonderful assortment of Oz memorabilia. His knowledge of film history and passion for the subject are infectious. Other club members who were particularly helpful include Ruth Berman, Michael Gessel, Barbara Koelle, Fred M. Meyer, John D. Nickolaus, Chris Shelton, and Gary Thompson.

Special thanks must also go to my colleagues at the Shubert Archive, who were a constant source of encouragement: Brooks McNamara, director; Maryann Chach, archivist; Reagan Fletcher, assistant archivist; and Sylvia Wang, archival assistant. Professor McNamara, who also served as my doctoral adviser at New York University, merits special thanks. His enthusiasm for the field of popular entertainments ignited my interest in this area, and his skills as an editor and critical reader are incomparable. In addition, Maryann Chach's acute understanding of the difficulties of trying to write a book while being employed full time was invaluable. Her support was essential to my completing this study.

I would also like to extend my thanks to Elaine Barber for her research assistance and her many offers of help; to Maria Endara for her retrieval of library materials; to Deborah K. Saunders for her support and advice; to Robert D. Rubic of Precision Chromes and Erika Ihara for their most able copy photography; to William K. Everson, Antonia Lant, Peggy Phelan, and Richard Schechner for reading and critiquing my manuscript at various points in its development; and to editors Douglas Armato and Maura Burnett and copyeditor Joanne Allen of the Johns Hopkins University Press for their astute suggestions.

Words are not enough to thank X. Theodore Barber for the unbounded support he provided me. He kept me on track when I threatened to veer off course, and he convinced me that I could carry this project successfully to completion. His perfectionism and high standards always pushed me to take that extra step. His research assistance was expert, and his patience as an editor is unsurpassed.

Finally, I would like to extend unlimited gratitude to my mother, Helen Swartz, and my uncle Myer Swartz, whose unfailing support and faith in me was a major factor in my completing this work. Their love and encouragement have helped to carry me through many difficult times. Although I can never truly acknowledge all they have done, I hope that in dedicating this book to them I make clear their vital contribution.

Oz before the Rainbow

Introduction

Off to See the Wizard

L. Frank Baum and *The Wonderful Wizard of Oz* (1900)

ENTION OZ, THE YELLOW BRICK ROAD, the Munchkins, the Scarecrow, or any of the other major images or characters from L. Frank Baum's *The Wonderful Wizard of Oz*, published in 1900, and chances are that most Americans will immediately recognize them. They are constantly referred to in all spheres of popular culture, including advertising, fiction, motion pictures, political cartoons, comic strips, greeting cards, popular music, and television shows. The fact is that the story occupies a unique position in the cultural fabric of this country.[1] But credit for this is largely due to the 1939 MGM musical film based on the tale. Given the shortened title *The Wizard of Oz,* that motion picture has probably been seen by more people than any other film (more than a billion at this point), and it has forever altered the public's knowledge and perception of Baum's original narrative.[2] So influential is this film that it, and not the novel, is generally the source of people's familiarity with the Wizard of Oz story.

And yet, Baum's narrative had a significant life prior to the release of the 1939 film. Ever since it was issued in 1900, in fact, the story has been on the minds and in the hearts of a great many Americans. Countless children grew up reading the book, which also spawned, among other things, a board game (1921), dolls (1924), and a display at the Chicago World's Fair (1933). But perhaps the main factor contributing to the foothold the world of Oz established in American popular culture in the first decades of the twentieth century was the many dramatic adaptations the story inspired.

In 1902 a stage version directed by Julian Mitchell took the country by storm. With a script by Baum at its core, this lavish musical extravaganza was still being staged with some regularity into the next decade. In 1908 Baum toured *Fairylogue and Radio-Plays,* a multimedia show that included several slides and brief motion pictures based on his book of 1900. The films had been made by the Selig Polyscope Company, a pioneer of the silent era. In 1910 that same studio produced another short motion-picture version of *The Wonderful Wizard of Oz.* Somewhat longer and more complete, it related the story in a series of amusing vignettes depicted with some interesting special effects. A feature-length silent film produced by Chadwick Pictures followed in 1925. The popular screen comic Larry Semon directed and starred in this free adaptation of Baum's tale. Semon played the Scarecrow in true slapstick style, while the Tin Woodman was impersonated by the then novice actor Oliver Hardy.

By the late twenties amateur theater groups were staging Baum's novel. In 1928 the playwright Elizabeth Fuller Goodspeed published a theatrical adaptation of the story aimed at the growing children's-theater market.[3] Issued by Samuel French as part of that publisher's Junior League play series, it became a standard in children's theaters throughout the country. Also by the late twenties, marionette versions of *The Wonderful Wizard of Oz* were appearing. One of the first was that produced by the Cornish Players of Seattle and staged by Ellen Van Volkenburg, one of the founders of the little-theater movement. Extremely faithful to the novel, this puppet entertainment, which toured many parts of the country, remained a staple of the Cornish Players through the 1930s.[4]

The year 1933 saw the first animated motion-picture version of the story, *The Wizard of Oz.* Produced by the Film Laboratories of Canada, it was directed by Ted Eshbaugh. The film was photographed in Technicolor and had a soundtrack. Legal problems prevented the film's release, however, although copies survive.[5] NBC broadcast a Wizard of Oz radio show three times a week from 25 September 1933 until 23 March 1934, sponsored by Jell-O and starring Nancy Kelly as Dorothy. The programs, in serial form, were based on Baum's original story, as well as on some of his later writings.[6]

The infiltration of the Wizard of Oz story into America's cultural bloodstream has been, then, no overnight process, and it certainly did not begin with the 1939 film. But because that film's grip on the public imagination has proved so strong, little attention has been paid to the earlier dramatic incarnations of *The Wonderful Wizard of Oz.* And yet the prevalence in their time of both Baum's original book and these early dramatizations suggests that even then the American populace was as preoccupied with Oz and its inhabitants as we are today.

The study that follows examines the beginning of the Wizard of Oz phenomenon as seen in the early examples of professional, live-action adaptation—namely, the musical of 1902, the Selig shorts of 1908 and 1910, and the Semon feature-length film of 1925. Along the way, we will encounter variable and surprising interpretations of elements of a tale we thought we knew well. Dorothy, for example, who in Baum's book is an innocent little girl, becomes first a young maid courted by a Poet, then again a child, then a flirtatious flapper who marries a prince and is crowned queen of Oz, and finally, in the MGM musical, a twelve-year-old girl just coming of age. And the Emerald City, which appears in Baum's book as a Victorian Orientalist fantasy and several times reappears in that guise in the adaptations, suddenly becomes a Middle European kingdom before emerging as an art deco world of splendor in the 1939 film.

The early adaptations are also fascinating in terms of the way they influenced MGM's *The Wizard of Oz* and laid the groundwork for its iconography. Although that film owed much to Baum's novel, the various pre-1939 dramatizations, as we will discover, left their stamp on it as well. They were the source of inspiration for, among other things, using the musical-comedy format to present Dorothy's journey, for adding the Kansas farm hands to the story, for having a snowstorm sent by Glinda save Dorothy and her companions from the deadly scent of the poppies, and for turning Dorothy's adventures into a dream.

A close look at these earlier dramatizations, then, not only will serve to place our own captivation with Baum's tale in a historical context but will allow for a much richer reading of the 1939 motion picture. Any discussion, however, must begin with a look at the landmark book of 1900 and the man behind its creation.[7]

⌁ Lyman Frank Baum is widely known as the author of *The Wonderful Wizard of Oz,* but his contributions to other spheres have been neglected by scholars. Only in recent decades have people begun to pay closer attention to the large body of work he left behind. If much of his *oeuvre* still is not regarded as fine art or great literature, his contribution to the world of American popular culture is almost unequaled. Baum was keenly interested in a popular audi-

Lyman Frank Baum, c. 1909.

ence, and he jumped from one endeavor to the next, with varying degrees of financial success.

Baum was born in Chittenango, New York, on 15 May 1856 to Cynthia Stanton and Benjamin Ward Baum. In 1860 his father made a fortune in oil and settled his family at Rose Lawn, a country estate just outside Syracuse. L. Frank Baum was not a healthy child; he had a congenital heart defect and was tutored at home in his early years. He was later enrolled in Peekskill Military Academy, but ill health saw him back home after a brief time. When he was only fourteen years old he published, with his brother Harry, a small newspaper called *The Rose Lawn Home Journal* on a modest printing press his father had bought for him. It was the beginning of his literary career.

Among his business enterprises, Benjamin Baum owned several theaters, and his sister, Katherine Gray, was an actress. It was not long before L. Frank Baum became interested in pursuing a life in the theater. The theater would, in fact, always be his first love, and it was to this field that Baum would repeatedly return throughout his life. Early in 1881 he studied acting, at the same time appearing under the name Louis F. Baum in productions at Albert M.

Palmer's Union Square Theatre in New York City. Later that same year he toured Pennsylvania with a repertory group, the Sterling Comedy Company. But Baum was not content to be just an actor; the end of 1881 found him in Richburg, New York, where, with the financial help of his uncle John W. Baum, he constructed Baum's Opera House to produce plays he had written. In March 1882, however, the theater burned down.

Later in 1882 Baum formed his own theatrical troupe and had his first taste of real success with a musical play of his own creation, *The Maid of Arran*, for which he wrote the book, the music, and the lyrics. He also starred as the character Hugh Holcomb in this Irish melodrama, based on an 1874 novel by William Black called *A Princess of Thule*. His uncle John acted as company manager, his aunt Katherine Gray played two different roles, and his cousin Genevieve Rogers served first as musical director and later as a performer. After its premiere in Gillmor, Pennsylvania, where his father owned an opera house, on 15 May Baum moved the play to the Grand Opera House in Syracuse, where he met with considerable success. From there, he toured the play through the United States and Canada, even making it into New York City for a week. Other plays written by Baum at about this time either were not produced or were not successful.

Also in 1882, Baum married Maud Gage, daughter of the famous suffragette Matilda Joslyn Gage. Although *The Maid of Arran* was still playing in 1883, Baum left the company because the life of a touring actor did not suit the newly married couple. That year they had the first of four sons, Frank Joslyn, and Baum joined his family's oil business in Syracuse, which marketed all grades of machine, engine, and cylinder oils, including a family-invented axle grease called Baum's Ever-Ready Castorine. Soon he was on the road selling the new lubricant.

The next few years brought catastrophes to the Baum family. In 1884 fire destroyed the Opera House in Gillmor, together with the costumes, sets, and scenery for *The Maid of Arran*. Then, in 1885 Benjamin Baum was injured in a buggy accident. He went to Germany for medical help, but while he was there his finances were mismanaged, causing him to lose much of his fortune. He died soon thereafter, in 1887. Meanwhile, business was slow for L. Frank Baum, who, in any case, was tired of selling oil and had little to keep him in the Syracuse area. As a result, in 1888 he relocated his family to Aberdeen, in the Dakota Territory, where Maud's brother and sister had already settled.

The area had been prosperous, but by the time the Baums moved there hard times were setting in. Inopportunely, Baum opened a variety store called Baum's Bazaar, which he was forced to close about fifteen months later. In

Program cover for *The Maid of Arran* (1882), L. Frank
Baum's first theatrical success as both author and actor.
Baum is pictured over his stage name, Louis F. Baum.

January 1890 he took over as editor of the *Aberdeen Saturday Pioneer,* which appeared until April 1891. The paper was a convenient outlet for the editor to indulge in creative writing and to discuss his various interests, including the growing women's movement and Theosophy.

With financial troubles in the Dakotas worsening, Baum looked to Chicago, and in the first half of 1891 he relocated his family there. The city was prospering and preparing to host the great World's Columbian Exposition in 1893. Baum's mother-in-law, Matilda Gage, who now had a strong interest in the occult, spent winters with the Baum family in Chicago. Baum and his wife shared her interest and invited Spiritualists to conduct seances in their home.

A brief stint for Baum as a reporter for the *Evening Post* was followed by two positions as a salesman, the second of which required him to travel extensively. While on the road, he did considerable writing, little of which was ever published. When he was not traveling, Baum also enjoyed telling stories to his sons. It was at this time that he began thinking of publishing books aimed at children. Through connections he had made at the Chicago Press Club, Baum obtained a contract to publish a set of stories based on old nursery rhymes. The book, called *Mother Goose in Prose,* was illustrated by the then up-and-coming artist Maxfield Parrish and was published in 1897.

Encouraged by the publication of the book—which was, however, only a modest success at best—and urged by his doctor to give up the life of a traveling salesman, Baum searched for a job that would enable him to remain in Chicago with his family. In the fall of 1897 he combined a longtime interest in window decorating with his talent for editing and writing and founded a trade periodical for window dressers called *Show Window.* It was the first in its field and proved to be highly successful.

In that same year, Baum privately published a book called *By the Candelabra's Glare: Some Verse,* a compendium of poems, some of which had previously appeared in newspapers. Perhaps most significant, this book marked Baum's first collaboration with William Wallace Denslow, the artist who would go on to illustrate *The Wonderful Wizard of Oz.*

Denslow had a varied background.[8] Born in Philadelphia in 1856, he was schooled at the National Academy of Design in New York. He illustrated several atlases before becoming a staff artist for a New York magazine, *Theatre,* in the 1880s, at which time he also designed costumes for several musical revues. About 1888 Denslow moved to Chicago, where he worked on the staff of the *Chicago Herald* and also designed several books. Next he had a brief stint with various newspapers, first in Colorado and then in California, but by 1893 he was back in Chicago working for the *Herald.* Once again he was illustrating

William Wallace Denslow working at his desk, c. 1900. *Father Goose, His Book,* which Denslow illustrated for Baum in 1899 and which became the best-selling juvenile book of that year, can be seen at right.

books, but now his drawings showed more polish and reflected his growing interest in art nouveau and Japanese art. At about this time Denslow joined the Chicago Press Club, where he began to befriend influential persons. In 1896 Denslow took a job as an artist with Rand, McNally and Company, for which he illustrated two books and more than a hundred book covers. And in the same year, he became involved with the Roycroft Shops of East Aurora, New York, which were inspired by William Morris's Arts and Crafts Movement.

Baum first met Denslow at the Chicago Press Club. After the publication of *By the Candelabra's Glare,* the two again worked together on *Father Goose, His Book,* a collection of Baum's children's poems, which became the best-selling juvenile book of 1899 and eventually sold more than a hundred thousand copies. The year 1900 was to be a highly productive one for Baum. With the success of *Father Goose,* he was besieged by publishers looking for a new work, and he published several more books for children. But although Baum was quickly establishing himself as a successful writer of children's literature, he was careful not to put all his eggs in one basket. His continuing work on the journal *Show Window* led to the publication of a book called *The Art of Decorating Dry Goods Windows and Interiors,* which was a trade standard for many years.

Most of all, however, Baum liked writing for children. As he would later say, "To please a child is a sweet and lovely thing that warms one's heart and brings its own reward."[9] Baum was now contemplating a full-length fairy tale. This tale, which was to become *The Wonderful Wizard of Oz,* supposedly began its life as a story for his sons and their friends. According to one anecdote, when Baum told his tale to the children, they asked him the name of the land his characters inhabited. The author looked all around the room in which he was seated, and his eyes fixed upon a filing cabinet whose bottom drawer was labeled "O–Z." Another story quotes Baum as telling his publisher about the completed manuscript: "I was sitting on the hatrack in the hall telling the kids a story, and suddenly this one moved right in and took possession. I shooed the children away and grabbed a piece of wrapping paper that was lying on the rack, and began to write; it really seemed to write itself."[10]

The truth of these tales of creation cannot be confirmed, but what is known for certain is that the resulting book, published in May 1900, did in fact move in and take possession of Baum's life. Indeed, so great was *The Wonderful Wizard of Oz*'s success that Baum, try as he might, was never able to escape the pull his fairyland exerted on both himself and his public.

In hindsight, the book's tremendous success comes as no surprise, although the publisher, George M. Hill, was hesitant at first. Part of the success was due to Denslow's numerous illustrations, including twenty-four full-page multi-color plates. Furthermore, all of the book's illustrations were linked by color to the text, with each region of Oz being represented by a different color, as outlined by Baum. Another unusual design element was the placement of the illustrations on the page. Drawings were found everywhere, sometimes over-lapping the text. The effect was humorous and lively.

The text itself was no more traditional than Denslow's illustrations. In his introduction to the fantasy, Baum explained that his intention was to create a whole new kind of children's tale:

> The old-time fairy tale, having served for generations, may now be classed as "historical" in the children's library; for the time has come for a series of newer "wonder tales" in which the stereotyped genie, dwarf and fairy are eliminated, together with all the horrible and bloodcurdling incident devised by their authors to point to a fearsome moral to each tale. Modern education includes morality; therefore the modern child seeks only entertainment in its wonder-tales and gladly dispenses with all disagreeable incident.
>
> Having this thought in mind, the story of "The Wonderful Wizard of Oz" was written solely to pleasure children of today. It aspires to being a modern-ized fairy tale, in which the wonderment and joy are retained and the heart-aches and nightmares left out.[11]

What Baum did was to create the first truly American fairyland, using lan-guage and imagery that would be familiar to the ordinary American child. And if he was not totally successful in fully omitting "bloodcurdling incident" and "heart-aches"—after all, one needs at least a small degree of these elements in order to create tension and sustain interest—the resulting story is full of action, imagination, humor, and unusual characters.

∿ *The Wonderful Wizard of Oz* begins matter-of-factly with the line, "Doro-thy lived in the midst of the great Kansas prairies, with Uncle Henry, who was a farmer, and Aunt Em, who was the farmer's wife." The little orphan girl's age is unspecified, but based on her actions and on Denslow's illustrations, she is probably about five or six years old.[12] There is no color or humor in the de-scription of Dorothy's home. In fact, there is nothing but gray prairie in all di-rections, and the one-room farmhouse in which she lives is rudimentary. Even Aunt Em and Uncle Henry are gray. They never laugh or smile. Baum tells us that it is Toto, Dorothy's dog, that makes her laugh and saves her from becoming gray herself. When a cyclone suddenly approaches the farm, all head for the cyclone cellar. But Toto jumps out of Dorothy's arms and hides under a bed.

to draw a crowd of people together and get them to pay to see the circus," he explained.

"Oh," she said; "I know."

"Well, one day I went up in a balloon and the ropes got twisted, so that I couldn't come down again. It went way up above the clouds, so far that a current of air struck it and carried it many, many miles away. For a day and a night I travelled through the air, and on the morning of the second day I awoke and found the balloon floating over a strange and beautiful country.

"It came down gradually, and I was not hurt a bit. But I found myself in the midst of a strange people, who, seeing me come from the clouds, thought I was a great Wizard. Of course I let them think so, because they were afraid of me, and promised to do anything I wished them to.

"Just to amuse myself, and keep the good people busy, I ordered them to build this City, and my palace; and they did it all willingly and well. Then I thought, as the country was so green and beautiful, I would call it the Emerald City, and to make the name fit better I put green spectacles on all the people, so that everything they saw was green."

"But isn't everything here green?" asked Dorothy.

"No more than in any other city," replied Oz; "but

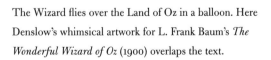

The Wizard flies over the Land of Oz in a balloon. Here Denslow's whimsical artwork for L. Frank Baum's *The Wonderful Wizard of Oz* (1900) overlaps the text.

The little girl runs to retrieve him, but before she can return to the cellar the house is shaken, lifted off its foundations, and slowly carried through the air like a balloon.

Many hours pass, and Dorothy falls asleep. She is awakened by a shock and runs to open the door. She cries in amazement at the wonderful beauty of the country she sees, a country where trees, flowers, and greenery mark a stark contrast to the world she has left behind. Three Munchkin men, dressed in blue, and the Good Witch of the North, an old woman in white, approach Dorothy and welcome her as a sorceress. They tell her that her house landed on the Wicked Witch of the East, thereby killing her and setting her subjects, the Munchkins, free. Dorothy also learns that the Land of Oz, the country in which she has landed, has had two good witches, one each in the North and the South, and one remaining wicked witch in the West. There is also the Great Wizard, who lives in the City of Emeralds.

The Wicked Witch of the East's legs, which had been sticking out from under Dorothy's house, shrivel up and disappear, leaving behind her magical silver shoes. The Good Witch does not know their exact power, but she gives them to Dorothy. When the little girl expresses her desire to return to Kansas, the Munchkins and the Good Witch at first do not know how to help her. Finally, the old woman takes off her cap, balances it on the end of her nose, and counts to three. The cap turns into a slate on which is written in white chalk, "Let Dorothy Go to the City of the Emeralds." The Witch tells Dorothy that this will be a long journey, which will be sometimes pleasant and some-times terrible. The old woman kisses the little girl on the forehead, and a round shining mark is left behind that will protect Dorothy throughout her travels. Next she is told that she will not have any trouble finding her way because the road to the City of Emeralds is paved with yellow brick. After saying good-bye, the three Munchkin men walk away as the Good Witch spins around on her left heel three times and disappears.

Dorothy washes, eats, changes into a blue-and-white gingham dress, and puts on the silver shoes before she and Toto start on their journey. She passes many farms, and at night stays with a Munchkin family. The next day, after walking several miles, she stops to rest and fixes her eyes on a Scarecrow, who winks at her. He begins to speak and complains that he is bored sitting up on his pole all day. Dorothy helps him down from the pole and tells him where she is going. The Scarecrow then explains that he is stuffed with straw and has no brains. He wonders if he might accompany her to the Wizard in order to ask for some. The two set off together.

As the two travelers journey on, Dorothy tells the Scarecrow that although

Kansas is dreary and gray, she still longs to return since "there is no place like home." They spend the night in a log cabin deep in the forest.

The next morning, while searching for water, Dorothy and her new friend come across a man made out of tin. He cannot move because his joints are rusted. Dorothy oils the Tin Woodman, and then he tells his story. He had been a woodman in love with a Munchkin maiden living with a crazy old woman who did not want the young girl to marry. The old woman bargained with the Wicked Witch of the East, who enchanted the woodman's axe. First, the axe cut off his left leg, but a tinsmith was able to replace it with a leg made of tin. Next, the axe cut off his right leg and then, in turn, each of his arms and his head. Finally, it split his torso in two. In each instance, the tinsmith made replacement parts, although he neglected to make the Tin Woodman a heart. After telling his story, the Tin Woodman decides to join Dorothy and the Scarecrow in the hope that the Wizard will be able to give him one.

The three friends now proceed through a dark and unfriendly forest. Suddenly a Lion jumps out at them and strikes the Scarecrow and the Tin Woodman. He is about to bite Toto, but Dorothy slaps him and scolds him. Backing down immediately, the Lion becomes timid and explains to the travelers that he is a coward. The Cowardly Lion then decides to accompany them to the Wizard so that he can ask for courage.

They journey on in peace until the Tin Woodman accidentally steps on and kills a beetle. He cries sorrowfully at having done so, and his mouth rusts shut. His new friends come to the rescue by oiling him.

The forest becomes rougher and rougher. The next day they come to a ditch too large for them to cross. The Scarecrow instructs the Tin Woodman to chop down a huge tree to place across the ditch as a bridge. Just as they begin to cross, they are confronted by two Kalidahs, fierce beasts with heads of tigers and bodies of bears. The Lion stalls them as the others cross over the ditch and then bounds across with the Kalidahs in pursuit. The Tin Woodman, however, destroys the bridge in the nick of time, and the Kalidahs are smashed on the sharp rocks at the bottom of the ravine.

Finally, the travelers leave the forest and enter rich, grassy farmland. But a wide river running across the road stops their progress. The Tin Woodman builds a raft out of trees, and the next day the friends board it. A strong current carries them off course, however. In trying to steer the raft against the current, the Scarecrow pushes hard on his steering pole, and it sticks to the bottom of the river. He remains clinging to it while the raft continues on without him. After this, the Cowardly Lion jumps into the water and uses his tail to tow the vessel to the shore. Dorothy and her comrades are in despair over the fate of the Scarecrow. But just then a Stork flies overhead. Discovering their dilemma, it flies out over the river and rescues the Scarecrow.

Now reunited, the group soon comes upon a large meadow filled with poppies, the scent of which will make one sleep forever. Before they are able to leave the meadow, Dorothy, Toto, and the Lion succumb. Because the Scarecrow and the Tin Woodman are not made of flesh, however, they are unaffected, and they carry the girl and her dog to safety. The Cowardly Lion, though, is too heavy for them.

Suddenly, the Scarecrow and the Tin Woodman encounter a wildcat chasing a field mouse. The Tin Woodman kills the Wildcat, and its intended victim turns out to be none other than the Queen of the Mice. Grateful to her rescuer, the Queen offers the Tin Woodman the servitude of her subjects. The Scarecrow thinks of a plan to save the Lion. While the Tin Woodman builds a cart, some of the mice gather string. The mice are then harnessed to the cart, and they pull the Lion, who has been lifted onto it, out of range of the poppies. Meanwhile, Dorothy and Toto have awakened, and it is not long before the Lion too regains consciousness.

The group resumes its journey and finally returns to the yellow brick road. The next day they reach the jewel-studded gate of the Emerald City. The Guardian of the Gates, who is dressed in green and has a greenish complexion, fastens green spectacles onto their heads and secures them with a lock and key. The spectacles are required by law for all inhabitants in order to prevent them from being blinded by the glare of the Emerald City. Dorothy and her friends then enter the city, where they discover that everything is green. Houses are made of green marble and emeralds, and even the food is green.

When the group reaches the door of the Wizard's palace, they are met by a soldier with long green whiskers. After consulting with the Wizard, he tells them that the ruler will see each of them individually on separate days. Meanwhile, they are shown to beautifully appointed guest rooms.

On succeeding days, each visits the Wizard in his throne room. To Dorothy, he appears as a giant floating bald head; to the Scarecrow, as a beautiful winged lady; to the Tin Woodman, as a strange and terrible beast; and to the Lion, as a ball of fire. To each of his suppliants the Wizard says the same thing—that he or she must kill the Wicked Witch of the West before he will grant any favors. Although they are upset, the four friends resolve to hunt down the Witch.

The following day, they set off. At the city gate the Guardian removes their glasses and tells them to head west, for once the Wicked Witch of the West sees them in her land, she will find them. In fact, the Witch does soon espy them with her very powerful single eye, and she sends a pack of forty wolves to destroy them. The Tin Woodman, however, beheads them all. Next the Witch sends out forty crows to peck out the strangers' eyes. This time, the Scarecrow first frightens them and then twists their necks. Now the Witch sends a swarm of bees. The Tin Woodman protects Dorothy and the Lion by dismantling the Scarecrow and scattering his straw over them. The bees arrive to find only the Tin Woodman. When they try to sting him, their stingers are bent and they die. Finally, the Witch sends her slaves, the Winkies, to kill the travelers. The Lion, however, frightens them off, and they return to their mistress's castle.

The Witch is furious, and using her magic gold cap, she summons the services of the Winged Monkeys, slaves to the power of the cap. Each owner of the cap may summon the Monkeys three times, and the Witch has already used the cap twice. The Monkeys are sent to capture the Lion and destroy the others. They throw the Tin Woodman on sharp boulders, scatter the Scarecrow's stuffing, and bind the Lion. When they see the mark of the Good Witch of the North on Dorothy, however, they are afraid to harm her.

Dorothy and the Lion are brought to the Wicked Witch of the West, who at first fears the little girl. But when she realizes that Dorothy does not know how to use the power of the silver shoes, she makes her a servant and threatens her with death. The Witch's castle is yellow, the predominant color of the western part of Oz. The Witch herself is mean but timid, afraid of the dark and of the Lion, whom she tries to starve into submission. Finally, the Witch tricks Dorothy out of one of her silver shoes by tripping her and then snatching it from her. Dorothy becomes so angry at being tricked that she throws a bucket of water on the Witch, who immediately begins to melt. After she has melted away, Dorothy takes back the silver shoe, which is all that remains of the Witch.

Dorothy frees the Lion and the Winkies, the native people of the West, whom the Witch had enslaved, and sets out to find her other friends. At length, with the aid of the Winkies, the Tin Woodman is repaired and the Scarecrow restuffed. After a few happy days at the palace of the late Witch, the travelers set out again for the Emerald City. Dorothy wears the Witch's magic cap.

Dorothy and her friends become lost, and several days pass. Finally, they summon the field mice with a whistle given to them by the Queen of the Mice. Arriving on the scene, the Queen and some of her subjects tell them that they are a long way from the Emerald City and suggest that Dorothy use the cap to summon the Winged Monkeys, who are no longer enemies. Soon the Monkeys are carrying her and her friends back to the Emerald City.

Once again the travelers are fitted with green glasses and shown to their rooms, but several days go by and they hear nothing from the Wizard. When they threaten to summon the Winged Monkeys for help, the Wizard at last agrees to an audience. This time the friends enter his throne room together. Now the Wizard is just a disembodied voice floating about the room. They demand that he keep his promise to help each get what he or she came for. The Cowardly Lion roars and scares Toto, causing the dog to knock over a screen. A bald old man is revealed who asserts that he is the Wizard. Dorothy and her companions call him a humbug, a label that both pleases and shames him. He explains how he used various tricks to assume the guises under which he previously appeared.

The old man tells Dorothy and her friends that he originally drifted to Oz from Omaha in a balloon and was proclaimed Wizard by the people. He built up the city and required its inhabitants to wear green glasses so that everything would appear to be emerald. All the time, he lived in fear of the late wicked witches. The Wizard insists that he is a good man but bad at his job, and he tries to convince Dorothy's companions that they already possess the qualities that they are trying to obtain from him. They are not satisfied, however, and the Wizard agrees to continue to help them if they will keep his secret.

The next day, one by one, the suppliants go in to see the Wizard once again. The old man fills the Scarecrow's head with "brains" made out of pins, needles, and bran; he puts a heart made of silk into the Tin Woodman; and he gives the Lion a green liquid to drink that he says is courage. He wonders to himself how he can help being a humbug when people are so gullible, believing that the impossible can be accomplished.

The Wizard decides to take Dorothy back to Kansas in a balloon, which he and Dorothy construct. On the day of their departure a large crowd gathers to see the little girl and the old man off. The Wizard, leaving the Scarecrow in charge of the Emerald City, gets into the basket and encourages Dorothy to climb in. Toto, however, runs after a cat, and as Dorothy goes to fetch the dog the balloon's ropes snap and the Wizard ascends without her.

Left behind, Dorothy summons the Winged Monkeys to take her to Kansas. But they are not allowed to leave Oz. Then the Soldier with the Green Whiskers is called upon to give advice, and he tells Dorothy to seek out Glinda, the Good Witch of the South, who rules over a people called the Quadlings. Once again, Dorothy's three friends accompany her on the journey.

On the second day of their travels, they encounter a dense forest guarded by a line of Fighting Trees that try to prevent their progress. With the help of the Tin Woodman and his axe, the group finally gets through. Soon they come to a high wall made of white china. The Tin Woodman builds a ladder so that they can ascend the wall, and once on the other side, they see before them a country made entirely out of china. The inhabitants, who also are made out of this delicate material, are diminutive, standing only about as high as Dorothy's knees. When the travelers reach the other side of the country, they again ascend the china wall, but as they leave, the Cowardly Lion's tail accidentally hits a church and smashes it.

Now back in the forest, with night approaching, they sleep. In the morning they encounter a group of animals holding a meeting in a clearing in the woods. The animals are discussing what to do about an elephant-sized spiderlike monster that has been terrorizing them. The Lion offers to kill the creature if the other animals will make him king. They agree, and the Lion finds the monster while it sleeps and beheads it. He vows to return for his title after he escorts Dorothy to Glinda.

The foursome now come to a steep and rocky hill. When the Scarecrow tries to ascend, a voice warns him to "keep back." Soon a strange, armless man with a flat head and wrinkled neck appears. He tells them that no one may cross the hill. When the Scarecrow defies him, the man's head shoots forward, his neck stretches out like a spring, and he rams the flat part of his head against the Scarecrow, who is sent tumbling. Then hundreds of similar Hammer-Heads appear on the hillside.

Dorothy decides to call the Winged Monkeys to help her and her friends once more. The Monkeys carry them to Quadling Country, where the rich countryside is predominantly red. After spending a night at a farm, they are directed toward Glinda's palace. Once at the palace, they find the Good Witch of the South seated on a throne of rubies. Glinda asks Dorothy what she wants and then vows to help the girl if she will give her the magic cap. Dorothy gives it to her, and Glinda asks Dorothy's three companions what they wish to do. The Scarecrow wants to return to the Emerald City and his rule there, the Tin Woodman wishes to preside over the Winkies in the West, and the Cowardly Lion wants to claim his title back in the forest. Glinda says that she will have the Winged Monkeys carry each to his desired destination and then, having thus used up the three commands that go with the cap, return the cap to the Monkeys, who will no longer be slaves to it. As for Dorothy, Glinda tells her that the silver shoes will take her anywhere she wants to go. She could have left Oz the first day of her adventure had she known about the power of the shoes.

After tearful farewells, Dorothy taps her heels together three times and says, "Take me home to Aunt Em." She lands on the prairie, right in front of a new farmhouse that Uncle Henry has built to replace the old one. The silver shoes, however, have fallen off during the trip home. Em quizzes Dorothy about where she has come from. "From the Land of Oz," says Dorothy. "And here is Toto, too. And oh, Aunt Em! I'm so glad to be at home again!"

⌒ It is easy to see that much of Baum's life influenced his fairy tale. The very idea of a journey filled with adventures may have been inspired by his own experiences as a traveling salesman. His yearning to return home to his family after days on the road may be reflected in Dorothy's longing to return home to Kansas. The abundance of objects, colors, and costumes in the story probably stems from Baum's background in both the theater and window dressing. This background also may be responsible for the personification and animation of normally inanimate objects. In fact, in his book *The Art of Decorating Dry Goods Windows and Interiors* Baum strongly advocated the use of mechanical movement to attract consumers to window displays.[13] The fantastic White City of the World's Columbian Exposition, which Baum visited, probably inspired the Emerald City.

The fact that Dorothy, Baum's leading character, is a strong-willed, self-sufficient girl whose main protector, the Good Witch of the North, and whose savior, Glinda, are women may reflect the author's sympathies with the women's movement. Furthermore, Baum had been familiar with scarecrows since his childhood in upstate New York, and one of his earliest writings is a six-line riddle-poem in the *Rose Lawn Home Journal* that has as its answer "Scare-Crow."[14] Even the oil that the Tin Woodman always needs was perhaps suggested to the author by his family's oil business. Finally, Baum's interest in Spiritualism is apparent in the encounters of Dorothy and her friends with the Wizard, a figure who, like a spirit, assumes different shapes and can even be no more than a ghostly disembodied voice. In addition, the slate of the Good Witch of the North that automatically tells Dorothy to go to the Emerald City may be a reference to the slates used by Spiritualists to receive messages from the "other side."

The Wonderful Wizard of Oz proved to be the best-selling children's book of the 1900 Christmas season, and it went through several printings.[15] The book's design and the easy appeal of the text to children account for much of its success. But perhaps equally important was the fact that adults also were quite taken with it. There is an element of the philosophical in Baum's story, evident, for example, in the theme that Dorothy and her companions already innately possess the qualities or powers they seek. And much of Baum's narrative and its accompanying illustrations work on several levels. Dorothy's adventure is, in fact, a symbolically rich tale open to multiple interpretations, and over the years scholars from a wide range of disciplines have found different meanings in the story. A sampling of these investigations of *The Wonderful Wizard of Oz* might help us to understand a novel that inspired so many stage and screen adaptations.[16]

～ Several critics have looked at *The Wonderful Wizard of Oz* from the standpoint of folk tale and mythology. Samuel Schuman points out that Northrop Frye's outline of the mythic pattern of comedy not only fits *The Wonderful Wizard of Oz* but puts the tale in a new context.[17] According to Frye, much comic literature since Aristophanes has a tripartite structure. It begins in a sterile wasteland (such as Kansas). From there, the action moves into the "green world," a magical environment full of unexpected phenomena (Oz). After being rejuvenated there, the comic protagonists return to the place from which they started, in a general mood of reconciliation.

Edward Hudlin maintains that the book follows very closely the structure of the heroic myth as outlined by Joseph Campbell. This structure too has three parts: departure, initiation, return.[18] Typically a hero (in this case Dorothy) leaves the ordinary world and journeys to a magical environment. There the hero meets with powerful forces and wins a significant victory. When the adventure is over, the hero returns to the everyday world possessed of the ability to benefit others.

In their examination of the female hero in fiction Carol Pearson and Katherine Pope look at Dorothy's adventures from a mythological and feminist perspective.[19] They show that in her quest for self-discovery the female hero has experiences that differ from those of her male counterparts. Dorothy kills the wicked witches, who represent society's negative view of the strong woman. She also meets the good witches, who stand for aspects of her own power. By unmasking the Wizard as a humbug, she discovers that she cannot rely on the traditional father figure to solve her problems. In the end, Dorothy realizes that she has the ability to save herself.

Some have interpreted *The Wonderful Wizard of Oz* from a spiritual and mystical perspective. Samuel Bousky believes that Dorothy represents each individual's higher spiritual plane, while Toto exemplifies the physical body. The little girl's desire to return home reflects the spirit's need to develop and reach maturity.[20] John Algeo views the tale as a Theosophical allegory, a reading founded on the fact that Baum was a Theosophist. The cyclone, or the cycle of birth and death, takes Dorothy from Kansas, the place of spiritual origin, to the Land of Oz, the illusory world in which we live. The Scarecrow, the Tin Woodman, and the Cowardly Lion are the mental, emotional, and physical bodies that Dorothy acquires on her journey into incarnation. The yellow brick road is the path to enlightenment, which leads to the Wizard, a guru, who is ultimately a sham, as are all teachers outside of ourselves. In the end, Dorothy returns home, or achieves Nirvana.[21]

Other critics have looked at the tale from a psychological point of view.

Carol Billman, for example, views *The Wonderful Wizard of Oz* as a testament to the power of positive thinking.[22] Oz is a land where those who believe in themselves succeed and where the Wizard's true power is to encourage human resourcefulness. In her study of alienation in modern society, Madonna Kolbenschlag cites Dorothy's adventures as a powerful metaphor for those who are emotionally adrift in the world.[23] Separated from the familiar, the orphan Dorothy must, through her own resources, conquer alien territory and find her way home. To reintegrate with society, Kolbenschlag suggests, we must forge our own way and combat the forces around us that have turned many of us into spiritual orphans.

For Sheldon Kopp the story is a psychotherapeutic tale.[24] Dorothy and her companions are patients seeking help from the Wizard, a therapist. When they reach the Emerald City, the Wizard holds an intake interview with each of them. He indicates that for him to help them, each must take an active role in his or her own cure. In the course of their therapy, Dorothy and the others realize that the authority figure, the Wizard from whom they seek help, is himself a person in conflict. Nevertheless, he aids them in realizing the innate powers they already have within themselves. Osmond Beckwith also gives a psychoanalytical interpretation to the book.[25] He views the story in terms of Baum's own psyche and sees Dorothy and her three companions as representing different aspects of Baum himself: innocent child (Dorothy and the Scarecrow), emotionally unstable adult (the Tin Woodman), and sexually unsure man (the Cowardly Lion).

From a Freudian perspective, Jerry Griswold interprets Dorothy's adventures as encounters with parentlike characters.[26] She acquires substitute parents (the Good Witch, the Scarecrow, the Tin Woodman, and the Cowardly Lion), competes in an oedipal struggle with female parental figures (the wicked witches), and is to some degree protected by a male parental character (the Wizard). Her final meeting with the "Good Mother," Glinda, shows Dorothy that she can be independent, that she herself possesses the power she needs to return home and be at peace.

The possible political and social symbolism contained in the Oz narrative has inspired yet other interpretations. Henry Littlefield suggests that *The Wonderful Wizard of Oz* is a parable of the agrarian-based Populist Party and the social and economic reforms it was advocating about 1900.[27] To Littlefield, harsh Kansas, for example, symbolizes the plight of the midwestern farmers who worked the hard land. The Tin Woodman, who was put under a spell by the Wicked Witch of the East, represents the dehumanization of the simple laborer by the evil powers of the eastern industrialists and politicians. Dorothy wearing the silver shoes and walking on the golden road to the Emerald City represents Baum's view of the silver issue of his day, namely, that the ordinary person wants a bimetallic monetary standard, which includes silver as well as gold, and is taking that message to Washington, D.C.

Barry Bauska sees the book as a response to the closing of the American frontier at the end of the nineteenth century.[28] America until then had seemed a land of unending expanse and promise. By 1900, however, there was little of the country that had not been explored, mapped, or settled. With a growing population, improving transportation systems, and developing mass media, America was, in effect, becoming smaller. The Land of Oz, on the other hand, was unknown and continually surprising. A type of utopia, it was a world of wonder where the American Dream was still alive.

Related to this interpretation is Tom St. John's view that Baum's novel reflects the American frontier experience.[29] For St. John, Oz mirrors the Black Hills of the Dakota Sioux, corresponding roughly to the present-day states of Kansas, Nebraska, North Dakota, South Dakota, and Montana, as well as part of Canada. Baum, of course, was familiar with this area, having lived in Aberdeen. The yellow brick road refers to the gold-rush pioneers who came to the Black Hills looking for quick wealth, while the Winged Monkeys satirize the Northwest Mounted Police.

In addition, St. John sees many ethnic references in Baum's tale. The Emerald City, he says, may point to Baum's interest in Ireland, the "Emerald Isle," and its people. (There were large communities of Irish in the Black Hills region.) Baum may be referring to the Chinese when he describes the Winkies, a people who live in the western part of Oz, where the predominant color is yellow. Their very name may be an allusion to the "slanty eyes" of Asians. Furthermore, the Wicked Witch of the West may be a negative portrayal of a black woman. Baum, describing her death, refers to her as "melting away like brown sugar," and Denslow depicts her as having pickaninny braids. St. John also sees references to the American Indian in the story. And interestingly, he likens Dorothy's adventures to Indian captivity narratives, which often involved an innocent young girl's capture, enslavement, and eventual escape.[30]

Similarly, William R. Leach draws parallels between Oz and Baum's America.[31] He argues, however, against those critics who see *The Wonderful Wizard of Oz* as an essentially agrarian story that celebrates farm life and such values as simplicity and hard work. For Leach, the tale is a reflection of urbanism and modern industrial society. There was a new and vibrant urban-based culture taking root in the late nineteenth century, and Baum was both a product and a supporter of it. The Emerald City, in this light, becomes the epitome of the wondrous new American city.

Furthermore, Leach argues, the abundant color in the book's illustrations and the many references to color in the text are the result of Baum's experiences with merchandising and advertising. Leach also discusses the ways in which Baum was influenced by new intellectual movements of his day, such as the mind cure, which emphasized the power of positive thinking; indeed, Dorothy, who rarely displays real fear, seems able to accomplish anything thanks to a positive mental attitude. Finally, Leach analyzes the Wizard as a trickster character who represents Baum's admiration for all the new forms of trickery and inventiveness in American culture, including advertising, commercial theater, and technology.

And there are still other approaches to *The Wonderful Wizard of Oz*. Stuart Culver provides a semiotic analysis that links the book to Baum's knowledge of window dressing.[32] He likens the Scarecrow, the Tin Woodman, and the Cowardly Lion, each of whom is lacking a particular quality, to display manikins designed to awaken desire in the shopper. To be human, according to Culver, is to feel desire. Once desire is erased and wholeness is achieved, humanity ceases. Thus, Dorothy's three companions seem humanlike only so long as they are searching for the attributes they lack.

Finally, Neil Earle, in his book *"The Wonderful Wizard of Oz" in American Popular Culture*, sees value in several of the interpretations outlined above and uses them as a springboard for his own ideas.[33] He finds the tale filled with meanings that stem from multiple themes and archetypes embodied in the text. He views Dorothy as a "Child of Grace," for instance—a metaphor for the innocent America of the original settlers—and Toto as an "Animal Helper" representing the instinctual side of human nature.

Most important, Earle quite reasonably argues that it is precisely because the book is open to so many interpretations that it has so fascinated the public and enjoyed such longevity. He accounts for the omnipresence of the Wizard of Oz story in our society by noting that "the commodities of mass culture, to truly enter the popular, must have the capacity to be invested with meanings before they achieve . . . iconic status."[34]

If Baum could never have predicted the many interpretations that would be applied to *The Wonderful Wizard of Oz*, he soon realized that his novel's success had changed his life forever. Putting aside his work on *Show Window*, he began to concentrate on the writing of children's books. In 1902 he achieved tremendous success with the first theatrical adaptation of *The Wonderful Wizard of Oz*. This, combined with the continuing sales of the original book, led Baum to respond in 1904 to his readers' ever-increasing demands for more of Oz. The result was *The Marvelous Land of Oz*, in which the Scarecrow and the Tin Woodman reappear, but neither Dorothy, the Cowardly Lion, nor the

Wizard. This book also was dramatized, but the resulting play, entitled *The Woggle-Bug*, was not a success.

Besides writing for children, Baum issued some books geared toward teenagers and still others toward adults. Nothing, however, met with as much success as his Oz stories, and in 1907 he brought out the third Oz book, *Ozma of Oz*. A fourth, *Dorothy and the Wizard in Oz*, followed in 1908, and in the same year he traveled with a multimedia Oz show called *Fairylogue and Radio-Plays*. *The Road to Oz* came out in 1909, and in 1910, *The Emerald City of Oz*, planned as the last volume in the Oz series. At the end of this sixth Oz book Baum had Glinda cut the fairyland off from the outside world by means of a so-called Barrier of Invisibility. Baum had grown tired of his fairyland and wanted to concentrate on new themes. He and his family relocated to Hollywood, California, where he settled into writing some new, non-Oz tales. The public's response to these was lukewarm, however; they wanted to hear still more about Oz.

In 1913 Baum reluctantly published the seventh Oz book, *The Patchwork Girl of Oz*. In the introduction he explains that he has reestablished communication with the now invisible fairyland by means of the wireless, and he formally proclaims himself "Royal Historian of Oz." For the remainder of his life, Baum regularly produced new Oz titles: *Tik-Tok of Oz* (1914), *The Scarecrow of Oz* (1915), *Rinkitink in Oz* (1916), *The Lost Princess of Oz* (1917), *The Tin Woodman of Oz* (1918), and two works published posthumously, *The Magic of Oz* (1919) and *Glinda of Oz* (1920).

In addition to the Oz works, Baum continued to write other books. And once again he met with some success in the theater, with the 1913 play *The Tik-Tok Man of Oz*, a musical based largely on *Ozma of Oz*. The next year saw Baum establishing the Oz Film Manufacturing Company with the intent of producing film versions of the Oz stories. The first of these, *The Patchwork Girl of Oz*, was not a success. The opinion of theater owners and producers at that time was that films aimed at children were difficult to sell. This attitude, in conjunction with legal problems experienced by Paramount, which had agreed to distribute Baum's film, led to the failure of *The Patchwork Girl*. Two more films with Oz themes, *The Magic Cloak of Oz* and *His Majesty, the Scarecrow of Oz*, were produced, but theater owners considered them children's films and distribution was a problem. Three non-Oz films aimed at adults followed, but the association of the Oz Film Manufacturing Company with children's film was too strong, and the company went out of business in 1915.

After Baum's death from heart failure in 1919, Maud Baum granted Ruth Plumly Thompson, a children's writer, the rights to continue the Oz chronicle.

In 1921 Thompson wrote the first of her many Oz books. Others wrote Oz books after her, and the occasional Oz tale continues to be written today.

Although more than forty Oz books have appeared in all, it is the first in the series, *The Wonderful Wizard of Oz,* that has endured and is known today all over the world. Many critics believe it to be the best one, and this may explain its popularity. But another factor in its continuing appeal has been the large number of successful stage and screen adaptations made of it.

The book itself is eminently adaptable to both media because it contains so many visual and theatrical elements. The book's visual aspects doubtless are due both to Baum's earlier work in the theater and his expertise as a show-window designer. In any case, his descriptions of the physical environments of Oz evidence a strong sense of color and design. There also is a great deal of vaudeville-style humor and physical comedy in the book. The Scarecrow and the Tin Woodman, in fact, display all the elements of a great comedy team. The Wizard himself is described as being a showman who has performed as a ventriloquist and a balloonist. Even the theatricality of the Spiritualist seance, with which the Baum family was familiar, makes its way into the book when Dorothy and her friends encounter the Wizard as a kind of spirit. Finally, the book is filled with dialogue that easily translates to stage or screen.

It should come as no surprise, then, that Baum was behind the first attempt to dramatize *The Wonderful Wizard of Oz,* a musical version of the book that premiered in 1902 and was being performed with some regularity as late as the teens.

PART 1

The Stage Musical, 1902–1918

Chapter 1

Collaboration and Conflict

The Wizard of Oz Takes Shape

WHO FIRST HAD THE IDEA of dramatizing *The Wonderful Wizard of Oz* is a matter of debate. Baum himself told three versions of how the musical came to be. In 1902 he claimed that he himself originated the idea of staging the work, inspired by the possibilities suggested by the unique characters of the Scarecrow, the Tin Woodman, and the Cowardly Lion. He maintained that he first tried a comedy but that after hiring the composer Paul Tietjens, he decided to turn his story into a comic opera. Later on in the creative process, he added, the producer Fred Hamlin and the director Julian Mitchell suggested making the show a musical extravaganza.

In an interview of 1905, however, Baum placed the credit elsewhere. "A lady suggested to me the idea of making the story into an American fairy extravaganza," he said, "a proposition so audacious that it nearly took my breath away." Still later, about 1910, he gave yet another version of the story: "The thought of making my fairy tale into a play had never even occurred to me when, one evening, my doorbell rang and I found a spectacled young man standing on the mat." The young man turned out to be Paul Tietjens, who did, in fact, become the composer of the musical. According to Baum, Tietjens suggested that Baum's book be made into an opera and that he be engaged to write the music.[1]

Probably the most accurate version of the musical's creation, however, can be pieced together from Tietjens's own personal diary, along with other evidence from the years 1901 and 1902.[2] Paul Tietjens was raised in St. Louis, where he became fairly well known as an up-and-coming concert pianist. He moved to Chicago to study and develop composition. He first met Baum in 1899, and the two began collaborating in March 1901 on a never-to-be-produced, non-Oz musical with two working titles, "The Octopus" and "The Title Trust." In June of that same year William Wallace Denslow heard some of Tietjens's music at a dinner party and suggested that the young man (Tietjens was only in his mid-twenties at the time) write the music for a play based on *The Wonderful Wizard of Oz.* Baum resisted this idea because he did not wish to work again with Denslow, for their collaboration on the novel had been somewhat unharmonious.[3]

Meanwhile, in the weeks that followed, Tietjens and Baum continued working on non-Oz projects but had no luck in getting anything accepted for pro-

The composer Paul Tietjens, c. 1900, just before he began collaborating with Baum on a stage version of *The Wonderful Wizard of Oz.*

duction. At Denslow's continuous urging, Tietjens, while visiting Baum at his summer home at Lake Macatawa in Michigan in the second half of July, tried to convince the author that a musical version of *The Wonderful Wizard of Oz* would be their best chance of having something produced in the near future. Baum finally relented and began work on the project. In fairly short order he drew up a scenario in five acts, and before long Tietjens had composed an opening chorus and several other numbers.

It was to comic opera that Baum and Tietjens turned for inspiration in preparing their musical. This popular form of entertainment had a comic plot and songs that, at least in the purer examples of the form, were linked thematically to the plot. It had grown in popularity in America during the nineteenth century and enjoyed a great vogue after the successful American premiere of Gilbert and Sullivan's *H.M.S. Pinafore* in 1878. Tietjens attended the theater regularly, recording his opinions of what he saw. He especially admired such comic operas as Gilbert and Sullivan's *The Pirates of Penzance* (1879) and Victor Herbert's *The Wizard of the Nile* (1895). In his diaries, Tietjens constantly expressed his desire to write a comic opera of real quality and make his mark with it.

Baum soon apprised Denslow of his plan to mount a Wizard of Oz musical, and Denslow, eager to participate in the project, began to shop around for a producer. He also came to Lake Macatawa to help prepare the show. In the early stages, at least, work on the musical proceeded smoothly. Baum's son Robert recalled his father's collaborating with Tietjens and Denslow at the lake, "the three of them cutting up like a bunch of school boys. Paul Tietjens would pound out a piece on the piano, and father would sing the words or perhaps do a tap or eccentric dance, accompanied by the ferocious looking Denslow."[4]

It was not long before difficulties arose, however. In early discussions the three men agreed that each would take a third of the royalty pool—Baum for the book, Tietjens for the score, and Denslow for designing costumes and advertising posters and for handling the business involved in actually securing a producer. The author and the composer would divide equally the additional profit from any sales of the music from the show. Denslow soon argued, however, that he and Baum should each receive two-fifths to Tietjens's one-fifth. Tietjens refused, and Denslow decided not to press the point.

Work on the musical continued, and the theatrical columnist Lyman B. Glover even wrote a small piece about it in the 5 September edition of the *Chicago Record Herald*. Shortly, though, old resentments between Baum and Denslow resurfaced. In his diary, Tietjens recorded that Baum wrote to him "decrying Denslow as usual" and that Baum no doubt had good cause for this. Tietjens did not elaborate, however.[5]

On 18 September a contract giving each man a one-third share was drawn up but not signed, as some changes were deemed necessary. On 20 September, probably because he was still angry over Denslow and Baum's attempt to reduce his share, Tietjens made his own demands. He did not believe that Denslow deserved a full third, and he demanded a half share for himself. The two men fought about it, but on 22 September Tietjens met with Baum and decided to go along with the contract "rather than to let *The Wizard* go by default."[6] Shortly after this, the three men signed the contract at the Chicago Athletic Club.

On 30 September Baum and Tietjens applied for a copyright on the show's music and lyrics. Meanwhile, Denslow was trying to find a producer for the work. Among those he approached was Fred Hamlin, a producer and manager at Chicago's Grand Opera House and one of the most important theatrical businessmen in Chicago at the time. Fred's father, John A. Hamlin, had made a fortune as the inventor and distributor of Hamlin's Wizard Oil, a favorite on the medicine-show circuit in the 1870s and 1880s.[7] In fact, it was reputedly the money made from sales of Wizard Oil that had allowed the elder Hamlin to obtain the Grand Opera House. Fred Hamlin invited Baum and Tietjens to dine with him in his apartment. Tietjens noted in his diary that Hamlin did not very much like either the book or the music of the Wizard of Oz show. Something about it must have appealed to him, however, because he expressed at least some interest. Perhaps it was simply that Fred Hamlin counted as a favorable omen the fact that the word "Wizard" appeared in the title of the show.[8]

In any case, he decided to call in the celebrated director Julian Mitchell, who had staged several shows that had played at the Grand Opera House. Mitchell was very much in demand. He had worked with Charles Hoyt and with Weber and Fields, and his specialty was the staging of elaborate musical numbers. According to Tietjens, Hamlin let Mitchell decide whether the Wizard of Oz show would be produced. For his part, Mitchell was dissatisfied with both the libretto and the score.

The script that Baum submitted to Hamlin and Mitchell has never been published. A surviving copy clearly shows the author's original dramatic vision, which was fairly true to the original novel but quite different from what later came to be produced.[9] The draft script begins with a dialogue-free prologue entitled "The Cyclone," set in a gray Kansas prairie, where we see Dorothy, Uncle Henry, and Aunt Em. A cyclone carries Dorothy and her house away. In the next scene, the blue "Country of the Munchkins," the Wicked Witch

Julian Mitchell, one of the most celebrated stage directors of his day, in a 1905 caricature. The inset photograph is from c. 1900, when he worked extensively with Weber and Fields.

of the East torments the Munchkins as all perform the "Opening Chorus." Suddenly the Kansas house falls on the Witch and kills her. The Munchkins greet Dorothy as a sorceress, but she explains in song that she is just "An Innocent Kansas Girl." The Good Witch of the North enters, instructs Dorothy to seek out the Wizard of Oz, and gives her the magical silver shoes of the Wicked Witch. The Munchkins sing "Farewell Sweet Stranger," and Dorothy sets out to find the Wizard. The girl then discovers a Scarecrow, who sings "A Man of Straw," lamenting his lack of a brain. He decides to seek the Wizard's help as well.

In the next scene, "The Road through the Forest," Dorothy and the Scarecrow are joined by the Tin Woodman, who sings "Oh, Love's the Thing," bemoaning his need of a heart, and the Cowardly Lion, who does not speak but acts fearful. Traveling on a road of yellow brick, the four friends dance and sing "The Merry-Go-Round," in which they rejoice in the help they expect to get from the Wizard.

Soon the foursome come upon a "Deadly Poppy Field," where the Poppies dance and sing "The Poppy Chorus." The scent of the flowers lulls Dorothy and the Lion to sleep. The Scarecrow and the Tin Woodman carry the girl out of the field as the Poppies sing the "Death Song," about how their scent can kill. The Queen of the Field Mice and her army then rescue the Lion.

Act 2 begins at "The Gates of the Emerald City," where the Guardian of the Gate, who has green whiskers, performs a drill and song, "I'm Here to Keep the People Out." When Dorothy, the Scarecrow, and the Tin Woodman (but not the Lion, who has simply dropped out of sight) arrive, he instructs them to put on green spectacles. The friends are now ushered into "The Throne Room of the Wonderful Wizard," where a chorus of the Wizard's Attendants— comprising astrologers, witches, necromancers, and sorcerers—sings an untitled song of caution about visiting the Wizard. Taking the form of a giant head, the Wizard himself appears and performs "The Wonderful Wizard of Oz." In response to Dorothy's request to be sent home, the potentate asks what she might do for him in return. The girl entertains him with "I Know," a number about Kansas. Then the Wizard, taking in turn the form of a lovely lady, a crablike beast, and a ball of fire, refuses to help Dorothy and her two friends.

Dorothy removes her glasses and realizes that they were a trick. She and her companions expose the Wizard himself as a fake. He in turn sings "When You Want to Fool the Public," about being a humbug. Next he mixes bran, pins, and needles to create brains for the Scarecrow and finds a heart for the Tin Woodman. He instructs Dorothy to go to Glinda the Good in the South for further help. The Wizard's subjects perform a "Minuet Chorus."

Soon thereafter, the Guardian of the Gate also questions the Wizard's powers. As a result, the ruler decides that it is time for him to leave the Emerald City. The Wizard, Dorothy, the Scarecrow, the Tin Woodman, and a chorus perform a finale song about fate. The act ends with a transformation scene change to the outside of the palace, where the Wizard is seen ascending in a balloon.

Act 3 opens with "The Forest of Fighting Trees." The Trees perform "Back," a song about how they attack their foes. Dorothy and the Tin Woodman enter, and he offers her his new heart in love. After she declines, he professes his love to a Forest Witch. Saying she is too wicked for love, she sings "I'm Freakishly Wicked" before exiting. The Trees now try to prevent Dorothy, the Tin Woodman, and the Scarecrow from passing. But after the Tin Woodman cuts a limb from one of them, the Trees all flee.

In "The Rocky Hill of the Hammerheads" the travelers confront the Hammerheads, who perform a "Laughing Chorus and Dance." Now wondering about the magic of her silver shoes, Dorothy removes them from her feet. Dorothy and her companions then perform a "Stocking Song and Dance" before she knocks together the heels of the shoes three times. This summons the benign Winged Monkeys, who bring the three friends to Glinda's palace.

At "The Ruby Palace of Glinda the Good" a female chorus of Bodyguards performs a march and chorus. Glinda then confers with her Wise Men (Socrates, Pericles, Sophocles, and Chumpocles) about the approaching guests. When the Tin Woodman arrives, he offers Glinda his heart, which she refuses. Similarly, she declines the Scarecrow's offer of some of his brains. She agrees, however, to send Dorothy home. The Scarecrow worries that his brains are not appreciated and will thus be as useless to him as was the pie to the hungry traveler. In explanation, he sings a comic number, "The Traveler and the Pie." For his part, the Tin Woodman discovers that Glinda's Captain of the Guard is his long-lost Munchkin love, who is about to take her place as Queen of the Munchkins. He is to be King of the Munchkins. When the Guardian of the Gate enters and asks the Scarecrow to rule the Emerald City in the Wizard's absence, the Tin Woodman advises his friend in a comic song, "Think It Over Carefully."

Dorothy states that she has no royal aspirations and performs the "Milkmaid's Song." She reasserts her desire to go home. After a "Grand Finale" in which there is much singing and dancing, Dorothy, upon Glinda's instructions, knocks the heels of her silver shoes together three times. A transformation scene returns her to the Kansas prairie and her aunt's embrace.

Baum's initial dramatization studiously captures most of the essential plot elements of his original book, but there are important differences between the two works. For one thing, the story was simplified for the stage. Plot elements in the novel that would have been especially difficult to depict theatrically, such as the river crossing, were eliminated. Likewise, the book's animal characters were either left out or downplayed. There is no Toto, probably because an actor wearing a dog costume would have been out of scale with Dorothy and the others. The Cowardly Lion barely figures into the action since, in keeping with the portrayal of animals in traditional pantomime, he is completely mute. Apparently, Baum did not think that he could develop and elaborate the character without recourse to dialogue.

There were changes to other characters as well. So that the story would be less specifically juvenile, Dorothy is no longer a little girl. Although her age is hard to determine, she is probably a young teenager. Her character, however, is not as well developed as in the book. She is not nearly so commonsensical nor so refreshingly direct. The Scarecrow and the Tin Woodman, on the other hand, play an even larger part in the draft script than in the novel. Perhaps recognizing their potential as a comedy team in the vaudeville tradition, Baum provided them with plenty of witty banter and comic routines. Finally, the character of the Wicked Witch of the West was eliminated altogether. In her place is the Forest Witch, who has no real importance to the story. She merely sings a comic number and has a brief interchange with the Tin Woodman. This has a major impact on the story, since without the Wicked Witch there is no real threat to Dorothy or her companions and thus no dramatic tension. One wonders why Baum chose to delete her.

For the most part, other changes to the story were made, one suspects, in an attempt to make the narrative more appealing to adults. First, a small romantic component was added. In the novel, the Wizard gives the Tin Woodman a heart made of silk, whereas in Baum's draft script he gets a heart from someone who had committed suicide over love. After he receives the heart, the Tin Woodman offers it in turn to Dorothy, the Forest Witch, and Glinda. In the end, he offers it to Glinda's Captain of the Guard, a character not in the novel, who reveals herself to be the Tin Woodman's long-lost sweetheart and accepts his offer. Second, an element of political conflict also can be discerned. In the novel, the Wizard is much beloved by his people, whereas in the dramatization the Guardian of the Gate questions the Wizard's power. It seems, in fact, that the Wizard has been keeping his balloon at the ready for that day when the people would find him out and attempt to overthrow him.

In general, the humor in the script is more mature in its appeal than in the novel. It includes many topical jokes, including many made by the Oz characters themselves—even though, of course, they are not supposed to be familiar with America. One typical example has the Tin Woodman wondering what he would do if he ran out of oil. "You wouldn't be as badly off as John D. Rockefeller," the Scarecrow reassures him. "He'd lose six thousand dollars a minute if that happened."[10] But this is not to say that children would not also find the show funny. The script plays up many of the humorous elements of the novel and adds much new comedy besides. Baum in fact invented new characters, Glinda's bumbling Wise Men, solely to get a laugh. Furthermore, although the dialogue contains much that is corny, it is very lively. Puns abound. The Scarecrow, for example, says to Dorothy, "I'm posted to scare away crows, and I'm ready to resign the job as soon as you can help me down." She responds, "To scare away crows? I thought there must be some caws for you being up there."[11]

Finally, Baum's sense of the theatrical clearly played a role in his adaptation. He was careful to keep in mind the unique properties of the stage. A dialogue-free prologue, for example, nicely sets the scene and creates a purely dramatic introduction to the play. Baum described the scene as a tableau, in reference, no doubt, to *tableau vivant,* a standard technique in the theater of the day, in which silent and motionless actors were arranged on the stage to depict a "living picture." But in Baum's theatrical treatment the actors move, creating a vivid sense of Kansas life disrupted by the fury of the cyclone. In addition, Baum included two dramatic transformation scenes, rapid special-effects scene changes designed to amaze audiences: the final scene of act 2, involving the Wizard's ascent in his balloon, and the end of the show, depicting Dorothy's return to Kansas.

Baum also added music and dance in such a way as to lend comic relief, advance the plot, and help develop characters. The lyrics are breezy and light-hearted and depend heavily on clever rhymes. Baum saw great opportunities for choruses in some of the book's minor characters. Thus, the Munchkins, the Poppies, the Fighting Trees, the Hammerheads, and Glinda's Bodyguards all are integrated into the musical as singing or dancing choruses that also add much visual appeal to the stage action. In addition, Baum created a chorus of Wizard's Attendants, characters not found in the book.

The musical numbers and the choruses reflect Baum and Tietjens's desire to make the Wizard of Oz musical a comic opera. In fact, like the best comic operas of the time, their show had a strong comic plot and well-defined characters. Its songs (except for the act 3 specialty numbers) also were integrated into the text: they arose from and commented on situation and character. In several ways, though, the show differed from a typical comic opera. First, although it included a romantic element, the action was not centered around a romantic plot, as was the case with most comic operas of the day. Second, at a time when most comic operas had a European setting, the show was decidedly American in theme and sensibility, as Baum's original book had been. Third, the plot and characters were unique and showed little influence from the stock traditions of the comic opera. And finally, although the show had elements designed to appeal to adults, it still was easily accessible to children, whereas most comic operas were geared to a largely adult audience.

Despite its innovations, Baum and Tietjens's musical remained essentially a comic opera. Julian Mitchell, however, had quite a different vision for the Wizard of Oz show. He saw it basically as an extravaganza, a lavish form of popular musical theater with a relatively loose structure that often had a fairy-tale theme. During the 1880s and 1890s David Henderson of Chicago had been a foremost proponent of the extravaganza, staging such spectacles as *Ali Baba, The Arabian Nights, The Crystal Slipper,* and *Sinbad the Sailor.*

At the start of the twentieth century the various forms of musical theater frequently crossbred with one other, creating various mutations and combinations. Indeed, the so-called extravaganza often was a mélange of elements from comic opera, farce comedy (broadly comic plays with interpolated songs strung together by a loose plot), pantomime (largely dialogue-free pieces with music that relied heavily on broad comedy, dance, and elaborate staging), spectacle (musical plays with loose plots and large casts that commonly involved exotic or fanciful locales and emphasized, above all, colorfully elaborate scenery, costuming, and special stage effects), vaudeville (collections of unrelated musical and other acts, including short sketches), burlesque (pieces that satirized either a famous literary work or current events, had comic songs and specialty numbers, and featured racily clad chorus girls who often played male roles as well as female), and minstrelsy (variety entertainments centered around African American or pseudo–African American song, dance, and comedy and performed by actors in blackface).

In essence, with the notable exception of the comic opera, many of the musical shows of the time, whatever they might be called, had little plot. The narrative, in fact, frequently was difficult to follow and was not necessarily unified. It was common for a predominant variety element, featuring a mixture of songs, dances, and other routines, to overwhelm whatever thin skein of a story ran through the entertainment. Furthermore, the songs were often extraneous, inserted into the text with little consideration about whether they arose naturally from situations or characters. The connections between action and song were tangential at best.

Julian Mitchell was unhappy with Baum's original script and wanted to rework it in line with a broader approach to musical theater, giving it a looser structure and enhancing the spectacle. A 1902 article explained that Mitchell had little interest in the project until the book itself was sent to him. At that point he wired Fred Hamlin: "Can see possibilities for extravaganza."[12] Furthermore, a pre-opening flier for the Wizard of Oz musical made it clear that the show was to be a loose amalgam of forms, including not only the extravaganza but also the comic opera, the spectacle, and the pantomime.[13] As for plot, Mitchell felt that in this type of entertainment it was more of a hindrance than a help. In fact, he once told a reporter that plots "are rather tiresome."[14]

During the last months of 1901, Baum, Tietjens, and Denslow entered into contract negotiations with Hamlin. It seems that from the start the producer insisted that Mitchell be included. Accordingly, in January 1902 all the men met in New York, where Mitchell was officially hired as a collaborator. Originally Hamlin had promised Baum, Tietjens, and Denslow a collective 6 percent royalty on the gross of every performance in addition to a 10 percent royalty on the net profits of each season. The final contract, dated 17 January, however, shows them agreeing instead to take 5 percent of the gross, with the other 1 percent going to Mitchell. In dividing their share of the gross, Denslow sacrificed the most, agreeing to take 1.25 percent, while Baum and Tietjens each took about 1.88 percent.[15]

Creatively speaking, however, it was Baum and Tietjens who sacrificed the most in this agreement with Mitchell, for the contract in effect required them to put the work largely into the director's hands. Tietjens states that after returning to Chicago, "Baum and Julian Mitchell worked together with much friction. It had been necessary to remodel the entire play, cutting out much of the music that had been written."[16] Additional collaborators also were called upon to help with revisions. According to Tietjens's diary, these were Glen MacDonough and Robert B. Smith, both librettists and lyricists. But a letter written by Fred Hamlin indicates that a third man, named Finnegan or Feinegan, also was called in, and programs from the show as it was finally produced indicate that A. Baldwin Sloane, Edgar Smith, and Nathaniel D. Mann worked on the music as well.[17]

Regarding April and May of 1902, Tietjens went on to say in his diary that "I again went to New York staying seven weeks and working with Julian Mitchell. What an awful time this was for me!" He had trouble composing anything usable, and the time was growing short. The production was scheduled to open in Chicago on 12 June. Tietjens wrote, "I called on MacDonough twice but did no work with him. In fact, I was in a state in which I was utterly incapable of work. I became frightened and barren of ideas in my vain efforts to conform to the style of music desired. The Finale of the second act was written in two days, before I had become in this state but after that I did little worthwhile." Tietjens concluded, "Never again, if I can possibly help it, will I tie myself down by contract to do a certain piece of work in a specified time. How often I woke in the night with a start and reckoned how much time still remained, how much time I had passed with so little accomplished."[18]

While in New York, Tietjens nevertheless found Mitchell to be very friendly. Besides securing him a room in a boardinghouse, Mitchell gave him "much valuable advice in the kind of work we were doing." In all, Tietjens found Mitchell to be "an extremely clever man, a hard worker, and withal pretty much of a gentleman." Tietjens returned to Chicago, and Mitchell soon appeared there as well. He arrived with the Weber and Fields Company, with whom he was still affiliated, toward the end of May, when they were scheduled to appear at Chicago's Grand Opera House. At this point, Tietjens's diary suggests, his relationship with Mitchell began to break down. Other problems arose too, and Tietjens wrote that with the preparations for the show in Chicago "his troubles began."[19] With these ominous words, the diary entries cease, and they do not resume until September 1903, when Tietjens was studying in Paris and living off his royalties from the Wizard of Oz musical.

Just exactly what these troubles were is impossible to say with any certainty. In part, Tietjens was probably referring to the logistics of putting together the massive undertaking the show had become under Mitchell's direction. The play featured a cast numbering at least sixty-eight people, and the opening was postponed twice.[20] In addition, Tietjens probably became increasingly upset that the musical was wandering farther and farther afield from his and Baum's original intent. A letter from Fred Hamlin to Townsend Walsh, the business manager for the show, suggests that Baum too was having trouble accepting what was being done to the show: "Impress on Baum when you see him that I won't do this thing without Mitchell. So he must not oppose him all the time and get him talking about quitting. We must have this thing quickly or not at all."[21]

A published interview with Baum dated 6 June 1902 makes no mention of any conflict but clearly indicates that much doctoring was taking place.[22] Baum noted in the piece that Mitchell had induced him to turn his tale into an extravaganza "on account of the gorgeous scenic effects and absurd situations suggested by the story." He went on to say that this was not an easy task since some of the situations in the book would be impossible to stage. So, Baum said, he had "selected the most available portions and filled up the gaps by introducing several new characters and minor plots which serve to throw the story of Dorothy and her unique companions into stronger relief." Baum, however, needed assistance in writing some of the dialogue since, he had been told, "what constituted fun in a book would be missed by the average audience, which is accustomed to a regular gattling-gun discharge of wit." About the collaborators brought in to revise his work Baum said that they had "peppered my prosy lines with a multitude of 'laughs.' Some of these I laugh at myself; some do not appeal to me so strongly."

The implication of this statement, as well as ones made by Hamlin and Tietjens, is that control of the show basically was taken out of Baum's hands. He certainly had some input into the process of revision, but his was not the final word. As a result, the show that premiered at the Grand Opera House on 16 June 1902—now called simply *The Wizard of Oz*—was only peripherally related to Baum's 1900 fairy tale and differed drastically from his original dramatization.

Chapter 2

What Pleases the People

The Script for the Chicago Opening

NFORTUNATELY, no script for *The Wizard of Oz*'s Chicago run is known to survive. We can surmise the action of the opening-night performance, however, from such sources as the program, the reviews, and the sheet and manuscript music. An extant script dating from 1903, when the show played New York, also helps to give a general sense of the action. But because the musical underwent changes following its premiere, it is not always possible to know to what extent this script reflects the show's original form.[1] The following summary reconstruction of the opening-night performance, then, is informed conjecture based on all the available evidence.

Act 1 begins with a pantomime scene entitled "A Kansas Farm," staged with musical underscoring. In a golden autumnal setting, farmers are busy with their work. Meanwhile, Dorothy Gale (a young woman of unspecified age) and her cow, Imogene, play, and a golfer looking for his golf ball flirts with a farm maid. A cyclone interrupts the activity and carries Dorothy and her house into the sky. In scene 2 the lights go up on the predominantly blue "Country of the Munchkins." Here a chorus of Munchkins dances around a maypole. A storm approaches, and they rush about wildly. The lights gradually go out and then come up to show, much to the Munchkins' amazement, Dorothy's house in the scene.

The Munchkin maiden Cynthia Cynch, the Lady Lunatic, now enters. The Munchkins accuse her of being a witch and causing the storm. The Good Witch of the North intervenes and explains that a house has landed on the Wicked Witch, killing her. After the Good Witch exits, Cynthia recounts her story: She had been a saleslady at one of the Land of Oz's largest department stores and was engaged to Niccolo Chopper, who played the piccolo. The Wicked Witch enchanted her fiancé, who is now missing. Mad with blighted love, Cynthia hopes to find him by going around humming his favorite tune, to which he is bound to respond. She now sings "Niccolo's Piccolo" (lyrics by Glen MacDonough, music by A. Baldwin Sloane), which tells how her lost love wooed her with his piccolo:

> Not with the sighing flute
> Sought he to press his suit
> Nor with the tinkling lute
> Came he zum-zumming
> Not on the light guitar
> Under the twilight star
> Could he be heard afar
> Tenderly strumming.
>
> But from his piercing Piccolo,
> My highly gifted Niccolo,
> Could charm with much celerity
> This melody divine.
> Defying fell malaria,
> He'd execute this aria
> With marvelous dexterity,
> Each night at half past nine.[2]

Cynthia leaves and the Good Witch enters, wondering about the origin of Dorothy's house. Sir Dashemoff Daily, Poet Laureate, then arrives on the scene. He announces that the cyclone has brought Pastoria, the rightful king of Oz, back to his homeland. It seems that years earlier a balloon had brought a man to the Emerald City from a mysterious place called the Earth. That man had lured Pastoria into the balloon and cut the ropes, causing the ruler to drift away. Meanwhile, the stranger had become king of Oz and was known as the

Wizard because of his mastery of mystic arts. The rightful king, aided by Briga-dier General Riskitt and the one-man Army of Pastoria, is now plotting a revolu-tion to recapture his throne.

Pastoria and his entourage enter. He will finance his revolution by selling, at speculators' rates, reserved seats to his coronation. Cynthia enters and asks Pastoria if he is her Niccolo. He says no and explains that he is the rightful king, who has up until now been forced to work as a motorman in Kansas. He sings "In Michigan" (MacDonough/Sloane), in which he rhapsodizes about a favorite state:

> In Michigan! In Michigan!
> I would that I were rich again!
> A ticket I'd buy,
> And away I'd fly
> To the far-off wilds of Michigan.[3]

Tryxie Tryfle is now introduced. She had been a waitress in the railroad station in Topeka. She and Pastoria met during the cyclone, became engaged, and were dropped in Oz. Always hungry, she frequently talks about food. Tryxie and Pastoria perform a song and dance entitled "The Man Who Stays in Town" (MacDonough/Sloane?) and then exit.

Dorothy and her pet cow, Imogene, now enter. The girl frets that she is lost and that her poor father will miss her. Seeing her house, Dorothy notices that a neighbor's door has blown onto her front porch. On the doorplate is the neighbor's name, Caroline Barry, and on the door is a note, a love song, "To the Princess Within." The Good Witch and the poet Dashemoff now arrive and assume that Dorothy is Caroline Barry. The poet tells the Witch that he loves the girl, and the Witch introduces herself and the poet to Dorothy. She also announces to the Munchkins that the girl is under her special protection and gives her a magic ring, good for two wishes. The ring will also serve to summon the Good Witch in time of need. Unfortunately for Dorothy, the ring's wishes are only effective in the Land of Oz, so Dorothy cannot wish herself home. Before she exits, the Witch suggests that the girl should journey to the Wizard of Oz for help in getting back to Kansas.

Dorothy tells Dashemoff that she is not Caroline Barry but Dorothy Gale. He is unhappy because he wrote his song (the one tacked to the door) for the wrong girl, but Dorothy says she likes it anyway and wishes that she knew it. Suddenly she does know it, having unwittingly used up the ring's first wish. She sings "Carrie Barry" (MacDonough/Sloane):

Airy, fairy, Carrie Barry, will you marry me?

I'm as much in love with you as any man can be;

Night and day for you always I pine, and pine, and pine;

Airy, fairy, Carrie Barry, say, will you be mine?[4]

The poet is called away by General Riskitt, and Dorothy is left alone with Imogene and a scarecrow on a pole. She wishes the scarecrow were alive and, again unwittingly, wastes the power of the wishing ring. The living Scarecrow now asks Dorothy to remove a golf ball from his ear. (The audience apparently is to assume that this is the golf ball lost by the golfer back in Kansas and that the cyclone carried it to Oz.) He then tells her how a farmer made him and did not put in brains. Dorothy helps him down from his pole, and he walks with wobbly legs. When she tells the Scarecrow that she is going to the Wizard to ask him to help her return home, he decides to go with her to request brains. Before he and his new friend exit, he performs "Alas for the Man without Brains" (Baum/Tietjens):

Tho' I appear a handsome man,

I'm really stuffed with straw!

'Tis difficult a man to plan

Without a single flaw.

Tho' you may think my lovely head

A store of lore contains,

The farmer each of skill displayed,

And quite forgot my brains.

When brains are lacking in a head,

It's usually the rule,

That wisdom from the man has fled,

And he remains a fool.

So, tho' my charms are very great,

As I am well assured,

I'll never reach my full estate

Till brains I have secured.

Alas! for the man who has little in his noddle, that he knows

He's under a ban,

And is called a rattlepate where'er he goes;

He always does the very thing he never ought to do;

He stumbles and he fumbles, and is aimless;

A lobster is he,

As anyone with half an eye can see.
You can hear them sneer and jeer,
For his wheels are out of gear,
And it's plain he'll remain quite brainless.[5]

In the next scene, "The Road through the Forest," Dashemoff meets Cynthia, who is still searching for her lost love. The poet ruminates on love in the song "Love Is Love" (Baum/Tietjens):

Though men are all protesting
In accents interesting
A love that's warmer than the summer sun
And passionately pleading
Their tender hearts are bleeding
And you are certainly "the only one!"
'Tis well to take their protestations
With a grain of salt,
They may have said the same sweet thing before,
For all their eloquence
Their pretty compliments
Are quite appropriate to state to ladies by the score.

Love is Love, and cannot be dissembled
Love is Love, and cannot be assumed.
When true love upon your lips has trembled
To its thrall you're quickly doomed!
Love is Love, its signet is devotion
Love is Love, that signet all may read
He who forges love must have a notion
Maiden's [sic] hearts are very innocent and soft, indeed![6]

After Dashemoff and Cynthia leave the stage, Pastoria and his army enter. While Pastoria poses to have his picture taken, roaring is heard offstage, followed by the appearance of the Cowardly Lion. Pastoria ends up taking the Lion's picture before the animal exits. General Riskitt then shows Pastoria a proclamation issued by the Wizard calling for Pastoria's arrest. Pastoria and his army exit.

Dorothy and the Scarecrow now enter and hear moaning from behind some bushes. The Scarecrow discovers that the source of the groans is Nick Chopper, the Tin Woodman, who stands rigid with a fife in position for playing.

Once the Scarecrow oils him, he begins to move and tells his story: He had loved a Munchkin girl named Cynthia, but the Wicked Witch, who forbade love in her domains, had enchanted his axe so that it cut off his arms, legs, and body, each of which a tinsmith then replaced with tin. The Tin Woodman's heart, though lost, had never been replaced. Dorothy invites the Tin Woodman to go with them to the Emerald City to ask for a heart. He accepts and then, accompanied by his new companions, performs "When You Love, Love, Love" (Baum/Tietjens):

> Oh, love's the thing that poets sing
> Their sweetest lays regarding;
> And none say nay to love's gay sway,
> Which wounds when not rewarding.
> Naught can allure the heart so sure
> As one swift dart from Cupid,
> And none, I know, would dodge his bow,
> Unless exceeding stupid.
> 'Tis love that makes the world go 'round
> And makes our lives worth living
> We all are lost till love is found,
> It's [sic] rare enjoyments giving.
>
> When you love, love, love in mad delirium
> When to love, love, love that's quite sincere you come
> There is nothing so divine
> There is nothing half so fine
> As the gladness of your madness
> When you love, love, love![7]

They exit.

Scene 4 reveals "The Poppy Field." The Poppy Queen and a chorus of Poppy Flowers sing "Poppy Chorus" (Baum/Tietjens):

> We are poppies in fairest splendor blooming fragrant always
> Through the mosses and the grasses looming
> Fascinations rare assuming.
> We delight when alone to pass the moments gaily at play
> Ev'ry petal graciously nods our many charms to display.
> For death like a breath, comes to all soon or late
> And mortals are the sport of a mischievous fate
> So welcome the peace that we bring to mankind
> It is happiness to dream on, with ev'ry care left behind.[8]

Dashemoff and Dorothy enter and are soon followed by Pastoria, Tryxie, Imogene, and the Lion, who are posing as members of a circus in order to escape the Wizard's police. The Poppies' perfume causes all to become sleepy and lie down. The Scarecrow and the Tin Woodman arrive and wonder how to wake Dorothy. In her sleep Dorothy calls for the Good Witch, who now appears through the power of the magic ring. She sees what the Poppies have done and is enraged. In vengeance, she calls down the North Wind and the King of the Frost. Snow falls, and the Poppies wilt and die. Then, during a period of darkness, the scene transforms to "The Poppy Field in Winter." A Snow Boy and Snow Girls, with a sleigh and a team of reindeer, are now seen upstage amid the falling snow. As the curtain falls, they are poised to rescue the slowly reviving sleepers.

Act 2 begins with a short scene set at "The Gates of the Emerald City." Private Gruph, the Guardian of the Gate, sings "The Guardian of the Gate" (Baum/Tietjens). Its lyrics emphasize the supposed power and glory of the Wizard and his capital city:

> So gorgeous is the city that if you are wise
> You'll use a pair of goggles to protect your eyes;
> Within his hand the Wizard holds your destiny and fate
> But I'm the man that guards the gate
> The guardian of the gate.
> The gate, the gate, the gate, the gate
> The glitt'ring, glist'ning gate!
> What e'er your name or your degree
> You must defer to my decree
> A person of authority
> The guardian of the gate![9]

Next, a contingent of Relief Guards, led by Leo, their captain, performs to a traditional soldier's marching song called "Hayfoot, Strawfoot." Dorothy, the Scarecrow, and the Tin Woodman now arrive and ask to see the Wizard. The Soldier with the Green Whiskers offers to escort them to Oz. But first the three friends contemplate the rewards that they hope to obtain from their visit in "When We Get What's A'Comin' to Us" (Baum/Tietjens). With their verses intertwining, they sing:

Dorothy: He's going to think!
               As quick as wink!
               I'll get to Kansas' sunny plains!
               I'll see the home that I adore.

Scarecrow:	When I get brains I'm going to think
	When I get brains I'm going to think as man ne'er thought
	before!
	I'll win all arguments quick as wink
	Philosophers all will take to drink because they don't
	know more!
	I'll get my brains!
	I'll life explore!
Tin Woodman:	He's going to think!
	As quick as wink!
	I'll get my heart!
	I'll love once more!
Trio:	When we get what's a'comin' to us
	We'll snap our fingers thus
	We won't do a thing but laugh and sing and skip the string
	and have our fling!
	When we get what's a'comin' to us,
	Our fortunes we'll discuss
	We'll not raise a fuss or kick up a muss
	When we get what's a'comin' to us.[10]

Sir Wiley Gyle enters. He is an old inventor who scorns all magical arts, and hence the Wizard. Warning the trio that the Wizard is a fake, he tells of his plans to overthrow him and take the throne for himself.

In scene 2 the action shifts to the predominantly green "Courtyard of the Wizard's Palace." Here chorus girls perform "Phantom Patrol," a march in which they appear and disappear. The Wizard's Wise Men, followed by Bardo, the Wizard's Factotum, arrive on the scene. Bardo introduces the Wizard of Oz. The ruler is surrounded by the imposing Princess Weenietotts, who is Pastoria's Angel Child, Gentlemen and Ladies of his Court, and Citizens of his land. The Wizard performs magic tricks for the assembled crowd. The chief trick involves a basket: the Wizard's confederate, the Soldier with the Green Whiskers, climbs into the basket; the Wizard then pours acid into it and runs it through with swords, but the confederate emerges unscathed in the end.

Wiley Gyle now tries to denounce the Wizard's tricks as fake, but no one listens and the old inventor is ejected from the palace. To entertain the excited crowd, the Wizard sings "Mr. Dooley" (William Jerome/Jean Schwartz). In several stanzas and choruses, the song boasts about the exploits of Dooley, whom no man, living or dead, could possibly surpass in greatness. One part of the song, for example, tells of Dooley's adventures with Teddy Roosevelt:

> This country never can forget forget we never will
> The way the boys at San Juan they went charging up the
>   hill
> Though Teddy got the credit of that awful bloody fray
> The hero who deserved it and the man who saved the day
>
> 'Twas Mr. Dooley, 'Twas Mr. Dooley
> Like a locomotive up the hill he flew
> Who drove the Spaniards back to the Tanyards
> 'Twas Mr. Dooley ooley oo.[11]

All except the Wizard exit. Cynthia now enters. She thinks that the Wizard is Niccolo and tries to convince him of the fact. He spurns her, and she fires a pistol at him. The Wizard catches the bullet in his mouth, throws it down, and runs off. Cynthia mourns her plight. Then, accompanied by a chorus dressed as witches and carrying brooms, she performs "The Witch behind the Moon" (Louis Weslyn/Charles Albert):

> Up behind de moon dere lives a nigger witch dat prowls
>   around at night,
> Comes a'ridin' down upon a broomstick when de moon
>   don't shine too bright;
> Keeps a'lookin' out for pickininies while she hums a hoo-
>   doo tune
> In de house you better stay,
> So you won't get in de way
> Of de witch behind de moon![12]

Dorothy now joins Cynthia, and the two sing "The Different Ways of Making Love" (L. Frank Baum/Nathaniel D. Mann). A trifle of a song, its lyrics compare the actions of maidens in love with those of little birds and pussycats.[13]

The Scarecrow and the Tin Woodman join Dorothy in order to meet the Wizard. After the Wizard enters, there is much bantering as he concocts brains for the Scarecrow and finds a used heart for the Tin Woodman. When the Wizard says he cannot help Dorothy, she laments having to stay in an awful country. The Wizard announces a great ball in honor of his having fulfilled the wishes of the Tin Woodman and Scarecrow, which he considers his greatest achievement. All exit.

The traveling circus (Pastoria, Tryxie, Imogene, and the Lion) enters. Bardo then arrives, only to learn that the circus does not have a license to perform. He goes to inform the Wizard that he has placed the troupe under arrest. Pastoria then tells Tryxie that he will take back the throne after proving the Wizard of Oz is a humbug. Cynthia appears briefly and threatens all who are assembled with an ax. When Bardo returns, he summons the circus for a royal performance. The circus leaves, but Tryxie lags behind. Alone on the stage with a chorus, she is asked what type of performer she is. She responds that she sings serio-comic songs and performs "Sammy" (James O'Dea/Edward Hutchison) as an example:

> Sammy, oh, oh, oh, Sammy,
> For you I'm pining when we're apart;
> Sammy, when you come wooing
> There's something doing around my heart.
> Sammy, oh, oh, oh, Sammy,
> Can't live without you, my dream of joy;
> Tell me, oh, oh, oh, tell me,
> You're only mine, my Sammy boy.[14]

The Wizard's Ball of All Nations takes place next, providing the context for several contiguous specialty numbers with an ethnic slant. The Tin Woodman performs "Connemara Christening" (Edgar Smith/A. Baldwin Sloane); the Scarecrow, "Spanish Bolero" (Smith/Sloane); the Wizard, "Wee Highland Mon" (Smith/Sloane); and Dorothy and Cynthia, "Rosalie" (Will D. Cobb/Gus Edwards).

After the ball, Pastoria and Tryxie plot to overthrow the Wizard. They give the Soldier with the Green Whiskers knockout drops, and Pastoria disguises himself in the man's clothes. Pastoria and Tryxie exit. Wiley Gyle, who has his own plan to dethrone the Wizard, now enters. Accompanied by a guard and several of the Wizard's subjects, he shows them that the supposed magic basket has a false bottom. Convinced that their leader is a fake, they all agree to rebel against him. After the others exit, Gyle nails up the bottom of the basket to spoil the Wizard's trick. Finally, Gyle himself leaves.

As a comic interlude, the Scarecrow and the Tin Woodman now enter and perform a duet entitled "The Lobster" (also known as "I Was Walking 'Round the Ocean") (Hugh Morton/Gustave Kerker). A nonsensical novelty song, it tells about a talking lobster salad on the bottom of the ocean and a woman who tries to eat a glass window pane. At the completion of the song, the two performers leave the stage.

Now Pastoria (in disguise), Tryxie, Gyle, and the Wizard and his court arrive on the scene. The Wizard asks for a volunteer—his plant—to assist him with another performance of his basket trick. Taking the place of the Wizard's confederate, Pastoria climbs into the basket. But the Wizard sees that the basket has been tampered with, and he pauses. Gyle taunts him to continue. When the Wizard refuses to proceed, Gyle incites the crowd against their ruler. Thus goaded to complete the trick, the Wizard nervously sticks a knife in the basket. At this point, Pastoria falls out and claims the throne. In celebration of the overthrow of the Wizard and the restoration of the crown to Pastoria, the ensemble now sings "The Wizard Is No Longer King" (Baum/Tietjens):

> The Wizard is no longer King,
> Away with him to prison
> We can't put up with such a thing,
> So clap him tight in jail!
> The law upon him we will bring.
> The people have arisen,
> Let no one further to him cling,
> 'Twill be of no avail!

Dorothy, the Scarecrow, and the Tin Woodman are hustled about by the populace as the new order's praises are sung:

> Peace and concord on us now shower their blessings
> No more will strife sound its warlike alarms
> Again will love with tender caressings
> Clasp us gently in its arms.

Amid all the celebration, the Wizard manages to escape in a balloon. The crowd continues to rejoice:

> Come join the frolic
> Come join the throng.
> We'll gladly frolic the whole day long!
> Rejoice for the Wizard is no longer king!
> All you maidens and youths come join in singing.
> Sing out, and let your voices loudly ring
> We'll shout hip, hip, hooray!
> The Wizard's surely down and out
> We now will make dear Pastoria king.
> Come join us and give him a rousing good cheer.

> All hail to Pastoria!
> All hail to Pastoria,
> The greatest monarch that we ever had,
> All hail! All hail![15]

The curtain comes down.

Act 3 takes place in the predominantly red "Domain of the Sorceress," otherwise known as Dreamland. Here Glinda the Good rules from a perch in the sky. Below her are Alerto, her page, as well as the Dreamland Youths, the Dreamland Maids, and the Cavaliers. Dorothy and her companions, who have come to ask Glinda for her help, are joined by the other principals. There is a general resolution of difficulties, including Cynthia's discovery of her lost love Nick Chopper (the Tin Woodman) and the promised return of Dorothy to her home. Amid feasting and celebration, a series of specialty numbers are performed. Dorothy and the chorus perform a romantic song, "I'll Be Your Honey in the Springtime" (Harry Freeman). The Wizard, who also has come to Glinda for help, sings "She Didn't Seem to Mind," also known as "She Really Didn't Mind the Thing at All" (John Slavin/Nathaniel D. Mann).

The Scarecrow and the Tin Woodman then perform yet another comic duet, a "cockney Negro song" called "That's Where She Sits All Day" (Frank Leo). The semi-nonsensical lyrics tell of a lazy woman whom one of the singers is about to marry. The real humor of the song, however, involves a series of bells that ring in the first verse but fail to sound in the second and third verses—to the increasing anger of the singers. The song begins:

> Boys, have you ever seen my Dinah?
> She's got thrown out of Carolina;
> She is as lazy as a coon can be—
> That's where she sits all day.
> The first time I met her it was at a church bazaar,
> I ask'd her if she'd be my little Uamvar,
> She said I'd have to get permission from her Pa—
> Papa said he'd only be too glad.
> Hark those bells! Hark those bells!
> I should like to call your notice to those bells.[16]

After this, the Scarecrow performs "The Traveller and the Pie" (Baum/Tietjens), a comic song about the misadventures of a traveling man. He narrates to a chorus:

> One day a weary traveller walked down a village street
> *Chorus:* Did he?

I think he did!

He thought he'd stop and ask a lady for a bite to eat
    Chorus: Did he?
I think he did!

He knocked upon a door and said in accents so polite:
"I'm very hungry and I hope you'll let me have a bite!"
"Oh, you shall have my pie!" the young wife answered
    with delight
    Chorus: Did she?
I think she did!

Oh, the weary hungry traveller!
The hungry, luckless traveller!
He took one little bite and next minute took to flight,
Oh, the weary luckless hungry traveller.[17]

The show ends with a finale performed by the entire cast.

〰 As produced, *The Wizard of Oz* was obviously very different from Baum's original dramatization and even more different from his original book, retaining only the bare bones of the story. The director, Julian Mitchell, likely demanded and orchestrated the changes—to the extent that the produced script should probably be credited more to him than to Baum or the other collaborators. In general, the Mitchell script displays little in the way of character development. The actions of the various characters in the play are painted in the broadest strokes. Dorothy has a much less significant role than in either Baum's novel or the first script. She is no longer the center of the action, but shares the stage with other principal female characters, such as Cynthia Cynch and Tryxie Tryfle. In addition, she is not formally introduced until well into act 1, and she spends a good deal of the play offstage. Furthermore, Dorothy is changed in other ways. Rather than being a little girl, she is probably a young teenager, but perhaps a bit older than in Baum's first dramatization since she is old enough to be courted by Dashemoff Daily. No longer an orphan, she mentions having a father.

The Scarecrow and the Tin Woodman are still dominant figures, but as characters they are more two-dimensional. Baum's script had made them into essentially a vaudeville team, and Mitchell carried this idea to the extreme. Here their vaudeville-type clowning rather than their vulnerable humanity is what is highlighted.

The role of the Wizard is much diminished in Mitchell's musical. In both the novel and Baum's original script the Wizard undergoes a series of marvelous metamorphoses. Here, he merely performs common magic tricks. Formerly a wondrous trickster character, he is now simply a kind of vaudeville performer. Not only is he in no way impressive or intriguing but he is not particularly likable. In both the novel and first script he is revealed to be a humbug, but he is still essentially beneficent. In Mitchell's musical the Wizard is portrayed as a conniving usurper of the throne rather than an ordinary man who finds himself, by chance, a wizard. Furthermore, when his own power is taken from him, the people of Oz are happy to be rid of him.

As in Baum's first script, there is no Wicked Witch of the West. Also eliminated were several characters that had appeared in Baum's original dramatization, namely, the Forest Witch, the Captain of the Guard, the Queen of the Mice and her army, the Fighting Trees, the Hammerheads, and the Winged Monkeys. Other characters that had played a role in Baum's first script were retained in an altered form. The Wizard's Attendants, for example, become, as they are in the novel, the Ladies and Gentlemen of the Court, while Glinda's Wise Men become the Wizard's Wise Men, and Glinda's Bodyguards become her Cavaliers.

Mitchell and his collaborators also introduced many new characters, several of whom served to change the story's focus. Cynthia Cynch, for one, plays a major role and figures significantly in the action from early in the play. As the Tin Woodman's former paramour, now mad with blighted love, she wanders through the show wreaking havoc. She is also a parody of *Hamlet*'s Ophelia, another woman driven mad by thwarted love. At one point, in fact, she recites her own version of Ophelia's famous mad scene from act 4, scene 5. Rather than referring to the properties of the flowers in her basket, as does Ophelia, she discusses vegetables and fruits: "Here are young spring onions,—they are for insomnia; here's a celery for remembrance,—and here are March strawberries—for—a dollar a box!"[18] Cynthia's lunatic ravings may have provided some comedy and even a bit of pathos, but she also served to complement Dorothy in an interesting way. Whereas the girl from Kansas wanders through Oz searching for her lost home, Cynthia goes looking for her lost love.

Pastoria, another of the newly created characters, is almost the polar opposite of Dorothy. Whereas the cyclone carries Dorothy away from home, it blows him back home. She is confused and innocent, while he is determined and manipulative. Also, the girl from Kansas is mistaken for a princess by the poet when he first meets her, while Pastoria is at first not recognized as royalty. Finally, Dorothy's quest is a purely personal one, while Pastoria's is entirely political.

The other major new characters are much less well defined than Cynthia and Pastoria. Dashemoff functions as a romantic element, a poet who can sing love ballads. Tryxie Tryfle, another romantic character, is little more than sexy decoration. Wiley Gyle is a disgruntled and bumbling old man who serves to add to the political intrigue. The minor characters who were added function basically as plot elements or, at worst, as set dressing. These include the Poppy Queen, the Snow Queen, and the Snow Boy and Snow Girls; the Wizard's attendant Bardo and Glinda's page Alerto; and the military and guard personnel, most notably, the one-man Army of Pastoria, commanded by General Riskitt; the Relief Guards and their captain, Leo; and the Phantom Patrol and their captain.

In creating the final musical, Mitchell and his associates also downplayed or eliminated several important themes that were present in Baum's earlier versions of the story. These include friendship, longing for home, self-discovery, self-reliance, and a young girl's process of maturation as she journeys on a voyage of discovery. In their place are several elements that either were not present or were not elaborated in Baum's novel and his preliminary script.

The idea of romantic love, for example, becomes much more prominent in the Mitchell version. In his original dramatization, Baum had expanded on the Tin Woodman's romantic plight; there, in act 3, the Tin Woodman offers his new heart to several women and finally finds his lost love in Glinda's Captain of the Guard. Mitchell, for his part, went still further with the romance theme in his attempt to make the story more adult. He and his collaborators eliminated the Captain of the Guard, who appears only toward the end of Baum's original dramatization, and in her place created the more central character of Cynthia to function as the Tin Woodman's lost sweetheart. Furthermore, Dorothy was provided with a love interest in the form of Dashemoff Daily. And finally, there are Tryxie and Pastoria, who met during the cyclone and immediately became engaged. Their amorous relationship becomes an element in the musical's comedy. In the context of these three romantic alliances, it is interesting to see Dorothy, Tryxie, and Cynthia as three different aspects of a woman in love. Dorothy represents the romantic virgin, Tryxie the seasoned sexual being, and Cynthia the victim of love gone wrong.

In the Mitchell version of the story, political intrigue and lust for power also become important themes. Baum's first script had small political touches, but Mitchell and his collaborators made these themes a focal point of the narrative, to the extent that Pastoria's and Wiley Gyle's quests for the throne almost overshadow the tale of Dorothy's search for a way back home. This alteration causes Baum's tale to lose a good deal of its uniqueness and to become more derivative of other contemporaneous plays and musicals. More important, it also renders the plot male-driven, whereas in Baum's original tale, as well as in his writings in general, it is females who propel the narrative forward—a fairly unusual thing for the time. Although the Good Witch of the North and Glinda retain some importance in Mitchell's production, their role is basically to resolve difficulties rather than to advance the plot.

The theme of mistaken identity running through the musical was another element supplied by Mitchell and his colleagues. In Baum's novel the people of Oz originally mistook the Wizard, an ordinary American man, for a wise and wonderful sorcerer. That circumstance served as the basis of his power henceforth and explained his actions in the tale. In Mitchell's script, however, the theme of mistaken identity is used as a plot device in a rather formulaic way. Cynthia is mistaken for a witch; Dorothy is mistaken for Caroline Barry; and Pastoria and the Wizard are both mistaken for Cynthia's lost love. Yet none of these situations really affects the main narrative; rather, they amount to a series of small asides that, in the end, are merely another example of the show's derivativeness since the mistaken identity theme was a common one in the literature and theater of the nineteenth and early twentieth centuries.

Although both Baum's novel and his original dramatization were thoroughly American in their sensibility and imagery, there was still a very strong sense that Oz was a mythical fairyland. Several of Mitchell's changes, however, largely blur the distinction between America and Oz. The sense of otherworldliness becomes lost. In the opening scenes, for example, the marked contrast between the gray of Kansas and the colorful landscape of Oz no longer exists. Mitchell's Kansas is a golden and picturesque portrait of a bustling farm disrupted only by nature's fury. This may make it easier to explain why Dorothy likes her home and wants to return there, but it also makes Oz, by contrast, less appealing and less magical. Furthermore, in the musical, Oz is often given American characteristics. For example, Cynthia, we are told, worked as a department-store clerk, hardly an occupation suited to a fairyland. Also, Pastoria scalps tickets to his own coronation as a way to finance his revolution—a parody of the ticket speculation that was well known to the Chicago theatergoing public of the time. And in the song called "Mr. Dooley" the Wizard sings about Teddy Roosevelt. Baum, of course, had included topical references in his dramatization, but many more are present in Mitchell's production.

Many of Mitchell and his collaborators' changes to the narrative probably were made with an eye toward practicality in staging. Instead of the Wicked Witch's magical shoes, for example, the Good Witch gives Dorothy a magic ring, a simpler property and one that is more easily explained, given that the dead Wicked Witch is not seen on the stage in this version of the tale and there is no opportunity for the Good Witch to take her shoes. Likewise, the yellow brick road was eliminated, most likely because it would have been a cumbersome recurring scenic device.

Mitchell altered many of Baum's animal characters too, primarily because of the restrictions and traditions of the stage. In Toto's place is Imogene the cow. This substitution was due, no doubt, to the difficulty of realistically portraying a small dog on stage. One cannot help but feel, however, the influence of Edward Rice's extravaganza *Evangeline*, which premiered in 1874 and played in various revivals for nearly thirty years. That show's cast of characters included a heifer that was a popular-culture icon for many years and would have been fondly recognized by audiences of *The Wizard of Oz*. As for the Cowardly Lion, he was retained, but as in Baum's original script, he is mute, in keeping with the pantomime tradition. Furthermore, even though he is here introduced before the Tin Woodman, he is even less significant a character than in Baum's first dramatization. There is nothing really distinctive about him, and little is made of his cowardice. He has almost nothing to do with Dorothy, the Scarecrow, or the Tin Woodman, but rather is used merely for comic relief, as part of Pastoria's circus. Finally, instead of an army of mice, it is a snowstorm, a standard stage device, that rescues Dorothy from the Poppies.

To a great extent, the various changes Mitchell and company made to Baum's original story serve to dilute the import of that tale. In fact, many of the interpretations that have arisen over the years to explain Baum's novel no longer hold true when applied to the musical. Obviously, for example, the idea that the story is a parable of Populist politics is no longer applicable. Gone is the picture of Kansas as a barren wasteland symbolic of the plight of poor farmers. Also eliminated are the silver shoes and the yellow brick road, which have been taken to symbolize the Populist monetary debates of the time. The view that Dorothy represents a spiritual orphan trying to find her true place in the world is invalidated too since she is no longer an orphan. In addition, Dorothy cannot be taken as a model for the power of positive thinking. Her character lacks real self-determination, and instead she is buffeted about by forces beyond her control. Indeed, she is only able to leave Oz by means of another cyclone, and not, as in Baum's original story, by power already in her possession.

Mitchell and his collaborators minimized much of the story's mythic impact as well. Dorothy is no longer a strong heroic figure in the mythic tradition since her quest is now almost peripheral to the story. She does leave behind one world to journey to another, but since her Kansas is idealized and homey, while Oz is Americanized, there is little contrast between the two. Furthermore,

Dorothy does not really learn anything on her journey, nor does she emerge a richer character for having made it. Finally, although her return home is promised at the end, the audience never witnesses it. With no indication of how Dorothy is able to reintegrate into her previous life, the mythic structure of the narrative is weakened, and there is no real closure to her adventure.

Mitchell did recognize, however, as Baum had in his first script, that the show had to include much humor if it was to succeed. The comedy in both versions is mainly of a popular and obvious variety, often pun-dependent and corny. There is little that is subtle or sophisticated. Some of the jokes in Baum's script did, in fact, make it into the musical that was finally produced, even though they were sometimes slightly reworded. When Dorothy tells the Scarecrow that she is seeking the Wizard to help her get back home, for example, he replies "What, to get back to Kansas? Dottie, why trifle with your luck?" And when Dorothy and the Scarecrow are oiling the Tin Woodman, he apologizes for his bad manners, claiming, "It's a long time since I've been in polite society and I'm still a bit rusty."[19]

Most of the jokes that Mitchell and company added were no more sophisticated. When a hungry Tryxie, for example, tells Pastoria to take her by the hand and lead her to a rare porterhouse steak, he replies, "But I am not playing for that kind of a stake."[20] Also, many of the new characters' names are puns that bespeak their function in the play: Dashemoff Daily, Wiley Gyle, General Riskitt, and Private Gruph. Baum liked puns, but he did not use them for names in either his book or his dramatization even though referential naming was common in the popular literature of the day. In fact, Dorothy's last name, Gale, a pun in its own right, appears for the first time in this Mitchell musical.

Baum was not averse to including topical jokes in his script, but in Mitchell's version they are even more numerous. A bit of political humor is injected, for instance, when the Wizard tells the Scarecrow he is giving him brains of the Mark Hanna variety. Hanna was a Republican senator from Ohio who was well known for his prolabor stance. After the Scarecrow receives the brains, he exclaims, "How I love the poor workingman."[21]

Some of the humor arises out of the action rather than the dialogue. The scene in which the Lion poses for his photograph and one in which Cynthia suddenly comes at several characters with an axe, for example, are clear instances of the absurdist humor that runs through much of the play. Absurdity is, in fact, one of the show's hallmarks. Logic is not a strong factor in the narrative, and what little plot there actually is often becomes hard to follow. Coincidences abound, and it is not always clear why things happen. In some cases the story is built up around, or grows out of, the costumes, the routines, and the music—a standard approach in the musical theater of the day. The idea of the three-ring circus, for example, seems to be little more than an excuse for interesting costumes and comedy bits involving the animal characters. Similarly, the business of Caroline Barry's doorplate merely sets the stage for a song.

Songs certainly were considered to be a large part of the show's appeal, and Mitchell made sure that there would be no shortage of musical numbers. There were twenty-eight in all on opening night, including four instrumental pieces by Tietjens and eight songs composed by Baum and Tietjens. Two of these songs—"Love Is Love" and "The Traveller and the Pie"—had been part of Baum and Tietjens's earlier non-Oz musical, "The Octopus."[22] The former, a love ballad sung by Dashemoff in act 1, did not appear in Baum's first dramatization of the Wizard of Oz story. The latter, a comic specialty number performed by the Scarecrow in act 3, did, but many of its lyrics were later changed for the version of the musical that was actually produced.

Of the other six Baum and Tietjens songs, three could be found in Baum's original Wizard of Oz script: "Alas for the Man without Brains," the comic lament sung by the Scarecrow after Dorothy wishes him to life, was a slightly altered version of the earlier "A Man of Straw"; "When You Love, Love, Love," the number led by the Tin Woodman when he is first discovered, was based on "Oh, Love's the Thing"—the first refrain and chorus are basically the same, but the second refrain is different; and "The Guardian of the Gate," sung by Private Gruph at the beginning of act 2, is essentially the same as the earlier "I'm Here to Keep the People Out." Despite a shared title, "Poppy Chorus" in the Mitchell musical is not the same as "Poppy Chorus" in Baum's script. The two songs are similar in sentiment but have completely different lyrics. "When We Get What's A'Comin' to Us," the act 2 number in which Dorothy, the Scarecrow, and the Tin Woodman contemplate the rewards they hope to obtain from the Wizard, and "The Wizard Is No Longer King," the act 2 finale, did not appear in any form in Baum's original dramatization.

For the most part, the Baum and Tietjens songs add to or comment on the plot, and their focus is clearly on the original story of Dorothy and her friends' quest. The show's other songs, used to fill out the production that Mitchell and his collaborators had devised, are less cohesive in nature. The lyricist and script doctor Glen MacDonough and the composer A. Baldwin Sloane contributed several songs to the show: Cynthia's "Niccolo's Piccolo," Pastoria's "In Michigan," Dorothy's "Carrie Barry," and probably also Pastoria and Tryxie's "The Man Who Stays in Town," an uncredited number. These focus on characters or situations not in Baum's original tale, and they do little to advance the plot as such. In addition, Edgar Smith and A. Baldwin Sloane provided three ethnic songs for the Ball of All Nations suite, which afforded major characters a moment in the spotlight: the Tin Woodman's "Connemara Christening," the Scarecrow's "Spanish Bolero," and the Wizard's "Wee Highland Mon." Two other songs that were written for the show—Baum and Nathaniel D. Mann's "The Different Ways of Making Love" and John Slavin and Mann's "She Didn't Seem to Mind"—were minor numbers.

All of the remaining songs in *The Wizard of Oz* were interpolations, either from other shows or from the world of popular music. Interpolating proven hits to give the characters who performed them a chance to shine was extremely common in musicals of the time. The comic song "Mr. Dooley," for example, the Wizard's first big number, had been a hit in *A Chinese Honeymoon,* a show produced earlier in 1902. It details the unsurpassable achievements of Dooley, an Irishman, who was originally a creation of the American humorist Finley Peter Dunne. A popular-culture icon of the day, the character was well known for his comic pronouncements on current events.

The interpolated songs usually had little, if any, connection to the plot of the show. The Wizard, for example, perhaps performs "Mr. Dooley" to suggest a comparison between himself, a humbug, and the Irishman, with his bluster and blarney. After Cynthia is rejected by the Wizard, she sings "The Witch behind the Moon," perhaps to imply that a woman spurned is like a witch, or perhaps not; the motives are unclear. Tryxie sings the sexy "Sammy" only to provide an example of the serio-comic song that is her specialty as a circus performer. Other interpolations, such as the Scarecrow and the Tin Woodman's nonsense ditty "The Lobster," have even less justification, except that they are meant to entertain the audience.

Ethnic songs were evidently considered to be an integral part of the Ozian landscape, even though, of course, there is no reason why the residents of that land would know them. A testament to the high regard in which the blackface minstrel tradition was still held were the several "coon" songs contained in the score of *The Wizard of Oz:* "The Witch behind the Moon," "Sammy," "Rosalie," "I'll Be Your Honey in the Springtime," and "That's Where She Sits All Day." And then there were the Scottish, Irish, and Spanish numbers in the Ball of All Nations suite.

In creating *The Wizard of Oz* musical, Julian Mitchell drastically altered Baum's original story and his dramatization. In fact, out of Baum's clear narrative he made what seems, in retrospect, to have been a crazy hodgepodge. Yet, the show turned out to be a huge hit with the public. Mitchell evidently knew what audiences of his day expected. Baum himself summarized the situation nicely in a letter he wrote in 1904 to the *Chicago Tribune* in response to rumors in the press that he was not happy with the stage version of his book. He said that at first "I was filled with amazement, indeed, and took occasion to protest against several innovations that I did not like, but Mr. Mitchell listened to the plaudits of the big audiences and turned a deaf ear to my complaints. . . . After 2 years of success . . . I now regard Julian Mitchell's views in a different light. The people will have what pleases them and not what the author happens to favor."[23]

The script, however, is only one part of a production, and in the case of *The Wizard of Oz*, it was the least of Julian Mitchell's contributions. The cast, the staging, the spectacle, and the promotion were what really drew audiences.

Chapter 3

"A Flare of Color"

The Chicago Premiere and the Midwest Tour

 N FEBRUARY 1902, when the major Chicago newspapers ran articles about the signing of contracts for the Wizard of Oz musical, Fred Hamlin was already making claims about the magnitude of the piece. "As regards expenditure for scenery, mechanical effects and dresses," said the producer, "I have given Mr. Mitchell carte blanche to spare no expense that will insure a spectacle to be recognized as a masterpiece."[1] In another interview he said that he intended to produce the musical "in as sumptuous and elaborate manner as money can assure."[2]

By early spring, newspapers were publishing frequent teasers and short articles about the show and the cast that was being assembled. In one such article Hamlin said he had found two well-known comedians to fill the roles of the Scarecrow and Tin Woodman, "upon whom most of the fun depends," but that he was not at liberty to state their names as they were then under contract to other managers.[3] But as other performers were hired, their attributes were trumpeted in the papers. A short article announcing the engagement of John Slavin as the Wizard, for example, listed some of his past successes and went on to say, "In his own peculiar line he has few superiors. The character of the Wizard should prove well adapted to his personality and extravagant methods."[4] Prospective audiences were also told that Anna Laughlin, who was to play Dorothy, had to be released from her recently signed contract with Martin Beck and the Orpheum Circuit in order to join the cast.[5]

The publicity often mentioned Julian Mitchell, stating that his participation was in itself an assurance of quality.[6] The costumes and sets were not left out of the advance press. "The costumes," one article revealed, "will come from a well-known New York firm [John Wanamaker], who have shown a positive genius in arraying the choruses of metropolitan productions in rainbow raiments of silk, twinkling firmaments of jewelry, and fleecy clouds of lace."[7] Lists of the various scenes of the production, along with the artists responsible for painting them, were published, and at least two separate interviews with the chief set designer, Walter Burridge, also appeared.

As the June premiere of *The Wizard of Oz* approached, the pre-opening literature became more elaborate, and posters went up to advertise the coming production.[8] In addition, an eight-page promotional booklet, replete with pictures of selected cast members, was distributed at the Grand Opera House. "Watch for the Date!" it advised, "*The Wizard of Oz* Will Arrive with the June Roses." Calling the show a "new musical extravaganza," it went on to say that the production "has been many months in preparation, and not only represents an unusual expenditure of money, but a proportionate expenditure of brains and talent. . . . Fully a hundred players will be employed in the production and the salaries paid them is in amount without precedent in the annals of summer shows." The booklet also pointed out that although *The Wizard of Oz* was based on a fairy story written for children, "it will be sufficiently spicy and alluring to engross a sophisticated Chicago audience. It is the ambition of the promoters to devise an entertainment that will appeal to play-goers of all ages and all degrees of intellect, to precocious juveniles and to senile cynics as well."[9]

The man responsible for generating much of this pre-opening publicity was Townsend Walsh, the business manager. Walsh was a man of many talents, and his previous work experience was extensive. A graduate of Harvard University, he had been at various times an actor, a drama editor for a newspaper in Albany, a reporter for the *New York World* and the *New York Dramatic Mirror,* and the business manager and advance agent for the actress Minnie Maddern Fiske. In 1901 he had become the press representative for Hamlin's Grand Opera House in Chicago, which led to his position with *The Wizard of Oz.* It was largely because of Walsh, a mastermind at publicity, that the show and its performers became household names.

Poster for the Chicago opening of the musical *The Wizard of Oz* in June 1902. The Poppy Girl costume depicted here is quite different from the one that actually appeared in the show. It is likely that the final costumes had not yet arrived when the artist designed the poster.

Julian Mitchell, the performers, and the scenic designers also were busy behind the scenes, scrambling to have the show ready for its first performance, which was scheduled for 12 June. Rehearsals were long and arduous. The hot Chicago summer was approaching, and theaters were not air-conditioned. And as was the custom, most of the performers were not paid for their services during the rehearsal period. Mitchell gave detailed directions to his actors—Edwin J. Stone, in the role of the cow, for example, was to moo in a frisky rather than a sorrowful way.[10]

For one newspaper Mitchell described his work with the chorus girls: Following discussions with the scenic artist and costume designer, he would begin to stage the girls' numbers. He did not consider it important for them to be able to read music. Instead, he would give the girls a typewritten lyric sheet at the first rehearsal and then "drum the airs into them by constant repetition." As the composer began to teach the girls the songs, Mitchell would observe and think about the staging, making notes on his own copy of the lyrics. "I mark on paper," he said, "just where every girl shall stand and her 'business' during the song. Later on I try to impress my ideas upon them, and carefully explain to them why they do this or do that. Some grasp my ideas at once. Others are not so quick, and require many rehearsals before my ideas are carried out to my satisfaction." "Day after day," Mitchell emphasized, "we rehearse the stage 'business.' Everything has been mapped out beforehand as a rule, but sometimes I figure out the 'business' of a song after the girls are on stage. This means constant rehearsals. It's one of the many reasons I fail to see that stagework should be regarded as a humorous pastime."[11]

For his part, Walter Burridge, the scenic designer, was hard at work with his creations. Well known in Chicago and New York for his work on such productions as *Arizona* (1900), *Francesca Da Rimini* (1901), and *King Dodo* (1902), Burridge maintained a studio in Chicago's Auditorium Theatre. The hydraulic paint frame on which he carried out his designs was said to be unique. The designer's work was painstaking. After reading the manuscript and discussing it with the author, Burridge began to visualize the settings. Once he had a clear idea of all the entrances and exits, he drew a ground plan of each act and all of its scenes. Then he constructed cardboard models for each scene, trying to achieve as much color accuracy as possible. The models and the ground plan for each scene were done on a scale of one-half inch to a square foot. Subsequently, Burridge used them to construct the final sets. The time allotted for their completion, however, was insufficient for him to work on all of the sets, and he assigned some of the scenes to assistants.[12]

The week before the 12 June opening was hectic. Three theaters were uti-

Julian Mitchell instructs the chorus on the last day of rehearsals for the Wizard of Oz musical (*Chicago Inter Ocean,* 15 June 1902).

lized in preparing the show. As Burridge and his assistants worked on the drops and the scenery at the Grand Opera House, Julian Mitchell rehearsed all the principal performers at the New American Theatre. Mitchell's brother Charles, the show's stage manager, rehearsed the chorus at the Studebaker Theatre.

Meanwhile, seats for the show went on sale on 9 June, with ticket prices ranging from $.25 to $1.50.[13] Newspapers reported brisk business. Before noon, the receipts exceeded $1,600.[14] Throughout the day there was a line at the box office, which recorded what supposedly was the largest sale for a local production in the history of the Grand Opera House.

Despite the good advance sale and the best efforts of the cast and crew, *The Wizard of Oz* was not ready to open on 12 June. A two-day postponement was announced. The official reason given was that Glen MacDonough was doing some last-minute tinkering with the libretto. When the show was postponed a second time, until Monday, 16 June, the newspapers announced that the costumes had been late in arriving and that, incidentally, "some of the performers were not sufficiently up on their work."[15]

Instead of signaling trouble to prospective audiences, the two postponements only served to further stimulate their curiosity. Still, the public must have been relieved to see the following advertisement in several 15 June newspapers: "Tomorrow Night . . . Sure Thing. Curtain Rises at 8 Sharp With a Kansas Cyclone—Don't Get Blown Away In It. A Charming Combination of Fun and Fancy! Harmony and Humor! Scenic Marvels! Cast of 75 People! Mostly Girls!

. . . Girls! Girls! Girls! Beauties! Beauties! Beauties!" And indeed, on 15 June a final dress rehearsal took place. Paul Tietjens's sister, Olga Dammert, recalled years later that the rehearsal had gone smoothly, although it had lasted well beyond two o'clock in the morning, the time she and her husband left.[16]

When *The Wizard of Oz* finally opened on 16 June, the Grand Opera House was thronged with people. Dammert, who attended, later recalled: "It was a huge well-dressed crowd, very enthusiastic and the weather fine—no misadventures. I have forgotten how many curtain calls. . . . The thing that impressed me was that the audience on leaving the theatre and for blocks and blocks on their way home whistled the songs of the opera. . . . My husband remembered every word of the whole score and sang it frequently."[17]

Baum's son Frank Joslyn Baum, who was about nineteen years old at the time of the opening, also recalled the excitement of that first night: "The house was packed, with people standing in the aisles at rear and behind last row of seats. . . . Father was dressed in an ordinary business suit. . . . He and mother were in one of the boxes while I, with my brother, had a seat on the lower floor. Father was very nervous before the show and tried very hard not to let it be evident—and aside from those who knew him intimately, none were aware of the fact."[18]

After the second act, according to his son, Baum recognized that the show was going to be a hit, largely because of the work of David Montgomery and Fred Stone, the actors who played the Tin Woodman and the Scarecrow. During intermission Baum went backstage to Fred Hamlin's office to recommended that the producer sign up the two actors for a five-year run. Hamlin agreed. Then, at the end of the show there was "a tremendous and insistent clamor of 'Author—author.'" At this point Baum slipped from his box and went onto the stage. There, said his son, he gave "a delightfully whimsical little speech of thanks." The text of Baum's speech was printed in the newspapers:

Kind friends, thank you for your enthusiasm. It is heart-warming. You have been generous enough to call for the author, but I do not need to remind you that he is only one of many whose efforts you are enjoying tonight. If you will pardon a homely comparison, our play is like a plum pudding, which combines the flavor of many ingredients. The author contributes only the flour—necessary, of course, but only to hold the other good things together.

What would *The Wizard of Oz* be without the spice of Paul Tietjens' wonderful music or the brilliant scenery of Walter Burridge; the skill of that master stage chef Julian Mitchell; the golden touch of Manager Fred Hamlin, and above all, our agile comedians Dave Montgomery and Fred Stone, and the plums and peaches of our talented stage company? All of us are happy you have enjoyed the show, and we hope that you and your friends will be back for a second helping.[19]

Baum's talk, according to his son, was enthusiastically applauded, and he had to reappear before the curtain several times. Afterward, "the house emptied very slowly as though the people hated to leave the atmosphere where they had been so enchanted."

That the opening night was a success with the audience is not in doubt, and word of mouth soon spread that a new hit had opened at the Grand. The critical response was generally positive. Many of the reviews, however, called for trimming, as the premiere lasted until 12:20 A.M. Changes were made almost immediately. Mitchell assembled the cast the following day and cut about forty-five minutes' worth of material. Gone entirely, for instance, was the character of Princess Weenietotts. By the end of June, the *New York Dramatic Mirror* reported, the final curtain was coming down at 11:15.[20] Over the next few weeks the performers continued to hone their roles. Several articles mentioned that the show was running much more smoothly than on the opening night and that the performances had improved.

The show sold out week after week. On some nights, as many people were turned away for lack of tickets as were admitted. Because of the extraordinary demand, tickets could be purchased four weeks in advance, which was unusual at the time. Even the summer heat was unable to deter crowds, and on the hottest nights the theater was filled to capacity. At the Wednesday and Saturday matinees too, "standing room only" signs were generally posted. As one newspaper remarked, "The bulk of the theatre-going population would apparently rather die of asphyxiation at the Grand than just manage to breathe elsewhere."[21] When the weather required, all twenty-four exit doors were kept open during the performance.

Needless to say, *The Wizard of Oz* was extremely popular with children and families. It broke attendance records at the Grand and became one of the most profitable shows mounted in Chicago up to that time. Its weekly gross receipts averaged more than $12,000, then a large sum, and it had more than recouped its production costs by the seventh week of its Chicago run. By the time *The Wizard of Oz* ended its engagement on 20 September 1902, after 125 performances in fourteen weeks, the show had been seen by 185,000 people, and gross receipts had amounted to $160,000. Only two performances saw box-office takes of less than $1,000, and the show never played to a losing house.[22]

The numerous reviews of the show, along with publicity pieces, programs, and manuscript musical scores, give us a sense of how *The Wizard of Oz* was staged during its initial run at Chicago's Grand Opera House.[23] Most critics noted the opulence and visual splendor of the production; Amy Leslie, for example, called the show a "gorgeous spectacle" with "resplendent costumes and scenic painting." "Money fairly drips from the gorgeous walls and skies of the Emerald City and the land of the Munchkins," she commented, "and from the costly robes of the pretty girls and amazing atmospheres of silver mists and golden lights. Lavishness combined with taste both cultivated and bountiful lock arms and fairly swagger imperially through 'The Wizard of Oz.'"[24]

The show's color scheme especially attracted the attention of the critics. The critic Leone Langdon-Key called the show "a flare of color. . . . Nothing in the palette of the scene painter was omitted, and the contrasts were not the delicate, shimmery type that fade from memory with a night's sleep. They were the indelible kind that will endure hot suds and a common laundry soap, and stand fast."[25] "Mr. Burridge has been venturesome," raved another observer, "in going out of the beaten path in the painting of his scenery, employing tones and tints that have not been used as often as would appear advisable and advantageous, the colors employed being always the same as, or at least in harmony with, the costumes of the people."[26] Although a wide array of colors was seen in the scenery, costumes, and lighting, the Country of the Munchkins was primarily blue; the Emerald City, green; and the domain of Glinda, red—in keeping with Baum's original conception.

The show's first scene, "A Kansas Farm," was painted by Fred Gibson from designs by Walter W. Burridge. It had a golden tint, augmented by the lighting, to reflect autumnal sunshine.[27] An extant newspaper photograph shows the farm scene as the cyclone is about to hit. A set piece depicting the front of the Gale farmhouse stands at the left side of the stage. It is two stories high with a dormer window, a chimney, and a porch. The front yard is enclosed by a white picket fence. Cut-out flats depicting trees and vegetation can be seen at either end of the scene. Hay wagons stand at the center of the stage near the rear. The painted backdrop shows flat farmland and the horizon.[28]

The following scene, "The Country of the Munchkins," was painted by Herbert Martin from designs by Burridge. A photograph of this setting reveals a large painted castle with turrets in the right distance and a small painted windmill slightly left of center. The outline of various forms of vegetation can be made out at the right. In the center of the stage is a large maypole. Little else of the scenery is visible in the cropped picture.[29]

The final scene in act 1, "The Poppy Field in Winter," painted by Burridge, had a setting of snow-covered vegetation, depicted through a backdrop and flats. Near the center was a ramp leading from the rear of the stage to the front. Down it came the sleigh that rescued Dorothy and her friends.[30]

The Orientalist "Courtyard of the Wizard's Palace," painted by Burridge for act 2, was quite ornate, probably inspired by W. W. Denslow's Moorish interpretation of the Emerald City in his illustrations for Baum's novel.[31] The painted backdrop shows a skyline of elaborate towers, turrets, and domes. Two large pseudo-Egyptian seated figures can be seen in the center of the drop. At the left was located a two-stepped platform on which sat the Wizard's throne. Above the throne was a decorated domed canopy ringed with large tassels.[32]

Unfortunately, no photographs are known to survive of the remaining scenes—"The Road through the Forest," painted by Gibson from designs by Burridge; "The Poppy Field" painted by Burridge; "The Gates of the Emerald City," painted by the Daniels Scenic Company from designs by Burridge; and "The Domain of the Sorceress" (also known as "Dreamland"), painted

"The Country of the Munchkins" (act 1, scene 2) (*Theatre Magazine,* August 1902). Dorothy stands at the far left, while Munchkins dance around a maypole. The Scarecrow can be seen in the center background.

by Burridge.[33] Several reviewers commented on the visual splendor of "The Domain of the Sorceress," the show's final scene. A built-up set lit with "hundreds of incandescents," it was a study in pink and rose, featuring Glinda's palace, with waving trees and lotus flowers.[34]

The scene showing the Kansas farm and the ensuing cyclone was one of several scenes repeatedly singled out by the critics. In fact, several articles warned prospective audiences to arrive at the theater on time so as not to miss the spectacular special effect of the storm. The scene's action was performed without dialogue, but there was musical underscoring. Dorothy and her cow, Imogene, played near her house. On the other side of the stage an old man read a newspaper. Farm hands worked in the field nearby, and women toiled over washpans. A horse with a hayrack was driven onto the stage, and some farm girls threw apples and wisps of hay at it. A golfer in search of a lost golf ball jumped over a stone wall, but instead of finding the missing ball, he began

Most of the cast assembles in "The Courtyard of the Wizard's Palace" (act 2, scene 2) (*Chicago Inter Ocean,* 22 June 1902). The characters in the foreground are (*left to right*): Princess Weenietotts (?), the Wizard, the Tin Woodman (wearing a sailor's outfit), Wiley Gyle, the Scarecrow, Dorothy, Pastoria, Tryxie, and Dashemoff.

flirting with one of the girls. Suddenly a rumble of thunder was heard, and the old man pointed toward an approaching storm. The horse was stowed away in the barn, and the people ran for cover.

The stage lights now slowly dimmed, and in a moment of total darkness, amid the sound of cymbals and kettledrums, a gauze screen was lowered. In the balcony, a magic lantern equipped with rotary slides was used to project the whirling cyclone onto the screen. In the original novel, W. W. Denslow had illustrated the storm lifting up the farmhouse, a cart, and some hay, but Julian Mitchell elaborated on this by also using the lantern to show Dorothy, her house, and Imogene—as well as all manner of other people, buildings, animals, and objects—flying through the air.

When the lights went up again, the scene had changed to the Country of the Munchkins, where a chorus of Munchkins, dressed in blue, were seen posed about a maypole. There was a brief dance before the cyclone approached and the Munchkins fled. The lights went out again, and when they came up, Dorothy's Kansas farmhouse, the worse for wear, now appeared in the midst of the Munchkins' country. This whole cyclone scene lasted between fifteen and twenty minutes.[35]

The scene in act 1 depicting the coming to life of the Scarecrow was also staged in such a way as to take the audience by surprise. While Dorothy and the chorus were singing "Carrie Barry," two stagehands dressed as farm hands quietly carried the Scarecrow onto the rear of the stage and placed him on a stile behind a set wall. Most of the audience was distracted by the musical number and did not pay much attention to the Scarecrow's arrival.

Fred Stone, who played the Scarecrow, took great pride in his ability to remain absolutely still for the duration of Dorothy's song, which often included several encores. One reviewer noted that "when Mr. Stone is first lifted on the stage and leaned against the stile very few believe that the figure is that of a live man. They think it to be a rag dummy, a veritable scarecrow, and nearly all of those in the audience who are witnessing the extravaganza for the first time are convinced that this manikin will presently be replaced, to the accompaniment of some hocus-pocus, by the real man so essential to the play. Thus, when Dorothy rubs the magic ring and the figure exhibits signs of life there is a gasp of astonishment all over the theatre."[36]

By far the most impressive and most admired scenes, however, were the two Poppy scenes at the end of act 1. Critics and audiences alike were rapturous about them.[37] After Dorothy and the Scarecrow discovered the Tin Wood-man, the three friends sang one of the show's hits—"When You Love, Love, Love"—close to the apron of the stage. At the conclusion of the number, they exited and the stage went dark. Next, the spectators began to see vague forms behind a gauze curtain. Rain fell gently, and as one newspaper reviewer described it, "through the rain we discern, faintly at first, a field of poppy flowers of gigantic size. The rain ceases, the sun rises, and a golden glow fills the atmosphere and emphasizes the scarlet of the flowers, which now, raising their heads in the grateful sunshine are discovered to be young and graceful women."[38] They sang the "Poppy Chorus."

Dorothy and Dashemoff entered. They were soon followed by Pastoria, Tryxie, the Cowardly Lion, and Imogene the cow, all four of whom were posing as a traveling one-ring circus. Pastoria, dressed as a lion tamer, and Tryxie, costumed as an equestrienne, engaged in some circuslike antics with the Lion and Imogene. The Poppies now began to sway their heads, and the characters onstage lay down in the field and fell asleep. The Scarecrow and the Tin Woodman entered, and Dorothy, in her sleep, summoned the Good Witch, who immediately appeared. Angered at what the Poppies had done, she railed against them for defying her power and called upon the cold winds of the frozen North to come and kill the flowers and revive the humans. Now a transformation scene began. As the Good Witch invoked the North Wind and the King of the Frost, shadows started to fall over the stage. Soon darkness covered the scene and snow came down. When light broke again, the flowers were gone, and the entire field was covered with snow. A team of reindeer hitched to a sleigh driven by a Snow Boy and Snow Girls was poised at the back of the stage. They stood ready to whisk the reviving Dorothy and her friends away to the Emerald City. The ensuing blackout marked the end of act 1.

The Poppy scenes were achieved through a deft blending of lights, costuming, and properties. The gauze curtain became totally opaque when the stage behind it was dark, and the rain, the snow, and the sunbeams that appeared at various points in the scene were projected on it. Revolving magic-lantern discs were employed for the effects, just as they had been in the cyclone scene. Most of the flowers were chorus girls wearing green dresses and large red poppy hats. But to make the field appear to be full of blooms, artificial poppies on wobbly green stems supplemented the living flowers. Stagehands made the artificial flowers sway by manipulating strings attached to them. Green grass and trees were suspended from the flies. As the frost was summoned and the lights became dim, the women of the Poppy chorus slowly sank to the floor until only their large red hats were visible. Then, when the stage went dark, they ran off, and the projected image of falling snow was seen on the gauze curtain. Drops were quickly raised to the flies and their all-white counterparts lowered to the stage while the reindeer team assumed its position. As the lights came back on, the snow gradually stopped and the audience suddenly found itself in the middle of winter.

The cyclone and the Poppy scenes framing act 1 were the greatest scenic triumphs that *The Wizard of Oz* had to offer. But the costumes, designed by Will R. Barnes and executed in New York by John Wanamaker, received much praise for their splendor and vibrancy and also were an important part of the show's appeal. Although W. W. Denslow apparently was not directly involved in designing them, several of the costumes, especially those of the Scarecrow and the Tin Woodman, were inspired by his book illustrations. To acknowledge his influence, beginning in August 1902 he was named in the program as the designer of the "character costumes."

The number of costumes in the production is not known, but we do know that there were more than 150 wigs alone.[39] The apparel of some of the characters is documented in photographs and newspaper reviews.[40] In act 1, for example, Dorothy wore an outfit that presented her as both innocent country girl and alluring young woman. It consisted of a short-sleeved, off-the-shoulder polka-dotted dress with a ruffled hem, a solid-colored apron at the waist, and a hat with trailing bands. Tryxie looked very much the part of the waitress. Her light-colored dress had a pleated and ruffled skirt that was mid-calf length. A ruffled apron ran down the front of her dress, dark stockings covered her legs, and a cap with a large bow sent a trail of fabric streaming down her back. Pastoria wore a motorman's uniform consisting of a short double-breasted jacket with matching pants, light-colored spats, and a tall brimmed cap.

In act 2 one of Dorothy's costumes consisted of an ankle-length dress, again worn off the shoulder, with ruffles and bows decorating the skirt.[41] Dashemoff's ensemble was one of the more ornate in the show, perhaps more fitting for a royal personage than for a poet laureate. It featured an embroidered, tight-fitting bodice adorned with tassels and jewels, as well as an ample ornamented floor-length cape. He wore tights and high-laced boots and a plumed, jewel-trimmed hat. Tryxie's equestrienne disguise included a sleeveless, tight-fitting embroidered tunic with a knee-length mini-pleated skirt over dark tights. On her head she wore an embroidered cap with a flap of silk falling down at the side. Wiley Gyle sported striped knickers, a velvet tunic tied with a large belt buckle, an oversized waistcoat, and turned-down boots. He wore a wig with sparse hair and also had whiskers under his chin.

As for the Wizard in act 2, his varied costumes tended toward the comical. One of his outfits consisted of a green magician's robe decorated with lobsters in repoussé. Over this he wore an elaborate cape with oversized hanging sleeves made to resemble lobster claws. A large pointed cap, also decorated

Neil McNeil as
Pastoria, the
motorman, and
Mabel Barrison as
Tryxie Tryfle, the
waitress. Here they
pose in their act 1
costumes.

Tryxie disguised as a
circus equestrienne
in act 2.

Stephen Maley as
Sir Wiley Gyle, a
conspirator bent on
exposing the
Wizard's hokum.

with a lobster design, adorned his head.[42] Lobsters, mentioned in the songs "Alas for the Man without Brains" and "The Lobster," were a recurring motif in the show, apparently because they were comical in their clumsiness. Another of his get-ups included an oversized light-colored tuxedo with tails, a dark vest, white gloves, and, on his head, a tiny derby. And for the Ball of All Nations he wore a traditional Scotsman's outfit complete with a tartan kilt. Throughout, his facial appearance was exaggerated to the point of being grotesque—he had a bulbous nose, a bald pate with wild hair at the sides, and a tuft of hair under his chin.

Little is known about the costumes in act 3. They did emphasize a rose palette, and Glinda wore a shimmering dress with lacework.[43]

The most unique and most popular costumes in the show were those of the Scarecrow and the Tin Woodman. Fred Stone, who worked on creating his own outfit, patterned much of his appearance on the way the Scarecrow had been described and illustrated by Baum and Denslow. He wore a blue shirt and blue trousers, both of which were stuffed with real straw so that bits of straw protruded from various parts of his body. Pieces of rope around his waist, wrists, and ankles; a large floppy hat; and oversized white gloves completed the outfit. His clothes, however, were much more tattered than those of the Scarecrow in Baum's book. Stone, in fact, worked hard to cover them with tears, patches, and repairs. "It took me three hours to get 'em so you could make consomme out of 'em," the actor said about his garments. "I tore and wore and smeared and mended till they began to show up right."[44]

Stone discarded as unsatisfactory the white circus-clown skullcap that he had been given and instead made himself a tight-fitting cap of chamois skin, which he painted pink with rough stitches and then varnished. Nightly, he covered his face with thick layers of a pinkish greasepaint, making sure to obliterate all traces of eyebrows and eyelashes. With black greasepaint, he first painted stitches around his face and head to simulate sewn cloth and then added circles for eyes, one much larger than the other, just as in Denslow's illustrations. In addition, he drew one eyebrow higher than the other. After painting a black triangle on his nose, he blackened his mouth so that it appeared to be merely a slit in the cloth.[45]

The Tin Woodman's costume was no less complex. Originally Julian Mitchell ordered a suit of armor for the character, but Dave Montgomery was not able to dance in it. So an outfit inspired by Denslow's illustrations was made from leather covered with silverine, a type of silver plating. For ease of movement there were openings at the elbows, shoulders, knees, ankles, and crotch. Through the openings could be seen the cloth covered with silver spangles that Montgomery wore against his limbs and torso. Disks indicated the joints, and silver boots and gloves covered his hands and feet. The funnel-shaped hat atop his head was made from real tin. Unlike the Tin Woodman drawn by Denslow, however, he also wore a biblike collar piece fitted around the base of his head. Montgomery used white greasepaint as a base for his face makeup and painted on a pair of irregularly shaped eyebrows. He drew streaks of black around his eyes, nose, and mouth and a large streak of red over his lips.[46]

In addition to their basic costumes, the Scarecrow and the Tin Woodman also had occasion to don other outfits on top of their basic ones. In act 2, for instance, for the number "The Lobster" they dressed in exaggerated nautical outfits. The Tin Woodman's outfit had typical white bell-bottoms, but the Scarecrow's featured unusual tights decorated with playing cards.[47]

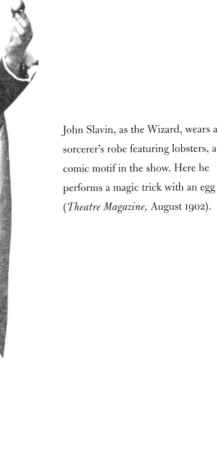

John Slavin, as the Wizard, wears a sorcerer's robe featuring lobsters, a comic motif in the show. Here he performs a magic trick with an egg (*Theatre Magazine,* August 1902).

The costuming of the choruses and minor characters was interesting as well. The Munchkin Maidens, for example, wore dresses of delft blue and white and pointed hats, while the Munchkin Youths sported blue short pants, long sashed overshirts, and wide-brimmed hats. The Snow Girls wore white satin dresses trimmed with sequins and a multitude of balls of white fur. The Ladies and Gentlemen of the Wizard's Court wore green pierrot costumes.[48]

The two animal costumes were commendable in their attention to detail but were strictly in the tradition of the great London pantomimes. The head of Imogene the cow was made of papier-mâché and had flexible jaws and oscillating eyes operated by a string. One reviewer called the effect "startlingly real."[49] The costume worn by Arthur Hill as the Lion was a much more elaborate affair. It reputedly weighed eighty pounds and was said to have been modeled after a study of a lion's head done by the artist Rosa Bonheur. The costume consisted of two pieces, a head and mane section and a large body section made from a lion skin. Hill's arms were fitted tightly into the front legs of the torso and could not be removed unless the head was first lifted off. The actor was able to peer out from the Lion's mouth, which could be opened by pulling a string. Other strings moved the eyes, ears, and tongue. (The sound of roaring was simulated from the wings by a stagehand who rubbed a large piece of resin up and down a stout cord fastened at one end to the center of a drumhead stretched over a barrel.) Hill stated that the Cowardly Lion was the most strenuous role he ever had to play because the costume was so heavy and elaborate.[50]

No matter how dazzling the costumes, it was the performers who carried the show. Dave Montgomery and Fred Stone, who had been an established comedy team before appearing in *The Wizard of Oz*, received the most attention. Audiences and critics alike were especially lavish in their praise for Stone's impersonation of Baum's brainless Scarecrow. They raved especially about his fluid movements and rubbery legs, which always seemed to be giving way beneath him. In Baum's original novel the Scarecrow trips over holes in the yellow brick road because he lacks the sense to walk around them. But Stone, in a brilliant interpretation of his part, had the Scarecrow flop all around the stage, as was appropriate for a creature without joints.

Amy Leslie summed up Stone's appeal: "His make-up, his wonderful command of every expression, every muscle, every queer tone and a perfect fusillade of brand-new steps, acrobatic tumbles and his famous repartee quick as a flash, were revelations, and his immense hit substantiated the suspicion that Fred Stone was the greatest burlesque comedian of the generation."[51] Audiences reportedly could not get enough of him when he was on stage. Writing years after the fact, noted critic Burns Mantle recalled that the Scarecrow was

John Slavin, as the Wizard, in two of his comical costumes:
his formal attire and his Scottish outfit for the Ball of All
Nations.

Fred Stone as the Scarecrow, David Montgomery as the
Tin Woodman, and Anna Laughlin as Dorothy showing
off their act 1 costumes in a posed studio photograph.

originally envisioned as a semi-pantomime role with little dialogue. However, after Stone's opening night success the character's lines were built up.[52]

A circus performer, acrobat, dancer, and minstrel performer, Stone first performed with minstrel comic Dave Montgomery in 1894. The two men were inseparable professionally for the next twenty-two years, until Montgomery's death in 1917. As a team they were a popular attraction in vaudeville before landing parts in the musical comedy *The Girl from Up There* in New York in 1901. The story of how they were engaged for *The Wizard of Oz* has several variants, but according to Stone himself, he and Montgomery were about to leave New York to appear in a pantomime in Liverpool, England, when he met Julian Mitchell on the street. Mitchell, who had directed *The Girl from Up There,* told him that he had him in mind to play the Scarecrow in a musical based on Baum's book but that the show was not yet firmly set for production. Once the team was in England, Mitchell wired them that he wished to engage Stone for the part of the Scarecrow and Montgomery for the character of Sir Wiley Gyle. Stone was anxious to play the role, but Montgomery was less than thrilled with his part because it offered little opportunity to perform specialties with his partner. He asked Mitchell if he could play the Tin Woodman instead, but the director thought he would not be right for the part as he conceived it. Nevertheless, Stone talked his partner into going back to America and giving the Oz musical a try.

Early rehearsals did nothing to change Montgomery's mind, however, and he complained to Stone. Finally, the two men went to Mitchell and told him that they would both leave unless Montgomery could play the Tin Woodman. Mitchell relented, and his decision turned out to be a crucial one.[53] If Montgomery's performance did not quite match the manic intensity of Stone's, it was nonetheless sensational. His broad grin and creaky movements rendered him at once funny and endearing. Amy Leslie called him the "gentlest philosopher" and labeled his contortions in the scene where his limbs are oiled "astonishing."[54]

The two men together were even more than the sum of their parts. Audiences went wild for their antics, and night after night they received more applause than anyone else in the cast. Their characterizations were regarded as new stage creations, the likes of which had never before been seen. "Montgomery and Stone," said the *Chicago Tribune,* "are pioneers in absolutely original comedy."[55] Another review added that the pair "have made personal hits which have seldom been surpassed in this sort of production. They have originated roles which . . . could have had very little in them at the outset that the librettist was responsible for."[56]

Other performers, of course, contributed to the evening's entertainment. On the whole, Anna Laughlin was much praised for her interpretation of Dorothy Gale. Laughlin was only about fifteen years old in 1902, but she was already something of a stage veteran, having performed in stock, vaudeville, minstrelsy, and musical comedy. "Miss Anna Laughlin," said Amy Leslie, "pretty as a doll and dressed exactly like one, all grace and spirit, earnest absorption and modest intentness, was a twinkling little star all by herself. Her songs were made delightful by her personality, her dainty feet, cunning ways and true small voice and by her becoming simplicity. Her comedy was trim and fetching and she shone a charming figure in every scene."[57] Others called her "exquisite," "captivating," "innocently naive," and "elfin."[58] But not everything about her was praised, in particular not her rather slight voice. Delancey M. Halbert, who reviewed the show's premiere, noted that her "nasal, tinny tones" were almost "painful at first." Hers was not the only poor voice, he felt. Halbert went on to note that "a serious defect in the organization is the absence of voices; in the feminine contingent there is not a single good singer."[59]

Helen Byron as Cynthia was, for the most part, seen as agreeable in terms of appearance, dancing, and acting and was praised for taking her part seriously, playing it as a legitimate role rather than as a stock musical-comedy turn. But her "trembly throaty voice" left a lot to be desired.[60] Her singing, in combination with Anna Laughlin's, produced what one observer called "such a concord of unmusical gurgles that one hardly knows whether to smile or to shrink."[61]

If *pretty* was the adjective most often used to describe Mabel Barrison, who played Tryxie, her voice fared less well. One reviewer claimed that "she will never take the prize in a vocal contest, even though she performed one of the most popular songs in the show, 'Sammy.'"[62] In the first part of August, Barrison left for another show, and Grace Kimball, who had been a chorus member, replaced her. Kimball received mixed reviews for her performance, although the consensus was that she had a better singing voice than her predecessor.

In classic burlesque style, Bessie Wynn played the male role of Sir Dashemoff Daily *en travestie*. Unanimously praised for her beauty and her shapely figure, she also was found generally wanting in the vocal department. "Shapely Bessie Wynn is the Poet Laureate of fairyland and does his looks credit," wrote one reviewer, "but poets should not be allowed to sing unless they have good voices and are well trained."[63] Aileen May, who played the Good Witch of the North, was spared a critique of her singing, as she, like Doris Mitchell in the role of Glinda, did not have a musical number. The critics, in general, however,

Grace Kimball as a Snow Girl, a character in the act 1 finale.

Arthur Hill poses with his Cowardly Lion costume, which was reported to weigh 80 pounds. The head supposedly was modeled after a study of a lion's head by the celebrated artist Rosa Bonheur.

felt that May declaimed too much. As for Mitchell, one critic noted that the tall, pretty performer was "studious, serious and spoke her lines with even music and charming calm."[64]

The musical numbers allotted to the female principals in *The Wizard of Oz* were mostly ballads and love songs, requiring some vocal skill, but most of the men's songs were comic specialties, for which good voices were not so crucial. Before the show's opening, John Slavin, who played the title role, was the top-billed star. He had been a favorite in vaudeville and musical comedy and was well known for his dialect comedy. But on opening night it was apparent to all that Slavin, playing the Wizard straight, was vastly overshadowed by Montgomery and Stone. Indeed, the critics who reviewed the opening found Slavin's performance disappointing but put much of the blame on the role, which they found lacking. However, the actor's rendition of "Mr. Dooley," which he performed with an Irish accent, accompanied by a buck and wing, was a hit with audiences. His rendition of "Wee Highland Mon," done with a Scottish accent, further allowed him to display his skill with dialects.

In a post-performance interview Slavin lamented: "I guess I haven't got the goods this time. They hardly knew I was there. If there is a man in this town who will 'write up' that part for me and make something out of it I'll pay him $200. Next week I'll try it in Dutch and Irish dialects. Maybe they'll like it better."[65] In subsequent performances he managed to gain better reception for his part by altering the makeup and by in fact playing the Wizard with a Dutch dialect (in the stage parlance of the time, the word *Dutch* was used to describe any kind of German accent).

Toward the end of August, Slavin left the show and was replaced by Bobby Gaylor. Celebrated as an Irish comedian, Gaylor changed the Wizard into a stage Irishman. He also reworked the character's makeup, replaced some of his predecessor's jokes with his own, and introduced a number of new verses into the "Mr. Dooley" number.[66] His first appearance in the role took the house by storm, and the critics praised both his dancing and his physical comedy. In reference to his performance of "Mr. Dooley," one reviewer remarked that "while Slavin's fine voice is missed Gaylor delivers the song with such simple humor and cleverness that encore after encore followed the lively Irish ditty."[67]

Reviewers generally considered the parts of Sir Wiley Gyle and Pastoria underdeveloped. In fact, they usually totally overlooked the performance of Stephen Maley in the small role of Gyle. As for Neil McNeil, who played Pastoria, they felt his part gave him little opportunity to shine. The actor reportedly was not satisfied with the role himself. When Slavin announced that he would be leaving the show to honor a previous commitment, McNeil, who was also

Slavin's understudy, probably expected to be awarded the part. Failing to get it, he also decided to leave the show. By 17 August Carlton King had taken over as Pastoria, but he was not favorably reviewed. One critic summed up the consensus about both him and his predecessor when he wrote, "Carl King has taken the place of McNeil and is about as bad a substitute as could be caught by a carelessly thrown net compassing the incompetent actors. McNeil was tolerably bad before he quit, but King is worse. At least the other man had talent if he did most inartistically grow slow and slovenly toward the last, when he knew he was going away."[68]

As for the animal impersonators, Edwin J. Stone, Fred's brother, received much praise as Imogene the cow. "The heavy lumbering walk of Bossy, the slowness with which she follows the heroine, little Dorothy, about the stage and the swaying motion of the head are all most closely reproduced," noted one reviewer.[69] In one particularly popular bit of pantomime Imogene nibbled on straw that she had pulled out of the Scarecrow.[70] As the Lion, Arthur Hill, who had been trained as a pantomimist in England, was also singled out as a clever and agile acrobat whose characterization was a favorite of children.

The singing and dancing choruses, who often joined in the numbers performed by the principals, were an important part of the show's spectacle. The primary appeal of many of these choruses—the Munchkins, the Poppy Flowers, the Phantom Patrol, the Ladies and Gentlemen of the Wizard's Court, the Dreamland Youths and Maids, and the Cavaliers—was that they were made up of beautiful women, and indeed, critics concentrated on their appearance more than any other aspect of their roles. Mitchell believed that the ideal chorus girl should weigh about 125 pounds, be about five feet, two or three inches tall, and have a good figure.[71] He made sure that the thirty-nine women who made up *The Wizard of Oz*'s chorus on opening night fit his ideal as closely as possible. Several articles boasted that Mitchell and Hamlin had secured for the chorus the services of the woman who had posed for artist Charles Dana Gibson's well-known book of illustrations *A Widow and Her Friends* (1901). She performed under the pseudonym Jane Blair because she claimed that she wanted to achieve success on her merits, not on past fame.[72] Many of the other women the producers engaged had recently worked with Anna Held or Weber and Fields.[73]

Mitchell also had firm ideas about how to best utilize these women. He believed that they should be more than just set dressing. Unlike a British chorus, which he described as "listless," American chorus girls should be "restless," that is, constantly moving "so that the audience, even if they did not hear a word, could get a sense of the lyrics" from their movements.[74]

Dave Montgomery *(left)* and Fred Stone *(right)*, c. 1902. The team had been performing together since 1895, but *The Wizard of Oz* established them as stars.

Although women played most of the minor male chorus roles, such as the Munchkin Youths, the Dreamland Youths, and the Gentlemen of the Wizard's Court, the opening night performance included ten men in the chorus. These men appeared, alongside female chorus members, as Farm Hands and as Citizens of the Emerald City, parts that required little, if any, singing and dancing. To add variety to the show, however, Mitchell included an all-male chorus, the Relief Guards, which performed a marching song.

The musical numbers in *The Wizard of Oz,* conducted by Alfred R. Moulton, were a primary focus of the production. One critic, in fact, remarked that the show was "but little different from a concert given in costume, amid gorgeous scenery, and accompanied by dancing and gesture."[75] Most of the numbers were not elaborately staged; that is, they did not involve large scenic changes or special effects. Rather, they were designed to showcase key performers and made abundant use of chorus girls. As was often the case in the period, they were not consistent musically, nor did they always blend smoothly into the play's action.

The numbers, of course, underwent changes over the course of the show's run. Within the first week, "The Guardian of the Gate," "The Different Ways of Making Love," and "She Didn't Seem to Mind" were cut to shorten the running time. "The Man Who Stays in Town" was gone by the beginning of the third week. At the producer's discretion, new songs were often added and old ones removed to keep the show lively and up-to-date and to attract repeat audiences. The interpolated numbers were especially malleable; sometime in August, for example, Montgomery and Stone substituted "Bloomin' Lize" (Matt C. Woodward/Benjamin Jerome) for "That's Where She Sits All Day." But even the Baum and Tietjens compositions were sometimes cut. About that same time, Bessie Wynn substituted "As Long As There's Love in the World" (James O'Dea/Edward Hutchison) for Baum and Tietjens's least significant song, "Love Is Love."[76]

The reviewers sometimes explained a song's style or how it was staged. One critic, for example, described "Carrie Barry" as a "popular waltz affair."[77] We are also told that the first song in the show, "Niccolo's Piccolo," was sung by Cynthia, backed by a whistling chorus, which presumedly imitated the sounds of the piccolo. A whistling chorus was also used for the Wizard's "Mr. Dooley" number. Stone executed a loose-limbed dance and clowned feverishly when he performed his first song of the evening, "Alas for the Man without Brains." Not only did the number provide an opportunity for Stone to show off his dancing abilities but the lyrics and dancing served well to introduce the Scarecrow and his plight to the audience.

Several reviewers singled out "When You Love, Love, Love," a trio and dance performed by the Scarecrow, the Tin Woodman, and Dorothy, as one of the catchiest and most popular numbers in *The Wizard of Oz.* Its staging was kept fairly simple; it was performed downstage in front of a drop while the big Poppy scene was being set up behind it. In fact, noting how the song was used as "filler" during the scene change, one reviewer complained, "It is somewhat astonishing that the biggest song hit in the presentation, 'When You Love,

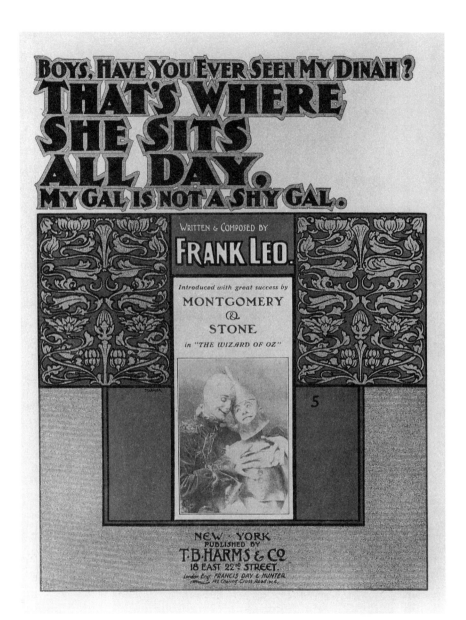

A sheet-music cover for "That's Where She Sits All Day,"
one of the Scarecrow and the Tin Woodman's big
specialty numbers in act 3. The piece was billed as a
"cockney Negro song," and like many musical numbers in
The Wizard of Oz, it came out of the minstrel tradition.

Love, Love,' has not been shaped around so as it should have more importance. . . . Mr. Mitchell should arrange to give it a chorus—a whistling chorus
if need be—and place his girls back of the three principals and lend it a swing."[78]

Montgomery and Stone's specialty duets were among the most popular
numbers in the musical. The two men worked well together, with the stiffer
Tin Woodman playing against the rubber-jointed antics of the Scarecrow.
Their duet "The Lobster," for example, a nonsensical novelty song that had
been a hit in *The Girl from Up There,* another show directed by Mitchell, was
full of "ridiculously amusing" comic action.[79] Their rendition of the "cockney
Negro song" called "That's Where She Sits All Day" (later replaced by "Bloomin' Lize") afforded them the opportunity to present a parody of an English
rendition of an American "coon" song.

A number of the show's songs and dances, in fact, had their origins in minstrelsy and black performance. In the Ball of All Nations, for example, Dorothy
and Cynthia accompanied "Rosalie" with a cakewalk. And in act 3 Dorothy
sang the coon song "I'll Be Your Honey in the Springtime" as she performed
a buck and wing. As several critics were quick to point out, Anna Laughlin, in
the role of Dorothy, was one of the very few soubrettes trained in this dance,
which was usually the domain of men.

"Sammy," yet another coon song, was probably the best-known song of the
show. It was not so much the song itself that appealed to audiences, however,
as the way Julian Mitchell staged the number. Mabel Barrison sang it backed
by a large female chorus. Performing in front of a large blue moon, they were
engaged in what one reviewer called "graceful and perhaps characteristic plan-
tation action."[80] Barrison and the chorus were directed to focus on an imaginary
man sitting in the upper-right box of the theater. While singing, they reached
out entreatingly, causing one critic to note that the song was performed "with
so much amatory gesture and such an excess of languishing facial expression"
that many spectators probably imagined that Barrison really was in love with
the man who happened to occupy the box.[81] It was not long before box E at-
tained a certain notoriety; any unknowing man who sat there ended up being
a great source of amusement for the rest of the audience.

The critics were mildly enthusiastic about Tietjens's instrumental music.
Fairly typical was the review that appeared in the *Chicago Evening Herald* the
weekend after the opening. "The principal music is by Paul Tietjens," it noted,
"and is of the popular order, sufficiently melodious and delicate to suit the
general fairy-like theme of the extravaganza without being startlingly original
or of a very high order. But it is pleasing and well written."[82]

Many of the show's songs, whether by Tietjens or other composers, were

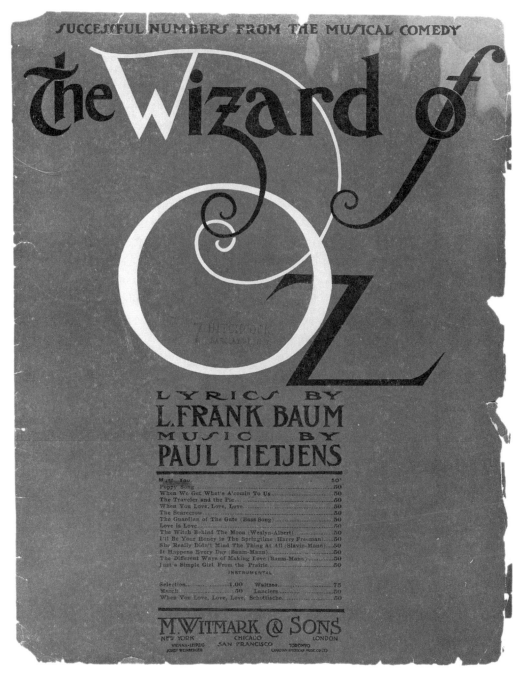

The sheet music for Baum and Tietjens's songs for *The Wizard of Oz* had a distinctive emerald green cover with a fanciful typeface. It was sold in the theater lobbies during intermission.

hits with audiences. During the show, it was not unusual for audiences to demand encores of their favorites. The flexibility of the show's book allowed for much improvisation in both music and dialogue. If the audience demanded it, the action could come to a stop while encores were performed, often repeatedly. Sheet music for many of the show's numbers was available for purchase from the ushers and in the lobby. Those songs written specifically for the show bore a distinctive emerald green cover with the title *The Wizard of Oz* in large, fanciful script across the page.

Although primarily an extravaganza, with its fairy-tale theme, loose structure, and lavish staging, *The Wizard of Oz* borrowed freely from other popular musical-theater genres. The mistaken identities, the political intrigue, and the romantic entanglements would have been quite at home in comic opera, while the show's broad approach to comedy was basically farce. Elements of pantomime were apparent in the Kansas prologue and in the animal characterizations. The sets and costumes, the special effects, and the transformation scenes, as well as the large cast and choruses, owed a considerable debt to spectacle. *The Wizard of Oz* also shared with vaudeville an emphasis on personality performers and specialty numbers, as well as on the use of vernacular language. Many of the show's songs, especially the interpolations, had clearly been designed for vaudeville in that they told a complete story.[83] The burlesque tradition could be seen in the assumption of male roles by women in tights and also in Cynthia's parody of Ophelia. Finally, minstrelsy's strong influence was clear in the show's coon songs and the choreography that accompanied them.

⌒ Early in its opening run the overwhelming success of *The Wizard of Oz* was readily apparent to Fred Hamlin. By the end of June he had already signed Montgomery and Stone to five-year contracts and Anna Laughlin for three years.[84] Hamlin also began to make plans for an extensive Midwest tour of the show, and at some point he decided to brave the rigors of New York City.

The tour began on Monday, 22 September 1902, almost immediately after the final Chicago performance, and was to end in late December. Full-week stands were scheduled for St. Paul, Minneapolis, Kansas City, Milwaukee, Detroit, St. Louis, Toronto, and Cleveland. Three-night stays were booked for Toledo and Omaha; two nights each in Memphis, Nashville, Louisville, Columbus, and Des Moines; and a night each in Topeka, Dubuque, Clinton (Iowa), Davenport, Lincoln, Sioux City, Cedar Rapids, Peoria, South Bend, Fort Wayne, and Dayton, as well as in Kingston, Ottawa, and London, Ontario.[85]

Touring such a large production and cast was no easy task. A special train carrying a dining car, as many as two sleepers and two day coaches, and three

HERE AT LAST!

MONDAY EVENING, NOVEMBER 3d,

The Great All-Summer Sensation from the Grand Opera House, Chicago.

Entire Original Production

including the same splendid cast, all of the magnificent scenery and the identical properties used in the remarkable record-breaking run in the "Windy City."

"The Wizard of Oz."

Lyrics by L. Frank Baum. Music by Paul Tietjens.
Scenery by W. W. Denslow.

Under the Management of **FRED HAMLIN.**

ACME OF SCENIC PAINTER'S ART.
A GORGEOUS FEAST FOR THE EYES.
STAGE PICTURES UNRIVALED IN BEAUTY.
DAZZLING IN THE EFFECT OF BRILLIANCY.

HEAR THE SONGS:

"The Guardian of The Gate,"   "Just a Simple Girl From The Prairie,"
"The Traveler And The Pie,"   "That Must Be Love,"
"The Witch Behind The Moon,"   "When You Love, Love, Love,"
I'll Be Your Honey In The Springtime,"   "Poppy Song,"
"The Different Ways of Making Love."

A SUPERB COMPANY OF ENTERTAINERS

including Bobby Gaylor, Helen Byron, Anna Laughlin, Bessie Wynne and

MONTGOMERY and STONE,

(THE TIN WOODMAN.)   (THE SCARECROW.)

The Greatest Hit in Years, Just Look at This!

During the **fourteen weeks** "THE WIZARD OF OZ" ran at the Grand Opera House in Chicago last summer it was applauded by approximately **135,000 people** and the gross receipts **amounted to $160,000.** At only two of the 125 performances did the takings fall below $1,000. These heretofore unheard of figures have startled the whole theatrical world. The tour of "THE WIZARD OF OZ," which was inaugurated in the north-west, has been a continuous triumph. Everywhere capacity houses have been the result. *WHAT DO YOU THINK OF IT?*

GET IN LINE EARLY FRIDAY MORNING.

Newspaper advertisement for *The Wizard of Oz* appearance at the Auditorium Theatre, South Bend, Indiana. The musical's post-Chicago/pre–New York tour of the Midwest in the fall of 1902 was a sellout.

baggage cars was needed. Hamlin announced to the newspapers that his weekly expenses would be about five thousand dollars and that *The Wizard of Oz* would need to play to capacity houses everywhere in order to make a profit.[86]

There were no major alterations to the cast on the tour, although some minor roles and the chorus saw changes. Some of the action had to be reblocked to accommodate the differences in venues that would be encountered on the road, and Mitchell, who had gone back to New York early in the show's run, returned to Chicago to hold several special rehearsals. In the course of the tour, substitutions were also sometimes made in the songs, especially those that were interpolations to begin with.

Cuts to the show were also made. The Wizard's much-encored "Mr. Dooley" song was eliminated within the first month of the tour, and there was a concerted effort to keep the encores for other songs to a minimum. The *Sioux City Daily Tribune* complained that although the large audience demanded encores, it was denied them.[87] And the critic in South Bend, Indiana, protested that many of the songs had been cut down to one verse, with the choruses and accompanying dances eliminated. Furthermore, that same writer added, some of the scenes and lighting effects that had helped make the show a success in Chicago had been completely curtailed.[88] It is quite possible, however, that cuts made in a given city were determined by the supposed caliber of the audience, the physical aspects of a particular theater, and the company's travel schedule. Critics in Omaha, Milwaukee, and Clinton, on the other hand, mentioned that requests for encores and applause extended the performance until about 11:30.[89]

In general, critics who saw the show on the road praised the physical production. A reviewer in Clinton, for example, wrote that the scenery and equipment surpassed anything ever seen there before.[90] Although the press continued to lavish praise on the performances of Montgomery and Stone, Anna Laughlin's singing voice seemed to be faulted more than in Chicago. Several other female principals, however, fared slightly better in the hands of critics than they had earlier.

In terms of attendance, the tour of *The Wizard of Oz* was wildly successful, and the show broke records at many of its stops. In St. Paul the *Dispatch* reported that "the audience filled the house, packed the aisles, and crowded the entrances, leaving none of the box seats empty. The gallery was a roaring cataract of vociferous enthusiasm."[91] In Clinton, 1,400 to 1,500 people crammed the Economic Theatre, including 120 who purchased standing room; about 300 had to be turned away.[92] In Memphis, the evening performance at the Lyceum was sold out by three o'clock in the afternoon, and "every foot of space in the rear and sides was used for standing room."[93] Likewise, the show broke records in Milwaukee and Cedar Rapids.[94]

The Wizard of Oz played a triumphant two-week return engagement at the Grand Opera House in Chicago beginning on Sunday, 28 December 1902.[95] Opening night found the theater packed, and many spectators had to stand. Amy Leslie reported that there was a "drowning welcome" for Fred Stone when he first appeared onstage.[96] All of the major cast members, in fact, were given a rousing welcome on their first entrance. The show was essentially the same as the one Chicago audiences had seen earlier in the year, with only a few changes. The first scene of act 2, "The Gates of the Emerald City," had been dropped. There was also a new Pastoria in the person of Gilbert Clayton, and a new Glinda, Ella Gilroy. By now, according to Leslie, the chorus had several vacancies and was less than stellar. This she expected to change when Mitchell returned to the Grand Opera House shortly to get the show ready for its engagement in New York City.

There were also several changes in the songs. Most important, Montgomery and Stone had two new numbers. Instead of "The Lobster," they now sang "Nautical Nonsense" (soon to be retitled "Hurrah for Baffin's Bay!"), with words by Vincent Bryan and music by Theodore F. Morse. This nonsense song with a nautical theme was lengthy and provided the comic duo with ample opportunity for comedy. The song begins:

> 'Twas on the good ship Cuspidor we sailed through
>   Baffin's Bay
> We tied her to the Ocean, while the Bulwarks ate some hay,
> The Captain said we'll tie the ship, whatever else be tied,
> And he drank a pint of gasoline with whiskey on the side,
> He had lost his breath, but soon it was restored.[97]

Also, Montgomery and Stone sang a new "cockney Negro song" in act 3, "Pimlico Malinda" (James O'Dea/Robert J. Adams).

Hamlin and Mitchell regarded the upcoming New York engagement as an extremely important next step for *The Wizard of Oz*. The show had done extraordinarily well in Chicago and the Midwest, but they knew that it would have to succeed in the East if it was to reach its full commercial potential. They also knew that the New York theatrical community looked down its nose at productions created in the "provinces." Abraham Erlanger, of Klaw and Erlanger, the legendary—and much feared—theatrical producers of New York City, had seen the show on its opening night in Chicago. According to Frank Joslyn Baum, Erlanger had enjoyed it but had "stated flatly it would never go in New York City because it was primarily a fairy tale and did not have enough suggestive material in the book and lyrics—which he thought the New York public demanded."[98] Although New York audiences and critics at the time were generally regarded as more demanding and sophisticated than those of the Midwest, Chicagoans competed sharply with New York and resented being considered unsophisticated. Hamlin and Mitchell realized that they would have to overcome New York's built-in bias, and they were determined to do so.

The Wizard of Oz was scheduled to be the inaugural production of the luxurious new Majestic Theatre, under construction at Columbus Circle in New York. But the theater was far removed from the main theatrical district, then located along Broadway in the upper thirties and low forties, which could prove to be an obstacle in the show's success. Nevertheless, Hamlin and Mitchell forged ahead and began to plan their strategy for an invasion of New York.

Chapter 4

"Something New under the Sun"

The New York City Engagement

B Y MID-DECEMBER 1902 Fred Hamlin and Townsend Walsh were preparing a massive publicity campaign for the New York debut of *The Wizard of Oz,* which was not scheduled to open until 15 January. On 12 December, Hamlin, in Chicago, wrote to Walsh, who was on the road with the show, informing him that fifteen hundred lithographs, one hundred stands, two hundred eight-sheets, and several hundred three-sheets, all advertising the musical, were already being shipped to New York. "This will be enough to start in with," assured Hamlin, "and you can tell after you get down there how many more you may need, if any." Ten thousand half-sheet snipes, or bills, also were ordered, and Walsh was told "to attend to the sniping personally and see that the town is plastered with them."

The producer warned Walsh that the show's venue, the Majestic Theatre, was a new house and that the manager there might not have had any experience in running a theater in New York. "Our success in New York will depend largely upon your efforts," Hamlin emphasized. "Don't let anything stop you between the time you strike New York and our opening night. After that you will have plenty of time to cut loose."[1]

A wall of posters at 36th Street and Fifth Avenue, New
York City, part of the advertising blitz for the show's
New York engagement.

A few days later, Hamlin wrote to Walsh to inform him that he and George H. Nicolai, the general manager of the Majestic, would share the cost of a quarter-page advertisement in the Christmas edition of the *New York Telegraph*. The copy would read: "Fred R. Hamlin's big extravaganza, *The Wizard of Oz*. 100 people, mostly girls." He instructed Walsh to insist that Nicolai and the rest of the management adhere to the usual custom regarding the placement of special billboard stands, whereby the producer paid for and supplied the posters, while the theater management paid for and supplied the locations for the posters. Most of all, however, he wanted things to proceed smoothly, and if Nicolai insisted that Hamlin share the expenses of the billboard stands, he would concede. "I don't want to be too stiff or antagonize them in any way," he concluded. "Everything must be perfectly friendly and amicable."[2]

On 24 December Hamlin wrote Walsh, who was arriving in New York about this time, reminding him about the terms of the financial agreement with the Majestic management. Nicolai and his associates had agreed to do two hundred dollars' worth of advertising each week. Hamlin shared equally any amount over that. The theater management was responsible for the costs of posting and distributing bills, while the producer furnished all printing. As to the show's weekly earnings, Hamlin would receive 60 percent of the first $6,000, 65 percent of the next $4,000, and 70 percent of any amount beyond that. The theater management would assume the cost of an orchestra of twelve persons, while the producer would share equally with management the expense of additional musicians. If weekly box office receipts should fall below $5,000 for two consecutive weeks, either party could post a notice stating that the show would close in two weeks' time.[3]

In the following days, Walsh received more letters from Hamlin regarding the New York advertising. Hamlin felt that it would be premature to focus the billing on Montgomery and Stone, even though they had scored a sensation in Chicago. He planned to feature them eventually but wanted "to let them 'make good' first."[4] In addition, concerned that New Yorkers would not know how to get to the Majestic Theatre, Hamlin instructed Walsh to include directions for getting there in all the snipes to be posted in streetcars.[5] Hamlin also had specific instructions about the wording of newspaper advertisements. The show, for example, could be described as an "extravaganza" but not as a "musical."[6]

As part of the advertising campaign, Hamlin and Walsh published an elaborate pamphlet heralding the opening of the new theater and its premiere production. Entitled *There Is Something New under the Sun,* it featured on its cover a Denslow drawing of the Scarecrow and the Tin Woodman.[7] The pamphlet was lavishly illustrated with photographs of the Majestic Theatre and performers from *The Wizard of Oz,* and it was filled with the sort of hyperbole that an experienced publicity man could offer. "The opening of the New Majestic Theatre will have a two-fold import for New York playgoers," the text began. "The occasion will not only signify the dedication of a handsome and artistic place of amusement, but it will mark the first presentation in this city of a new extravaganza, *The Wizard of Oz,* which has been in preparation and represents an unusual expenditure of brains and talent." The pamphlet went on to assure prospective audiences that the show would be "a new departure in the field of extravaganza, and consequently an agreeable relief from the bombardment of inane musical comedies which have held the board in recent seasons."

In addition to working on the publicity, Hamlin was also arranging for new costumes and scenery for the New York show. Julian Mitchell, meanwhile, was working on revisions to the script. The two men conducted their activities at their base in Chicago and were not to arrive in New York until 10 January. Until that time, Walsh would be their representative in New York, and he was responsible for making sure that the Majestic Theatre was made ready for the show. The entr'acte curtain had to be hung; the first row of seats had to be removed so that the orchestra would not have to be placed below the stage; the bridge from which the scenery was painted had to be taken down; the new scenery had to be brought in; the gauze curtain used for the special transformation effects had to be hung; and the lights had to be installed.[8]

In a harried state, Mitchell warned both Hamlin and Walsh that he would not open as scheduled unless everything was in perfect shape. On 3 January 1903 he wrote to Walsh: "I would rather have the stage ready and in perfect condition for our opening Thursday night than all the billing and press notices in the world. I can win out if I have a good performance the first night, better than I could if I had a million lithos and as many press notices."[9]

Apparently Mitchell was not able to resolve all the behind-the-scenes problems as the scheduled opening approached; in the end, he had to postpone it. The opening, which finally took place on 20 January, however, was an important occasion. One reviewer noted that "the audience was a brilliant one . . . and between the acts there was an air of social happenings of an intensity that is seldom surpassed in the heart of the Rialto."[10] Reporters made much of the fact that the Majestic was so far uptown; one even referred to it as the "north pole of the Broadway theatrical world."[11] But the theater was highly praised with regard to its architecture, its decoration, and its amenities. The design of the house was quite advanced for its time, boasting, among other things, an auditorium without pillars or columns to obstruct the sightlines of the audience.

If the new Majestic received unqualified raves from the critics, *The Wizard of Oz* itself was not so fortunate. The opening-night reviews were on the whole mixed, certainly nowhere near as enthusiastic as those at the Chicago debut. Some critics, however, did find the show enjoyable. A number praised the work of Montgomery and Stone. Acton Davies, of the *New York Sun,* for example, could not imagine what the show would have been like without them, for "from start to finish they carried the entire performance on their shoulders."[12] And in general the reviewers liked the costumes and the scenic effects. The *New York Times,* referring to David Belasco, the New York producer famous for innovative and realistic staging techniques, said the show had "no end of Belasco gorgeousness of scenic effect." "One would go a long way," the same critic continued, "before finding as pretty effects of costumes and dance, cyclones and snowstorms as are to be seen at the Majestic."[13] "Such scenery and such costumes as are rarely seen, even in these days of elaborate productions," another reviewer commented, adding that the show "has never been excelled in its class in this city. . . . It is an entertainment that will please children of all ages, from six to ninety-six, and should easily run the season out to overflowing houses."[14] Acton Davies also commended the show's cleanliness and the fact that the libretto was "singularly free from vulgarity and Tenderloin jokes."[15]

Overall, however, for every positive comment there was a negative one. The very same reviewer who perhaps praised the sets and Mitchell's staging, for example, may also have harshly criticized the book and the music. The comedy especially came under heavy attack, and more than one critic lamented the constant use of old jokes and even older puns. Some of the criticism had a condescending tone, probably due in large part to the New York prejudice against shows that were created out of town. According to Alan Dale:

> The piece itself is absolutely inexplicable. It is of year Dot and carry one. It is Chicago, in its early days. . . .
>
> Evil comedians with infamous puns, rough and uncouth horse-play, jokes that Noah would have routed out of the Ark, and a "juvenile" story that no modern juvenile would tolerate are served up energetically and with wondrous audacity. . . . It is an astonishing affair with which to besiege Central Park, but it is useful for it puts us on good terms with ourselves and shows us how vastly superior we are. There are road productions—and road productions. . . . But "The Wizard of Oz" is in a class by itself. It is the very essence of "the road."[16]

Kate Carew concurred: "In most important respects, 'The Wizard of Oz' fairly reeks of London, Ont., and Paris, Mich. You are asked to shriek with merriment at a cow and a lion that would be voted out of date at any village hall entertainment. There is no striking novelty in ensemble singing or dancing, the chorus is employed chiefly in marching and countermarching in good old Amazon fashion, and many of the principals are irritating persons with cave-dweller traditions of comedy."[17]

But audiences did shriek with merriment. "Not for seasons," said one critic about opening night, "have I heard such genuine and continuous shouts of laughter as echoed throughout the marble corridors of the new Majestic Theatre."[18] And the laughter continued night after night. Much to the consternation of the critics, *The Wizard of Oz* became one of the biggest hits of the season. Originally scheduled for only five weeks, the show was extended indefinitely. Even though seats could be purchased up to eight weeks in advance, people were being turned away nightly.[19]

The receipts for the first twenty-two weeks averaged $12,000 weekly, and the show's financial grosses were setting the theatrical world on its ear.[20] Many spectators saw *The Wizard of Oz* more than once. One newspaper article written late in the run mentioned that the theater was always filled with people who had seen the show before and who whispered to their companions what was about to take place onstage.[21] Even in the heat of the New York summer audiences came. By the time the show ended its run on 3 October, it was the longest-running musical of the season.

Despite the critics' reviews, Hamlin and Mitchell apparently knew quite well what New York audiences wanted—and that it was similar to what Chicago audiences had appreciated. The script used for the show's debut in New York, however, differs in a number of ways from the script used in the Midwest.[22] In act 1, for example, the maypole dance of the Munchkins was eliminated, while a duet featuring Tryxie and Pastoria was added shortly after the former's entrance and before the "Carrie Barry" ballad. Tryxie tells Pastoria how much she likes the circus, and then the two sing "When the Circus Comes to Town" (James O'Dea/Robert J. Adams). Dealing with a town's excitement at the arrival of the circus, the song did absolutely nothing to advance the plot; it only served to establish a rapport between Tryxie and Pastoria. In addition, a song entitled "That Is Love" (or "That Must Be Love"), by Maurice Steinberg, was now Dashemoff's love ballad to Dorothy. Finally, eliminated from the end of the act were the sleigh and team of reindeer, which in the Chicago show had stood at the ready to whisk Dorothy and her friends away after they awoke from the sleep of the Poppies. Instead, the Snow Queen and her entourage stand triumphantly at the rear of the stage. When Dorothy revives, she kneels down in respect, and the curtain falls.

Act 2 was now set in a single location, "The Courtyard of the Wizard's Palace," since the opening scene, "The Gates of the Emerald City," had been

The conclusion of act 1 of *The Wizard of Oz* as revised for its New York premiere in January 1903. Here, in the snow-covered Poppy Field, we see, downstage *(left to right),* Pastoria, the Cowardly Lion, the Tin Woodman, Dorothy, the Scarecrow, Dashemoff, Tryxie, and Imogene. The Snow Queen stands upstage with her arms raised.

cut by the time the show played Chicago in December. In addition, New Yorkers were to see other changes. The character of Wiley Gyle was modified so that he was no longer an inventor but simply a conspirator. Furthermore, where the Wizard had formerly sung "Mr. Dooley," he now sang "On a Pay Night Evening" (John W. West/Bruno Schilinski). The setup for the number begins with the Wizard's performing some magic tricks for his subjects and then asking Bardo, his Factotum, to pass the hat. When he is told that the people have no money until payday, he sings this comic song about the joys of getting paid. Performing with his usual Irish brogue, he is accompanied by a chorus of the working class, girls armed with pickaxes and tin dinner pails.

The Ball of All Nations suite also was moved to an earlier place in the act, immediately after the Wizard gives the Scarecrow brains and the Tin Woodman a heart. Following the suite, Pastoria and his traveling circus enter. Then Dashemoff arrives on the scene looking for Dorothy, his love. At this point, the poet performs a song that was added to the show for its New York run, "I Love Only One Girl in the Wide, Wide World" (Will D. Cobb/Gus Edwards). In it, Dashemoff testifies that although there are dozens of women he could have, he

In act 2 the Wizard performs "On a Pay Night Evening" along with a chorus of workers carrying lunch pails and pickaxes.

loves only one and will be true to her. The next song to be performed is Tryxie's "Sammy," which in the Chicago production had appeared earlier in the act.

Act 2 still concludes with the revelation that the Wizard is a fake. He no longer escapes in a balloon, however. Instead, he and Wiley Gyle are taken prisoner as Pastoria, now claiming the throne, sings "Star of My Native Land" (Glen MacDonough/A. Baldwin Sloane). This song replaced "The Wizard Is No Longer King."

The most changes occurred in act 3, which was totally rewritten for New York. It was now set in "The Borderland, Dividing the Kingdom of Oz from the Dominions of the Good Witch," representing the frontier of Pastoria's kingdom. At stage left is a bridge leading to the domain of Glinda, the Good Witch. At the start of the act, Pastoria's Royal Guards march across the stage. During the march one guard takes a position as a sentry at the bridge. Alberto, Captain of the Guard, also remains behind. Then a chorus of Cooks, Waitresses, and Laundresses performs MacDonough and Sloane's "Opening Chorus." After they finish the number, Alberto questions them because he is trying to capture some escapees from Pastoria's jail. They say that they are out looking for work. Alberto informs them that there is a large reward for the escapees and that they should read the royal proclamation posted near the bridge for a description of the criminals at large.

While they read, the Scarecrow and the Tin Woodman enter, having escaped from Pastoria's prison. The former is wearing a top hat and some ragged white clothes apparently stolen from a clothes line, while the latter is disguised as a burlesque chauffeur in white livery. They determine that they must make it across the bridge. At about this point in the action, they perform the "cockney Negro song," called "Pimlico Malinda" (O'Dea/Adams). Then, when they try to cross the bridge, they are asked to pay a toll, which they cannot afford. The sentry becomes suspicious, and they are locked in a cage at stage right. The cage, several feet off the ground, is formed by a tangle of trunks and vines.

A file of guards now enters. They are escorting the Wizard and Wiley Gyle, who are dressed as convicts, complete with ball and chain. Pastoria, wearing royal purple robes, follows close behind. He has a bandage on his face, apparently from an injury suffered when he took part in the Wizard's basket trick. The two prisoners are to be Pastoria's new street cleaners, and they are given brooms as the new king gloats over their misery. Tryxie and the Lion enter, and there is some comic business with the Lion. The Wizard and Wiley are now escorted off to clean the sewers. Tryxie is unhappy about Pastoria's ascending to the throne because he has become pompous. She and Pastoria break up, and they exit at opposite ends of the stage.

Now Dashemoff and Dorothy enter. They also have escaped from Pastoria's prison and are on the run. About to try to cross the bridge, they discover the imprisoned Scarecrow and Tin Woodman. The Tin Woodman has a plan to set the Scarecrow free. He will use a pair of scissors to cut up his companion. Then he will pass the pieces through the bars of the cage and down to Dorothy, who can carry them to safety and sew them back together again. Dashemoff, meanwhile, will create a diversion by sprinting across the bridge, thereby forcing the sentry to chase him. When the poet does just this, the chorus of Cooks, Waitresses, and Laundresses enters to watch the pursuit. They ask Dorothy if she knows who has just run across the bridge. She says that he is her sweetheart and that the two of them are wandering minstrels: he writes the songs, and she sings them. She then sings a song of love, "Honey, My Sweet" (Henry M. Blossom Jr./George A. Spink).

By this time the Tin Woodman has finished cutting up the Scarecrow, and he drops the pieces of the straw man out to Dorothy one at a time. She places them in her basket. Cynthia enters, and Dorothy tells her what she is up to. Alberto now arrives on the scene. He sees Dorothy and Cynthia carrying the basket filled with the pieces of the Scarecrow and orders a guard to throw the contents into the river. Next, realizing that a prisoner is missing from the cage and that the sentry is not at his post, Alberto runs off in a panic, leaving the keys in the lock of the cage. The Tin Woodman lets himself out. He and the two women retrieve the pieces of the Scarecrow from the river and carry them over to the sentry box. They begin to put him back together, piece by piece, but on seeing guards approaching, they flee in different directions. The Tin Woodman comes back and finishes reassembling the Scarecrow, who steps out of the sentry box. The two friends exit.

A guard enters with the Wizard and Wiley and puts them to work cleaning the area. Cynthia and the Tin Woodman also arrive. She asks him to play on her piccolo, which he does. Realizing that they were formerly lovers, they embrace. The Scarecrow enters, soon followed by Dorothy and Dashemoff, who has managed to outwit the soldiers. Suddenly Pastoria and his guards enter. He declares them all prisoners and calls for his executioner. A headsman with an axe and two attendants bearing a block enter. Pastoria orders the men to the block and the women to the prison. Dorothy begs for mercy and in desperation calls for the Good Witch of the North. The Good Witch appears and calls on Glinda to spread darkness across the land so that the victims might escape the tyrant and to send the spirits of the air to bear Dorothy back home. On hearing this, Pastoria, fearing another cyclone, declares Dorothy and all of her companions free to depart whenever they wish. The curtain falls.

The climax of act 3. Pastoria's executioner stands at the
ready as Dorothy cowers. To the left of the executioner
stand the Scarecrow and Dashemoff, and at the far left is
General Riskitt flanked by the Wizard and Wiley Gyle
in convict uniforms. To Dorothy's right are the Tin
Woodman (dressed as a chauffeur), Cynthia, Pastoria,
and Tryxie.

The new act 3 had almost nothing to do with Baum's original novel beyond the fact that in both, the Scarecrow is taken apart and then reassembled and Dorothy wants to return to Kansas. Furthermore, it did little to advance the story developed in the first two acts of the musical. One wonders, in fact, why Mitchell and Hamlin considered it an improvement over the version seen in Chicago. The theme of political conflict becomes the central focus, played out in the struggle between Pastoria's new regime and the Wizard and his perceived supporters. The restored king is a mean and pompous character who wants to enslave or kill anyone who opposes him. His new power corrupts him, and his fiancée, Tryxie, rejects him for it. The Wizard and his associates, meanwhile, are reduced to being either chain-gang convicts or escapees. The political conflict, however, does not overwhelm the theme of romantic love, which also is important in the revised version of the third act. The theme is centered around the relationships between Dorothy and Dashemoff and between Cynthia and the Tin Woodman.

The motif of the working class, alluded to in other parts of the show—such as the number "On a Pay Night Evening" in act 2—is prominent here. The chorus of unemployed Cooks, Waitresses, and Laundresses provides lively color and situates the action in a kind of populist landscape made up of blue-collar workers in search of ideal jobs. Furthermore, the Wizard and Wiley Gyle are not merely prisoners; they are forced to labor in a street-cleaning detachment. In general, however, the working class is presented here merely as a source of entertainment and color for a primarily middle-class audience.

Beneath its surface comedy and high jinks, however, the new act 3 does possess a certain mythological power. The Borderland becomes a kind of liminal area where roles are reversed or changed: The former Wizard is now a prisoner, while Pastoria, the former motorman, is now king. And the Tin Woodman and the Scarecrow assume new personas through their disguises. Furthermore, the dismantling and reassembling of the Scarecrow becomes, in a way, a death-and-rebirth archetype similar to that found in many nature myths. And finally, like many myths, the story is built around a motif involving the duality of nature. The cyclone, a destructive force at the start of the play, becomes a positive entity that will return Dorothy to her home. In addition, the tangle of wisteria vines and trunks, beautiful to the eye, also functions as a means of entrapment. Even Pastoria, who becomes a symbol of nature when his name is taken as a play on "pastoral," represents this duality; in the early part of the story he is a sympathetic victim, but by the end he has become an abusive tyrant.

In the course of the New York run the script underwent additional modification.[23] By February, for example, Wiley Gyle's first entrance had been moved up from act 2 to act 1, scene 3. New jokes and routines also were introduced from time to time to keep the show fresh. On 13 July a chorus of sailor lasses made their debut as an accompaniment to the Scarecrow and the Tin Woodman's "Hurrah for Baffin's Bay!" number.[24]

In addition, of course, new songs were introduced. Act 3 seemed especially vulnerable to song changes. By the show's second week, "Pimlico Malinda" had been replaced by "Must You?" (Harry Boden and David Montgomery [the Tin Woodman]/Bert Brantford). It was a comic specialty primarily for the Tin Woodman, although the Scarecrow joined in the performance. It turned out to be a smashing success that was identified with Montgomery for years afterward. Thematically unrelated to *The Wizard of Oz*, the song tells the story of a henpecked man abused by his wife. In the last verse, the man tries to wine and dine a show girl, only to be abused by her as well and then sent back to his spouse. Also by the second week, the Montgomery and Stone number "That's Where She Sits All Day," which had been performed in the Chicago production of the musical, had been introduced as the show's final song.

By mid-March the Scarecrow's "The Traveller and the Pie" had made its triumphant return to the show, replacing act 3's opening chorus number performed by the Cooks, Waitresses, and Laundresses. *The Wizard of Oz* now ended on a very strong note, with four big specialty numbers. Audiences were sent home with a bang. Too much of a bang, perhaps, because June found "That's Where She Sits All Day" eliminated from the show. Also in mid-March, Cynthia's big number in act 2, "The Witch behind the Moon," was replaced by a song entitled "Things That We Don't Learn at School" (also known as "There's a Lot of Things You Never Learn at School") (Ed Gardenier/Edwin S. Brill). Each verse of this comic ditty describes a situation in which book learning proves to be less valuable than street smarts.

It appears that most, if not all, of the sets were repainted for New York, and several of them were redesigned as well.[25] The scene called "A Kansas Farm" was credited to Fred Gibson, working from designs by Walter W. Burridge, and "The Courtyard of the Wizard's Palace" was credited to Burridge, as they had been in the program for the Chicago production. This suggests that they were similar in both the Chicago and New York versions of the show. Photographs of these scenes from both productions, indeed, indicate that the sets remained substantially unchanged. "The Road through the Forest," which in Chicago had been designed by Burridge but painted by Gibson, was now credited to Gibson alone, so some alterations may have been made. "The Country of the Munchkins," "The Poppy Field," and "The Poppy Field in Winter" retained the same titles they had had in Chicago but were painted and appar-

The Scarecrow performs his comic specialty "The Traveller
and the Pie" with the chorus of Cooks, Waitresses, and
Laundresses. The Tin Woodman watches from the cage.

ently redesigned by a new scenic artist, John Young, who had his headquarters
at the Grand Opera House in New York. Young also created the setting for
the new final act, "The Borderland, Dividing the Kingdom of Oz from the
Dominions of the Good Witch."

Surviving black-and-white production photographs provide a sense of the
appearance of the new sets.[26] "The Country of the Munchkins" had a basic
rustic setting. The painted backdrop depicts a hilly countryside. An abundance
of trees and vegetation, in the form of cutouts and flats, appears on both sides
of the stage and also in the upper part of the proscenium opening. To the
left stands Dorothy's house, transported there by the cyclone, in a somewhat
dilapidated condition: the shingle roof is falling in, and the pillars holding up
the front porch are giving way. "The Road through the Forest" has a painted
backdrop showing a road flanked by trees and, in the distance, hills and more

trees. Flats and cutouts of vegetation stand on either side of the road. "The Poppy Field," which also has a painted backdrop, cutouts, and flats, depicts a dense grove of oversized poppies that fill the entire proscenium space. (The "living" Poppies stretch across the stage and mingle with the set so as to produce a three-dimensional effect.) "The Poppy Field in Winter" shows the same locale but with snow covering all the vegetation.

Whereas act 3 in the Chicago production, "The Domain of the Sorceress," had been a study in rosy tones, the new scene that replaced it, "The Borderland, Dividing the Kingdom of Oz from the Dominions of the Good Witch," featured lavender scenery, costumes, and lighting. The scene took place in a wisteria grove. Photographs show a backdrop depicting a fortress on a hill. On both the left and the right sides of the stage are giant trees in the form of flats reaching from floor to ceiling. Slightly to the left, toward the rear, is a large three-dimensional tangle of trunks and wisteria vines. To the right are a guard house surrounded by vegetation and a bridge leading off the stage.

"A Kansas Farm" and the approach of the cyclone (act 1, scene 1). Dorothy's house is partially visible at the left.

The Orientalist decor of "The Courtyard of the Wizard's Palace." Here the Wizard *(left)* banters with a mustached guard as Wiley Gyle *(right)* and the inhabitants of the Emerald City look on.

The sets were painted in rich hues, and lighting was important to help achieve truly vibrant colors. Many lighting changes took place in the course of the production. And in April, James Finn, the electrician for the show, introduced an electronic switchboard of his own invention to control these changes. Before this, calcium light operators had changed the colors of the lights by hand, and Finn's revolutionary device, one of the first of its kind, received considerable publicity.[27]

As for the show's special effects, New York audiences, like those in Chicago, were impressed by the cyclone and the Poppy scenes. In addition, New Yorkers were amazed to see, in the new version of act 3, the Scarecrow being cut up and then reassembled. This was done using traditional stage-magic techniques such as had also been employed in a popular nineteenth-century French fairy spectacle, *Les Pilules du Diable,* in which a character was dismembered in a train explosion and then put back together again.[28] While Dorothy sang "Honey, My Sweet," Fred Stone as the Scarecrow, shielded by the Tin Woodman, slipped out of the cage and was replaced by a collection of dismantled body parts. He also secretly made his way into the sentry box and hid himself behind strips of black masking covering the doorway. When Dorothy, Cynthia, and the Tin Woodman were ready to reassemble the Scarecrow, they brought the set of body parts over to the sentry box. Then they began to place the pieces one by one into the box. As they did so, the parts were passed out of the back of the box, while sections of the masking were removed to reveal the corresponding parts of the living Scarecrow. All the while, Dorothy and her companions were careful to shield parts of the box from the view of the spectators so that the trick would not be revealed. The Scarecrow's bright white costume stood in sharp contrast to the black interior of the sentry box, and piece by piece he seemed to return to life. By the time the last limb was restored, he was ready to step forward out of the box.[29]

The show's wardrobe also made quite an impression in New York. Made from luxurious materials, including silk and velvet, it was colorful, whimsical, and highly ornamented with lace, feathers, and jewels. The costumes of both the Cowardly Lion and Imogene the cow were basically unchanged from Chicago, as were the Poppy costumes. The primary costumes and makeup of the Scarecrow and the Tin Woodman remained the same as well. The other costumes used in the show were mostly new, with Caroline Siedle responsible for designing many of them for New York. Fortunately, some of Siedle's sketches, in color, survive. These, along with extant black-and-white production photographs, give us a good sense of the costumes seen in the show.[30]

Most of the principal characters changed their costumes in the course of the

"The Country of the Munchkins" (act 1, scene 2), in which the Good Witch *(center)* introduces Dorothy *(left)* to Dashemoff *(right)* as Munchkin Youths and Maidens look on. Dorothy's house, battered by the cyclone, can be seen at the left.

"THE WIZARD OF OZ"

Pastoria *(crouching)* and his assistant, General Riskitt *(recoiling in fear),* encounter the Cowardly Lion in "The Road through the Forest" (act 1, scene 3).

performance. Dorothy, for example, wore a simple, brick-red country dress with a white ruffled apron covered with red polka dots in the first act. A bonnet tied at the chin matched the apron's pattern, while red shoes matched the shade of the dress. She more strongly looked the part of a demure farm girl here than she had in Chicago. In later acts Dorothy's clothes became more elaborate to suit the fantasy world of Oz. In the second act she had a fancy dress in mint green, worn off the shoulder. It had a laced bodice and a wide border of ruffles at the hem. Small white flowers and ribbons decorated the dress, and a large flowered headdress completed the outfit, which was much more extravagant than its Chicago counterpart. In the same act, for her cakewalk number, Dorothy sported an unusual harlequin-like outfit in white with black polka dots and stripes. It consisted of a blouse, belted at the waist, and asymmetrical short pants, with one leg shorter than the other. On one side she wore a black glove and a black stocking; on the other, a white glove and a white stocking with a black garter. On her head she had a pointed cap that continued the patterns on her outfit. In the final act Dorothy wore a knee-length dress with puffed short sleeves and a pleated skirt over a ruffled petticoat. The bodice was decorated with a purple diamond-shaped pattern.

Other principals wore their share of striking costumes in the course of the production. In act 1 the Good Witch of the North, for example, had a full-length trailing gown with a beaded net overlay. Dashemoff wore a blue, thigh-length slotted tunic that was belted at the waist and laced up at the front. A small pouch hung from his waist, a cape was draped over his left shoulder, and he wore a billowy blue cap. Siedle originally designed tall boots as part of the outfit, but these were eliminated, apparently to reveal more of the legs of the actress who played this male role. Tryxie, for her part, donned a contemporary waitress's uniform, which was fancier than the one she had worn in the Chicago production. An ankle-length light blue dress with laces up the side was trimmed with ruffles at the top and around the sleeves, and a flowing white pleated apron ran down the front. She wore a ruffled cap on her head.

In act 2 the Wizard sported a largely green outfit of satin knickers, a vest decorated with shamrocks, and a similarly decorated fur-trimmed, thigh-length jacket. On his head he wore a large pointed crown. This costume was more regal and less comical than anything he had worn in the Chicago production. When Wiley Gyle appeared in the same act, he wore striped tights, a short jacket with an exaggerated collar and trim and ruffled sleeves, and a pointed cap. For her sexy "Sammy" number Tryxie wore a green fancy dress awash with embroidery, sequins, feathers, and fur. It was low-cut and had a flouncy skirt. She also wore a large feathered and sequined hat with a streamer flowing down her back.

In act 3 Pastoria, now a king, donned royal robes. He wore a thigh-length jacket trimmed with ermine, satin shorts and a satin tunic, a fancy collar, and a hat that seemed to be a cross between a crown and a motorman's cap. In the same act, Cynthia appeared dressed in a manner befitting Shakespeare's Ophelia, whom she was meant to parody. She had a full-length flowing robe, the hems of which were decorated with a leaf pattern. A large purse hung from her waist. Her long and somewhat unkempt hair was adorned with flowers.

Some of the most creative and attractive costumes were worn by the choruses. In act 3, for example, the costume of the Royal Guards was an elaborate, highly decorated affair in varying shades of purple that consisted of a pinched-waist tunic over a full-sleeved shirt and an ample jeweled cape. A decorated sword hung from a belt at the waist, and the headdress was trimmed in jewels

In "The Poppy Field" (act 1, scene 4), Dashemoff and
Dorothy meet up with the traveling "circus," comprising
the Cowardly Lion, Pastoria, Tryxie, and Imogene.

and feathers. Also in the same act, the Cooks had an especially whimsical outfit, a long-sleeved tunic with a kettle decoration at the waist and short pants with stripes at the hem. The accompanying hat was circular with a flat top and had silverware protruding around the perimeter of the brim.

When *The Wizard of Oz* made its debut in New York it featured the same principal performers who had been in the show during its final run in Chicago, with the exception of Edith Hutchins, who took over the role of the Witch of the North. Paula Edwardes, a well-known star, had been hired to replace Grace Kimball as Tryxie since Hamlin and Mitchell had not been entirely satisfied with Kimball's performance and felt that she was not sufficiently well known to New York audiences. Edwardes, however, was suddenly taken ill before the New York opening, and Kimball was reinstated.[31]

Most of the New York reviewers applauded the work of Montgomery and Stone. The critics and general public enjoyed their musical numbers, such as "Hurrah for Baffin's Bay!" For that song the Scarecrow wore a bizarre costume consisting of bell-bottomed sailor's trousers decorated with playing cards, a striped shirt with puffed sleeves, a scarf tied at the neck, and a sailor's cap. The Tin Woodman donned a more traditional sailor's suit, but the sleeves and the trousers were designed to fit badly. At one point in the number Montgomery and Stone played small drums that hung from their necks, and at another point they sat in a small sailboat adrift at sea.[32]

The reception of the other principal performers tended to be more mixed. One critic, for example, felt that Anna Laughlin as Dorothy was a "really graceful dancer" and "displayed more dramatic ability than any other member of the cast," but another said that she had a voice of "emory-paper calibre" that could "ignite any match."[33] Still another called her "a chubby little soubrette" who sang her songs "as if she were about to choke."[34] The one performer who fared much better in New York than in Chicago was Bessie Wynn as Dashemoff. Evidently she had worked herself into the role and had endeavored to improve her voice. A typical review noted that she "sang and acted sweetly . . . and deserves to become a favorite."[35] Also, as had been the case in Chicago, most critics were enchanted by Julian Mitchell's chorus girls. "There are acres of them," wrote James Montague, "young, slim, ox-eyed (peroxide, also), tall, short, blond, brunette, all pretty, all lively, all engaging."[36]

In February, Lotta Faust joined the cast in the role of Tryxie. Faust was an up-and-coming musical-comedy actress who had begun her career in 1897 at age sixteen. She had moved to increasingly larger roles prior to her engagement as Tryxie, and her debut in *The Wizard of Oz* was a great success.[37] "Sammy" became even more popular than before, and pieces frequently appeared in the

Lotta Faust as Tryxie Tryfle in
her act 2 fancy dress.

Lola Gordon playing one of the Cooks in act 3. Her whimsical costume includes silverware in her hat and an embroidered kettle on her bodice.

The Scarecrow in his outfit for "Hurrah for Baffin's Bay,"
a specialty number that became one of Montgomery and
Stone's most enduring classics.

papers about embarrassed young men seated in the "Sammy box." The former Tryxie, Grace Kimball, remained with the show but played lesser chorus roles.

About the same time that Lotta Faust joined the cast, Helen Byron, who played Cynthia, left. One newspaper account said that the producers chose not to renew her contract, while another had her traveling to Europe to join her sister.[38] Jeanette Lowrie took over the role and stayed until September, when Allene Crater assumed the part. Both women were generally well received, but the latter made a bigger impression on Fred Stone. He had seen her perform some years before in Denver, and since then she had appeared in several musical comedies. Stone and Crater now began a romance that would lead to marriage in 1906.[39] Another female performer, Bessie Wynn (Dashemoff) left the cast at the end of April or the beginning of May and was succeeded briefly by Edith Yerrington and then more permanently by Gertrude Mac-Kenzie, who assumed the role about mid-June.

As for the males in the cast, Owen Westford replaced Gilbert Clayton in the role of Pastoria sometime in March, and ill health forced Edwin Stone, who played Imogene, to leave the show at about the same time. The part of the cow was taken over by Joseph Schrode, who had been with the show in smaller roles since its inception. Perhaps most important was the exit of Bobby Gaylor about 15 June. His replacement as the Wizard was James K. Wesley, another Irish comedian, who had been successful in European vaudeville and on the Keith circuit in the United States but was not particularly well known in America.[40]

For all of the show's strengths and weaknesses, two prime factors made *The Wizard of Oz* the talk of New York in 1903. The first was the team of Montgomery and Stone. New York audiences, it seems, just could not get enough of these two performers. As the show's run continued, the attention lavished on them in articles and advertisements served as an ongoing testament to the public's interest in the duo—and as effective promotion for the show. Even after fifteen weeks of performances audiences' enthusiasm was undiminished. Noting the numerous encores they were still required to give, one newspaper reporter wrote, "For example, Fred Stone is recalled regularly for three versions of his Scarecrow song. David Montgomery is called upon likewise for as many repetitions of the Tin Woodman's love song. The nautical duet of Montgomery and Stone in the second act wins six encores, and the burlesque parody of the cockney coon song never satisfies the audience until the two comedians have sung and danced themselves completely out of breath."[41] Another reporter observed that "there are no 'Johnnies' about the stage door of the Majestic Theatre, in spite of the fact that Julian Mitchell selected the chorus. Their place has been usurped by the small boys, who foregather to greet the appearance

Allene Crater as Cynthia Cynch, the Lady Lunatic. Fred
Stone met and married the actress during the run of *The
Wizard of Oz.*

of Stone and Montgomery, the Scarecrow and the Tin Woodman. Every day Stone, especially, is greeted with shouts and familiar tugs at his coattails, and he seldom gets to his cab till he has scattered a handful of coppers. Hero worship is not quite dead yet, after all."[42]

The other hero in the story of *The Wizard of Oz*'s success in New York was Townsend Walsh. From the moment he began his pre-opening publicity campaign to the moment the show ended its long run, Walsh made sure that the musical was always in the public eye. The masterful campaign that he conducted at Fred Hamlin's urging never allowed interest in the show to flag. Besides the posters and snipes that covered the city and the advertisements in newspapers and magazines, there were countless special features, articles, and small news items about the show, many of them planted or encouraged by Walsh. These ranged from news pieces about embarrassed gentlemen in the "Sammy box" to articles about milliners who were designing hats based on those worn by the Poppy chorus.[43]

One newspaper published an "imagined" dialogue between Dorothy, the Scarecrow, and the Tin Woodman to introduce the characters to those who had not yet seen the show and then summarized the action.[44] Another related the story of a masher who left roses and a love note to Anna Laughlin backstage. He instructed her to wear one rose as a signal to him in a certain part of the show. The Scarecrow, however, rebuked the masher onstage by feeding the rose to Imogene the cow. The embarrassed and rejected man supposedly fled the theater.[45] In addition, numerous newspapers ran short pieces about Stone's plight in act 1 one night when he felt like sneezing as he hung motionless on the pole before the Scarecrow comes to life. He was able to suppress the sneeze for what seemed to him like an eternity.

Nothing that kept the show and its cast in the spotlight was considered too trivial. One chorus girl, Nancy Poole, merited mention in the news because she became engaged to be married via telephone, while another, Georgia Barron, was touted in the press as the "Cucumber Girl" because she ate cucumbers for her complexion. Several short articles made much of the fact that Emily Fulton, another member of the chorus, held a Green Tea party for Bobby Gaylor and eight of her fellow chorus girls. Yet another chorus girl, Nellie Payne, was said to have inherited a large amount of money and to be about to leave the country. Lotta Faust, it was reported, regularly had flowers thrown at her following her rendition of "Sammy." An article entitled "Poppy Queen a Drug Victim" recounted how Anna Fitzhugh, who played several small roles, mistakenly used chloroform to clean her gloves and promptly fainted.[46]

Reports also appeared saying that both British and French managers were interested in staging *The Wizard of Oz* in Europe.[47] (There is no evidence, however, that the show was ever mounted abroad.) And in one of Walsh's most original moves, a copy of the payroll sheet that cast members signed for their paychecks, showing the imaginative and often comical ways in which the performers signed their names, was reproduced in *Stage*.[48]

During the summer, when the show was still playing even though other theaters had closed because of the heat, the advertisements boasted of the Majestic's excellent ventilation system and the musical's longevity. "Cool as the Catskills," read one advertisement, noting that *The Wizard of Oz* was the "All Winter, All Summer, All Year Round Success."[49] In fact, newspaper filler constantly planted here and there mentioned that *The Wizard of Oz* was worth repeated viewings and that many people were seeing it more than once.

In June, several of the musical's performers and backstage personnel formed a baseball team. They played the teams of other shows and received much publicity.[50] Another sports-related story that received a good deal of press was the visit to the show on 15 August of the Irish yachtsman Sir Thomas Lipton and two hundred members of the Larchmont Yacht Club. Lipton was quite a celebrity at the time because of his recent attempts to win the America's Cup, and the press followed his every move. Several newspaper articles spoke of his upcoming visit to *The Wizard of Oz,* and it was mentioned that special events were planned in connection with it. Irish flags were to be hung all around the theater, and small flags were to be distributed to the audience. The act 2 finale, "Star of My Native Land," was retitled "Flag of My Native Land," and its lyrics were changed to suit the occasion. In addition, Lotta Faust was to sing a special version of "Sammy," entitled "Tommy," which she would direct to Lipton, seated in the "Sammy box." Newspaper stories about the performance were numerous, and the crowd was supposedly wild with excitement. Lotta received bouquets of roses, and at the end of the show Lipton gave a speech and kissed all of the chorus girls.[51]

Another of Walsh's publicity schemes—of a sort common in the period— entailed the distribution of souvenirs to commemorate landmark performances. For the 100th performance, on 15 April, for example, audience members received a metal jewel box with a three-dimensional Cowardly Lion on the top. For the 125th performance they were given picture books, and for the 200th and 225th, collapsible silver drinking cups.[52]

Hamlin and Mitchell must have been more than satisfied by the phenomenal success of *The Wizard of Oz* in New York, and they were prepared to take advantage of it. The two men had already foreseen an extensive cross-country tour for the musical, as well as the formation of a second company that would go

Townsend Walsh, the business manager of the show and
the orchestrator of its publicity campaign, greets the
Scarecrow in this publicity shot.

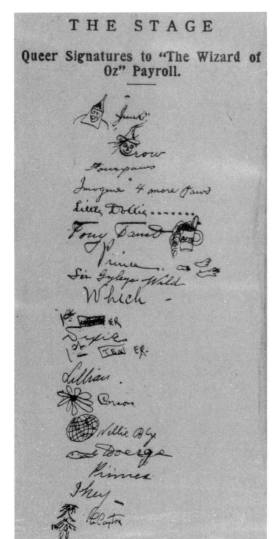

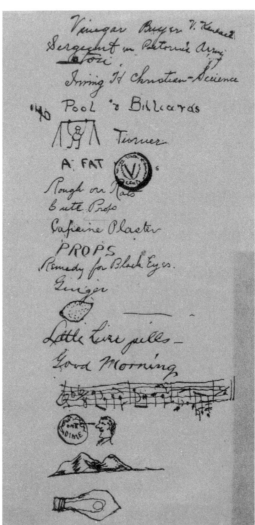

Townsend Walsh submitted to *Stage* magazine the playful payroll signatures of the show's cast—a fine example of Walsh's inventive approach to publicity. The humorous autographs include those of Anna Laughlin, who signed as "Little Dottie . . . . . .''; Arthur Hill, who signed as "Fourpaws"; and Joseph Schrode, who signed as "Imogene 4 more paws."

out on the road. In fact, on 17 December 1902, based on the show's success up to that point, Hamlin had already contracted with Baum, Tietjens, and Denslow for the creation of the second company.[53]

It was not until the spring of 1903, however, that Hamlin and Mitchell's future plans for the 1903–4 season began to take shape. In March, Hamlin wrote to Walsh from Chicago instructing him "to get busy with the newspapers all over the country."[54] By April brief casting announcements for the second company were appearing in newspapers. The Swor Brothers, Bert and John, minstrel comedians who were fairly well known for their blackface comedy, were cast in the key roles of the Scarecrow and the Tin Woodman. Isabel D'Armond, who had been in the Dan Daly Company with Anna Laughlin, was hired to play Dorothy. John Swor and D'Armond, in fact, had the opportunity to perform in *The Wizard of Oz* before the second company was actually formed. Beginning in July, Swor replaced Montgomery when he took a seven-week vacation from the show. D'Armond, for her part, substituted for the vacationing Lotta Faust during the first two weeks of July and then replaced her in the first part of August when she had her summer break.

Because of the success of *The Wizard of Oz*, Hamlin and Mitchell also made plans to produce other musical comedies. Early in the New York run of the show, they formally entered into a business partnership to create new joint productions. Under their agreement, Hamlin would provide financing and direct the tours of the shows. Mitchell, for his part, would decide which shows to do, put together the companies, and direct the productions. They established an office at Chicago's Grand Opera House and later added a second office in New York's Knickerbocker Building.[55]

Babes in Toyland was the first extravaganza produced by Hamlin and Mitchell to capitalize on the popularity of *The Wizard of Oz*. It also would be a hodgepodge of music, spectacle, and vaudeville-style comedy, but it had one special advantage in that the accomplished composer Victor Herbert had agreed to provide the score. The musical made its debut at the Grand Opera House in Chicago in the summer of 1903, and like its predecessor, it triumphed. Hamlin and Mitchell decided to bring the new show to the Majestic in the fall of 1903, announcing that it would directly follow *The Wizard of Oz*, which they hoped would soon tour America.

Chapter 5

The Wizard Deluxe and Redux

The Cross-Country Tours and Beyond

N THE SUMMER OF 1903 the musical *The Wizard of Oz,* which had already achieved much success with its premiere in Chicago and its subsequent tour in the Midwest, was enjoying continuing popularity during its New York engagement. Over the course of the next several years, as vast numbers of people across the country had an opportunity to attend the play, it would become further ingrained in the public consciousness. As an institution, it would stand on its own terms and be appreciated and loved in its own right, side by side with its source, Baum's original novel. From this point on, in fact, both Wizard of Oz narratives would serve as inspiration for future stage and screen adaptations.

Once *Babes In Toyland* had been scheduled to follow *The Wizard of Oz* at New York's Majestic Theatre, Fred Hamlin and Julian Mitchell made their final plans for sending the Baum musical on its grand tour of the country. Both the first company, with the original cast, and the second company would tour the East, the Midwest, and the South and also venture into Canada. For the most part, the first company would play major cities, while the second would appear in lesser cities and towns. But only the second company would tour the West.[1]

The second company's physical production was basically the same as that of its more prestigious counterpart. The costumes again were based largely on the designs of Caroline Siedle, with the drawings of W. W. Denslow inspiring the wardrobe of several key characters. The scenery also was similar, but now the scenic company of Cook, Donigan and Lewis was responsible for "A Kansas Farm," "The Courtyard of the Wizard's Palace," and "The Borderland." Fred Gibson produced "The Country of the Munchkins" and "The Road through the Forest," and Walter Burridge, "The Poppy Field" and "The Poppy Field in Winter."[2] (It is possible that the Burridge drops were not new, that they were simply those that had appeared in the original Chicago production of the musical and were now being used a second time.)

On 7 September 1903, while the first company was still playing the Majestic in New York, the second company made its debut at the Montauk Theatre in Brooklyn. In an unusual move, Hamlin and Mitchell decided to send four key members of the first company—Montgomery, Stone, Anna Laughlin, and Jeanette Lowrie (Cynthia)—to Brooklyn to perform in the new company, thus making it a bigger attraction. In exchange, their counterparts—the Swor Brothers, Isabel D'Armond, and May Taylor—were given the opportunity to prove themselves on Broadway with the original company at the Majestic.[3] By the time the second company played its next date, in Bridgeport, Connecticut, the new cast was complete and intact for the first time.

The first performances at the Montauk Theatre, a matinee followed by a show on the same night, were both sold out, and the evening show ran late because of the numerous encores.[4] A reviewer who attended the opening-night performance said that the production was a lavish one that compared "favorably with the original." Noting that the orchestra had been increased in size to meet the demands of the production, the same critic felt the show was assured success "when more confidence, more voice, and more ability is acquired by the members of the cast other than the four leaders."[5]

With the cast complete, the second company appeared in Bridgeport beginning on 14 September. One critic there liked all of the leading performances, mentioning especially that May Taylor, as Cynthia, was "excellent" and that Arthur Larkin, as Pastoria, was "also good." The chorus, however, was a different matter: it was "decidedly disorderly and careless" and in desperate need of discipline.[6]

On 21 September the show reached Albany, where a critic noted that it was "a very complete duplication of the original production." The Swor Brothers, the reviewer concluded, were "accurate copies of Montgomery and Stone and distinctly clever as the most memorable comic element in the extravaganza."

Also singled out for praise was Arthur Larkin, along with L. J. Wyckoff as Imogene, C. Ray Wallace as the Cowardly Lion, and Daniel Barrett as the Wizard. Admiring Isabel D'Armond, the same critic called her "chubby, charming, and juvenile, with a sweet, small voice and a pair of light, fantastic feet."

Unlike previous reviewers, however, this one felt that May Taylor, although lovely, had a poor singing voice, a criticism he also applied to Madge Ryan (Tryxie) and Mildred Elaine (Dashemoff). But the review ended on an upbeat note: "Neither voice nor personality are as important to a production of this sort as gorgeousness and frolic, and while there was small vocal talent in the cast and few familiar names, nobody who had gone to *The Wizard of Oz* to be diverted went home disappointed."[7] Other regional reviewers varied in their level of enthusiasm, but the awareness of *The Wizard of Oz* around the country was high, and attendance was for the most part good. Furthermore, in general, the smaller the city or town, the better the show's reception.

Meanwhile, the original company was still playing to crowded houses in

The Wizard of Oz on tour: the show's large cast waits to board a train. Townsend Walsh, holding a walking stick, is seated front center. Dave Montgomery, holding a dog, sits in the same row, to the right. Beside him, at the end of the row, is Anna Laughlin. Fred Stone, wearing a derby, appears in the uppermost right corner.

New York but was preparing to embark on an extensive tour. The first stop was to be the Garrick Theatre in Philadelphia, on Monday, 5 October 1903, just two days after the show's final performance in New York. September was to be a busy month for the producers of the show as they made plans for the tour. On 24 September, for example, Fred Hamlin wrote with some urgency to Townsend Walsh about the advertising campaign on the road. "Be sure to advertise original New York cast *big* and *often*," he advised.[8] On 29 September Charles Mitchell, the stage manager, wrote to Walsh asking him to arrange for help in mounting the show when it arrived at its first stop. The entire production had to be transported on Sunday, 4 October, and installed in Philadelphia the next day, ready for the evening performance. Much advance planning and manpower would be needed to do this, and Charles Mitchell's almost frantic tone provides a clear picture of the daunting magnitude of touring such a large show. He outlined his precise requirements as follows:

> *Sunday, to take in show*
> 6 men for scenery
> Property man, assistant and 3 clearers
> *Monday to put on show*
> 12 men for scenery
> Property man, assistant and 3 clearers
> *To man show at night*
> 24 men/6 on a side and 12 in the flies.
> Property man, assistant and 5 clearers.

Tell carpenter we will want a *clear stage, above*, and *on stage*. We will require 50 sets of [electrical] lines. . . . If they don't happen to have lines where you want them it doesn't take them long to run them if they have them. We carry everything in the prop line with the exception of the perishable stuff, which is easily gotten when we get in town. We will require 11 operators in Phila. and *ten* on the one nighters. Have as many dressing rooms as they can possibly scrape up. . . . I'll see you on Monday or possibly Sunday and we can talk over the much dreaded one nighters.[9]

With the exception of a song change here and there, the show presented by the first company on tour took pretty much the same form that it had in New York. Reviews were mixed, but audiences turned out in droves, and encores were frequent. Montgomery and Stone created a sensation wherever the extravaganza played. Boston was especially enraptured with the musical; it played the Boston Theatre from 30 November 1903 until 2 January 1904.

But the Montgomery and Stone company was not without its share of problems. A Chicago engagement scheduled for 17–23 January 1904, was abruptly canceled, for example, when all the theaters in that city were shut down following the great Iroquois Theatre fire. To fill the void, at the last minute the company was booked into the Princess Theatre in Toronto and the Grand Opera House in Hamilton, Ontario. Then, toward the end of February, Fred Stone developed a throat problem and had to miss most of a week's engagement in Pittsburgh. At first, Julian Mitchell, who was with the company at the time, wanted to cancel performances. Fred Meek, the show's manager, insisted, however, that Stone's understudy, George Field, go on as the Scarecrow. Mitchell finally agreed. After Field's first performance in the part, Meek wrote to Townsend Walsh, who was in Washington, D.C., preparing for the show's arrival the following week, "Field played the part and did remarkably well under the circumstances. No one knew the difference, who had not seen the performance before. J. Mitchell is here and wanted to close but I knew this fellow could pull through, and we did not make any announcement."[10] Whether Pittsburgh audiences were ever informed that the Scarecrow was not being played by Fred Stone is a matter of conjecture, but in a letter to Walsh, Fred Hamlin, in New York, reported that Stone's absence from the cast did "not seem to have hurt business to any extent" and that the Pittsburgh week would probably bring in more than $14,000.[11]

Both the first and second companies proved to be lucrative. In his diary, Paul Tietjens, who received 1.88 percent of the gross of every performance, recorded the amount he earned each week from the musical. His royalty share for the period from 6 December 1903 to 2 January 1904, for example, indicates that the first company was grossing between $11,096 and $16,681 per week, a huge sum for the time. The Swor Brothers company did less well but was still profitable, grossing between $3,774 and $4,535 per week during the same period. It played less prestigious venues, of course, but its expenses were not high.[12]

A look at the routes of both companies for February 1904 shows just what touring meant during the earliest years of the twentieth century and, more specifically, reveals Hamlin's different plans for the two companies.[13] The first company began the month in Missouri, playing St. Louis and Kansas City on 1–6 February and 7–13 February, respectively. Engagements then followed in Louisville, Kentucky; Indianapolis, Indiana; and Pittsburgh, Pennsylvania, on 15–17, 18–20, and 22–27 February. Then, on 28 February, the show was in Washington, D.C., for a seven-day stay. In general, as this schedule shows, the first company did much traveling, but for the most part it appeared in major cities, often staying at a particular venue for several days.

Meanwhile, the beginning of the month found the second company in Illinois, playing Monmouth, Galesburg, and Peoria on the first, second, and third, respectively. Then the show moved to Missouri, where it appeared in Hannibal, Moberly, and Sedalia on the fourth, fifth, and sixth. Two engagements followed in Kansas, at Fort Scott on 8 February and Pittsburg on the ninth. The company then returned to Missouri, performing in Joplin and Springfield on the tenth and eleventh. Arkansas then saw the show. There it was staged in Fort Smith on 12 February, Little Rock on the thirteenth, Pine Bluff on the fifteenth, Hot Springs on the sixteenth, and Texarkana on the seventeenth. For the remainder of the month, the company was in Texas, playing Denison on 18 February, Dallas on 19 and 20 February, Fort Worth on the twenty-third, Waco on the twenty-fourth, Austin on the twenty-fifth, and San Antonio on 26 and 27 February. Obviously, the second company had a particularly grueling schedule, made up mostly of one-night stands. With some exceptions, it generally played smaller cities and towns.

By the end of February the producers of the *Wizard of Oz* were preparing to bring the first company back to the Majestic Theatre in New York in a new edition. The musical's successor there, *Babes in Toyland,* had done well, but New Yorkers were anxious for Baum's show to return. On 26 February, John Flaherty, the manager of the Majestic Theatre, wrote to Townsend Walsh: "We love the *Babes* here," he said, "but we are impatiently sniffing the air at the approach of *The Wizard.* That first night will be a gala occasion. Julian has me all jollied up about those ten new musical numbers." Flaherty went on to discuss how the show would be advertised, asking Walsh to "grind out some stuff" to be sent to the various dramatic editors.[14]

After one-week engagements in Baltimore and Newark, the first company of *The Wizard of Oz* returned to the Majestic Theatre on 21 March 1904, and it remained there for several weeks. Known as the second edition or the edition de luxe, it was a tremendous hit all over again. One newspaper account of the opening night described the enormous welcome afforded the cast. "Mr. Fred Stone must have felt like shaking hands with himself a great many times after the curtain fell on the second edition of 'The Wizard of Oz,'" the critic began. "No greater welcome has ever been accorded an American artist in any line of work. From the moment the gallery saw him first . . . there was such a pandemonium of welcome from all parts of the theatre that the actors could scarcely hear themselves speak." The critic added that Dave Montgomery "got a big salvo all to himself" and that other performers, including Anna Laughlin and Lotta Faust, were similarly welcomed.[15]

The show's new edition saw several significant cast changes: May De Souza assumed the role of Dashemoff, and Charles Swain, that of the Wizard. At least one reviewer considered Swain a great improvement over his predecessor, James Wesley.[16] Although no major alterations were made to the basic script, judging from a program of 4 April, many of the show's musical numbers were changed.[17] Pastoria's song "In Michigan," in act 1, was deleted. In its place, Cynthia was given a new number that directly followed her "Niccolo's Piccolo." Entitled "The Tale of the Cassowary" (Will D. Cobb/Gus Edwards), this comic specialty tells of a missionary who becomes stranded on a desert island, where he is eaten by a cassowary, which in turn is eaten by a cannibal.

Next, Tryxie and Pastoria introduced a new duet called "Down on the Brandywine" (Vincent Bryan/J. B. Mullen) to replace their former number. It was a romantic "coon" ballad sung in southern dialect. "Carrie Barry" and "Alas for the Man without Brains" were retained, but following them came two new numbers for Dashemoff, "I Love You All the Time" (Will R. Anderson), and "Mary Canary" (Edward P. Moran/Seymour Furth). Both of these were sentimental love ballads. Act 1 finished as before with "When You Love, Love, Love" and the "Poppy Chorus."

In the next act, the Wizard had a new comic specialty called "The Tale of the Red Shirt" by two songwriters known only as Brackett and Medor. Cynthia was given a new act 2 specialty as well, entitled "It's Enough to Make a Perfect Lady Mad" (also known as "'Twas Enough to Make a Perfect Lady Mad"). Written by Bryan and Mullen, it was apparently created with *The Wizard of Oz* in mind, for unlike most of the other new songs, it related to some degree to the character who sang it. The first refrain and chorus speaks of Cynthia herself and refers to her past with Niccolo:

> My sweetheart had a pickle farm, and played the piccolo,
> And when a pickle grew too high to pick, you know,
> He used to blow the piccolo,
> Upon his little piccolo some awful tunes he'd play,
> My dog Napoleon heard them and grew thinner ev'ry day,
> My dog was quite a cunning little elf,
> When the piccolo would blow, he'd blow himself.
>
> 'Twas enough to make a perfect lady mad,
> My poor old dog grew bony as a shad,
> It nearly broke my aching heart, to see Napoleon's bony part,
> That music spoiled the nicest nap I had,
> 'Twas enough to make a perfect lady mad.[18]

The song's remaining five refrains and choruses pertain to women not in the play and describe ridiculous mishaps that befall them.

The "edition de luxe" of *The Wizard of Oz* in 1904 was special primarily because it contained several new musical numbers. To play up this aspect of the show, a new cover was designed for the sheet music.

Changes also were made in the suite formerly known as the Ball of All Nations and now called the Dance of All Nations. The Wizard still performed his "Connemara Christening," but the Scarecrow discarded his "Spanish Bolero" for an Italian dialect song called "Good-bye, Fedora" (James O'Dea/Robert J. Adams).[19] The Tin Woodman's "Wee Highland Mon" was retained, but it was followed by a new selection for Dorothy called "Under a Panama" (Bryan/Mullen). Finally, a dance number entitled "An Afternoon Tea" was added to the suite. With lyrics by Edgar Smith and music by A. Baldwin Sloane, it afforded Dorothy, the Scarecrow, and the Tin Woodman a second opportunity to perform together. (The first was "When You Love, Love, Love" in act 1.)

Following the Dance of All Nations, Tryxie and Dashemoff each sang a song. Not only was the order of their numbers reversed in the new edition of the show but the songs themselves were new as well. "Johnny, I'll Take You" (Cobb/Edwards) replaced Tryxie's "Sammy" but harkened back to the original song. As with "Sammy," Tryxie addressed the new number directly to a man seated in one of the boxes. In addition, she even referred to Sammy in the chorus:

> I've lost my honey, my ready money,
> I must find another like him, wonder where I'm going to
>   strike him,
> You're just his size sir
> You've got his eyes sir
> If I can't have my Sammy
> Then Johnny I'll take you.[20]

In her customary encore, Tryxie also usually included at least one verse of "Sammy." Dashemoff's new song was a love ballad, also by Cobb and Edwards, called "I Never Loved a Love As I Love You" (also known as "I'll Never Love Another Love Like I Love You").

Next, the Scarecrow and the Tin Woodman were given two comic duets in place of "Hurrah for Baffin's Bay!" The first was called "The Nightmare" (Bryan/Mullen), and the second, with words by David Montgomery (the Tin Woodman), was titled "I'd Like to Go Halves in That." In act 3 the extremely popular "The Traveller and the Pie" and "Must You?" both were retained, but Dorothy had a brand new number with which to close the show, "The Sweetest Girl in Dixie" (O'Dea/Adams).

Although over the course of the next several years additional songs would be added and old ones removed, these new numbers amounted to the largest revamping that the show would ever undergo at one time. And this strategy worked to the advantage of *The Wizard of Oz*, for while the musical had done a fair amount of repeat business during its initial run in New York, audiences now had even more reason to return to see the show a second time. Business was brisk, and the edition de luxe remained at the Majestic until 2 May, when it moved to the New York Theatre for another three weeks. Located in the Times Square theater district, the New York Theatre apparently attracted new audiences that previously had not ventured up to the Majestic.

On 23 May 1904, following the New York run, the new edition made its debut at the Grand Opera House in Chicago. By June there had been several more song changes, suggesting that some of the numbers introduced in New York had not been successful. To replace his two songs in act 1, Dashemoff was given two new numbers, "Only You" (Frank Keesee/Charles Zimmerman) and "When the Heart Is Sad" (Hollister/Zimmerman). Then in act 2 the Wizard returned to singing "On a Pay Night Evening" instead of "The Tale of the Red Shirt," which had been introduced in New York, and Dorothy was back to "Rosalie" instead of "Under a Panama."[21]

This Chicago engagement, in fact, was the first time the extravaganza had returned to the city of its creation since its New York premiere in January 1903. Critical opinion was mixed regarding the many changes the show had undergone. The reviewer for the *Chicago Record Herald,* who had never been a great fan of *The Wizard of Oz,* found this most recent version even less satisfying. "From Broadway it has acquired an unsavory bluntness," he wrote, "and its journey into the countryside has accented its crudity."[22] The critic for the *Chicago Journal,* on the other hand, found the show "much more spirited, coherent and enjoyable than it used to be."[23]

Audiences' reaction to the new version of the show was also mixed. Percy Hammond, the business manager for this engagement, wrote to Townsend Walsh in New York that the "Broadwayized" musical "does not seem to go as well as the old one, the new songs, with one exception, being dead ones so far as Chicago is concerned." "At that," he noted, "we are doing twice the business of any other house in town."[24] The musical did, in fact, extend its run at least once, playing until 9 July, at which point the cast took its first summer vacation in two years. And the second company, which had assimilated most of the new edition's changes, also took a summer break.

By the last week in August both companies were on the road again. The Swor Brothers, now accompanied by Blanche Powell Todd as Dorothy, began their new season with a one-night stand in Peoria, Illinois, on 26 August, while Montgomery and Stone returned again to New York City for a successful two-week engagement at the Majestic Theatre in Brooklyn beginning 29 August. The first company then took the edition de luxe to the Boston Theatre in Boston, where it played to capacity houses for five weeks, and the second company took the play to California for the first time, with engagements in San Francisco (19 September–2 October), Los Angeles (6–8 October), and other locales. The critics for the *San Francisco Chronicle* and the *Los Angeles Times* found the musical wanting, however, and especially criticized the cast.[25] Acknowledging that California was still considered something of a backwater at the time, the reviewer for the *Chronicle* noted, nonetheless, that "Messrs. Hamlin and Mitchell should have found better people than they had, even for a Western company."

After another stint on the road, the Montgomery and Stone company returned to New York again on 7 November. This time the show played at the Academy of Music, on Fourteenth Street. It remained there through the end of the year and broke the house's attendance records. On Election Day alone a special matinee and an evening performance together netted $5,014.[26]

Programs reveal that the musical again saw a few changes in its songs. Dashemoff was down to one solo in act 1, "I Love You All the Time." Furthermore, by 12 December "The Nightmare" and "I'd Like to Go Halves in That" were no longer in the show. Now, in their place, the Scarecrow and Tin Woodman were singing the familiar "Hurrah for Baffin's Bay!" as well as a new song, "Marching thro' Georgia" (Vincent Bryan/Charles Zimmerman), a parody.[27] As usual, occasional bits of dialogue were also changed. Fred Stone, for example, added new jokes to the matinee performance of 24 December in honor of the staff of the publishing firm of Doubleday, Page and Company, who were attending the show as a Christmas theater party. He noted, among other remarks about the company, that one Page made a whole book and that Mr. Page's chauffeur was writing an autobiography.[28]

During this New York engagement, on 27 November, Fred Hamlin died at his home in that city. He had been ill for two months, but his death was evidently sudden.[29] Julian Mitchell, along with the business manager, William Gray, however, would carry on with the business affairs of the Hamlin and Mitchell firm. As a result, the touring plans for the two companies of *The Wizard of Oz* were little affected, although for the most part the firm's plans for future projects died along with Hamlin.

The show continued to be successful during the second half of the 1904–5 season. When the first company played a return engagement at Philadelphia's Garrick Theatre on 13–18 March 1905, the *New York Clipper* noted that the show was "welcomed by filled houses" like those that had greeted the earlier run.[30] Encores in Washington, D.C. (20–25 March), Brooklyn (3–8 April), and

Next Monday, September 12

FRED R. HAMLIN'S magnificent production of the musical extravaganza,

THE WIZARD of OZ

The original Cast, including

MONTGOMERY and STONE and All the Old Favorites

EDITION DE LUXE
of this Famous Spectacle

The Realistic Cyclone	*The Wonderful Scarecrow*
The Gorgeous Poppy Field	*The Tin Woodman*
The Glittering Snow Scene	*The Cowardly Lion*

And all the features which have made the "Wizard" famous, together with numberless new ones.

The whole under the personal stage direction of

JULIAN MITCHELL

☞ The "Wizard" played a record-breaking engagement at this theatre last season and it is expected that on this occasion the success will be more than duplicated.

Advertisement for the musical's engagement at the Boston Theatre in 1904 emphasizing that the edition de luxe contained new features as well as old favorites. With this notice the show's producer hoped to attract those who had already seen the show as well as newcomers.

Toronto (17–22 April) also drew good houses. At the end of April, however, both companies decided to call it quits for the season.

The first company returned to the road on 6 September 1905, and the second company resumed its tour thirteen days later. As the show continued to tour, cast changes became increasingly frequent. Most important, Anna Laughlin did not return to the Montgomery and Stone company for the 1905–6 season. In the first weeks of the season the part of Dorothy was assumed first by Blanche Powell Todd (from the Swor Brothers company) and then by Mabel Barrison (who had played Tryxie in the original Chicago run of the show). Finally, Mona Desmond took the part until the last several weeks of the season, when she was replaced by Belle Robinson.[31]

In addition, of course, new jokes and new numbers were always being added. A program from 11 September, when the first company was playing the Majestic Theatre in Brooklyn, lists the new songs then in the show. In act 1, Cynthia was given a comic fable song entitled "The Tale of a Monkey" (Vincent Bryan/Leo Edwards) in place of "The Tale of the Cassowary." Furthermore, the Wizard once again had a new number for his act 2 entrance, "Julie Dooley" (Frank R. Adams and Will M. Hough/Joseph E. Howard). Another Irish dialect song, it had originally appeared in the show *His Highness the Bey*, earlier in 1905.

In the Dance of All Nations, the Scarecrow had a new number called "Sitting Bull" (Bryan/Zimmerman). For this comic song, Fred Stone was costumed as an American Indian chief and was surrounded by a chorus of girls dressed as Mexicans, cowgirls, and squaws. He followed the song with "Green Corn Dance," a so-called "spineless," or loose-limbed, dance which was so strenuous that when it was done, according to a publicity release, his dresser had to give him an alcohol rubdown before he could go back on stage.[32]

Following the Dance of All Nations, Tryxie and Dashemoff each had new solos, and the Scarecrow and the Tin Woodman had two new duets. Tryxie sang "The Tale of a Stroll" (George Totten Smith/Byrd Dougherty and Benjamin M. Jerome), a romantic ballad that had been introduced in the comic opera *The Royal Chef* in 1904. Dashemoff's new ballad was "My Own Girl" (Bryan/Edwards). The Scarecrow and the Tin Woodman's first new duet was "Football" (Bryan and Zimmerman). The sport was under attack at the time because of its excessive violence. At the beginning of the 1906 football season, in fact, rules would be enacted that would tone down the game. Montgomery and Stone's parody of the game's violence involved stunts so rough that doctors were kept on hand at every performance.[33] Costumed in football gear, the pair clowned around with a football as they sang:

Just bring along the ambulance
And call the Red Cross nurse,
Then ring the undertaker up and make him bring a hearse;
Have all the surgeons ready there,
For they'll have work today,
Oh, can't you see the football teams,
Are lining up to play?

Football, Football,
That's the game for me,
Break his hip, hip! hip hurrah,
Kick him in the knee.
Soak him on the five yard line,
We must have 'em lame,
Football, Football,
It's a gentle game.[34]

The comedy team's second new duet was "Marching through Port Arthur" (Bryan/Zimmerman), a replacement for "Marching thro' Georgia."

So once again *The Wizard of Oz* was trying to revitalize itself with new material. And once again the strategy worked to a large degree. Stone's "Sitting Bull" and "Green Corn Dance" caused a special sensation and inevitably demanded encores. But an even bigger sensation was caused by Montgomery and Stone's "Football" routine. It was the talk of the town wherever the show played, and it received much attention in the press. A review of the routine's debut in Philadelphia mentioned that it "literally convulsed the audience to screams of laughter."[35]

Twice during the 1905–6 season the show's first company returned to New York City, and both times it proved successful. For its one-week engagement at the West End Theatre in Harlem in September, the *New York Clipper* reported, the musical held "unusual drawing power."[36] On opening night the house was full, and most of the seats were already sold for the remainder of the week. *The Wizard of Oz* also prospered during its four-week stay at the New York Academy of Music in October and November, where a big opening-night audience gave Montgomery and Stone a "tumultuous welcome, and howled with glee over their new travesty on football."[37] A subsequent three-week run in Boston also was well received, and when the show returned to Chicago to begin a Christmas run, audiences were as appreciative as ever. Of opening night there one reviewer noted, "There was a genuine reunion . . . in the Grand, a big audience and Montgomery and Stone being the principal participants. The

Tin Woodman and the Scarecrow had come home again and there was not the slightest doubt of the sincerity of their welcome. Twice the audience practically stopped the proceedings of 'The Wizard of Oz' to acclaim the two popular comedians."[38]

But despite this continued success, all was not as it had once been. For one thing, a glut of other shows attempting to capitalize on the popularity of Baum's extravaganza had saturated the market in recent years. Such musical spectaculars as *Babes in Toyland* (1903), *The Pearl and the Pumpkin* (1905), and *Wonderland* (1905), which had met with varying degrees of success, had made *The Wizard of Oz* much less of a novelty than it once was. The show's fortunes became increasingly dependent on Montgomery and Stone. It was because of them that audiences kept flocking to the show, a fact borne by the second company, which played fewer and fewer engagements as the 1905–6 season wore on.

For their part, Montgomery and Stone were eager to call it quits. Their roles were demanding, and they had worked almost continuously for more than three years. In February 1906 Stone published a short article explaining to the public his frustration at playing the same role over and over. He mentioned that he had transformed himself into the Scarecrow "something like fourteen hundred times," and although he was gratified by his character's continuing popularity, he longed for change. "Imagine," he wrote, "the tedium of donning the scarecrow's raiment, contorting one's physiognomy into the blandest vacuum, squeaking instead of articulating every time you open your mouth, and gyrating for three hours as no mortal man ever does in order to create the illusion of a thing of straw and patches endowed with breath and life."[39]

The two comedians must also have been making their feelings known to Julian Mitchell and William Gray. In a letter of 18 December 1905 to Townsend Walsh, Gray mentioned that the new manager of the Grand Opera House in Chicago wanted to add a matinee for the Sunday before New Year's Day. But, Gray noted, "we are unable to force matters with Montgomery and Stone. They simply will not do anything more than the contract calls for, nor will the inducement of extra money have any effect upon them."[40]

Not long after this, in fact, the comedy team's contract itself became a matter of dispute. By March 1906 the two stars were seeking to break it. Their original agreement with Fred Hamlin bound them exclusively to the producer's services for a period of four years, with an option for a fifth. Now Montgomery and Stone announced their intention of leaving at the end of the present season, which was the fourth year of their contract. Gray and Mitchell realized, however, just what a loss this would mean to *The Wizard of Oz*, and on 31 March

One of William Wallace Denslow's full-color plates from the
first edition of *The Wonderful
Wizard of Oz* (1900). Here Dorothy and her companions consult
with Glinda.

Anna Fitzhugh as a Poppy Girl in
the 1902 musical extravaganza
The Wizard of Oz.

Poster for the New York stage production of 1903, showing the Scarecrow (as a Spaniard), Dorothy, and the Tin Woodman (as a Scotsman) performing at the Ball of All Nations. The ball was held in celebration of the Wizard's having given the Scarecrow a brain and the Tin Woodman a heart, but it was really just an excuse to provide each of the major cast members with a chance to perform an ethnic specialty number.

The act 1 transformation scene depicting the rescue of Dorothy from the spell of the Poppies was a sensation wherever *The Wizard of Oz* played. The Poppies shown in this poster for the 1903 New York production comprised a mixture of set pieces and chorus girls dressed as flowers.

Poster from 1903 showing the Tin Woodman (dressed as a chauffeur) and Dorothy reassembling the Scarecrow. Part of the new act 3 that was devised for the musical's New York premiere, this stage trick was one of the show's most elaborate special effects.

Most of the costumes for *The Wizard of Oz* were redesigned for the New York premiere of the show in January 1903. Four of Caroline Siedle's costume sketches for the production are shown here: (*top, left*) Dorothy in her Kansas dress, act 1; (*right*) Dorothy in her fancy dress, act 2; (*bottom, left*) Tryxie as a waitress, act 1; (*right*) a Royal Guard, act 3.

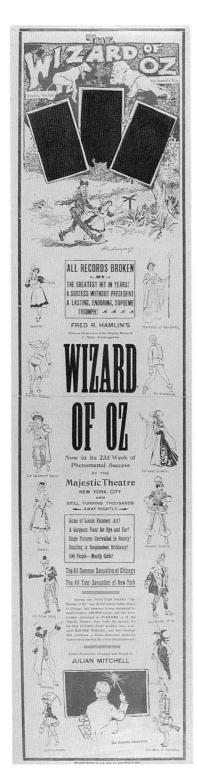

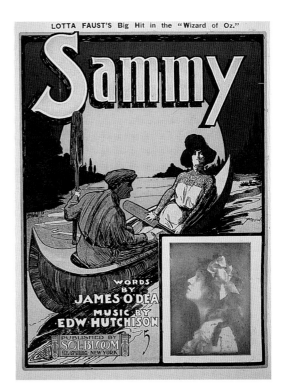

Sheet music for Tryxie Tryfle's "Sammy" song (1903). In the show, Lotta Faust as Tryxie sang the song while suggestively entreating whatever man happened to be seated in the upper righthand box. The number became one of the most notorious in the production.

Broadside heralding the musical's twenty-fifth successful week at New York City's Majestic Theatre. In an era when a theatrical long run was more the exception than the rule, the *Wizard of Oz*'s continued success, even during the heat of the New York summer, was something to be trumpeted.

Poster advertising Hurtig and Seamon's touring production, c. 1907. Tryxie stands on the Cowardly Lion's tail, as the Scarecrow and Tin Woodman look on. Hurtig and Seamon, who purchased the production from the Hamlin estate in 1906, took *The Wizard of Oz* on tour across the United States through the 1908-9 season.

Dorothy with the Scarecrow, the Tin Woodman, the Cowardly Lion, and the Hungry Tiger (a character from Baum's book *Ozma of Oz*) in a slide from *Fairylogue and Radio-Plays*, Baum's multimedia lecture tour of 1908.

French poster for the Semon film, 1925. Larry Semon was known as Zigoto in France, where the comedian had quite a large following.

Dorothy and her traveling companions about to enter the deadly poppy field. The snowstorm with which Glinda kills the poppies in the MGM film was suggested by a similar construct in the 1902 stage version of *The Wizard of Oz*.

Magazine advertisement for the MGM release, 1939.

Poster featuring the Scarecrow and the Tin Woodman's "Football" satire for the edition de luxe appearance at the Academy of Music, New York City, in October 1905. This number became an immediate sensation wherever the show played. It was said that a doctor was on hand at every performance because Montgomery and Stone's parody contained stunts that were extremely rough.

Poster for the engagement at Ford's Theatre, Baltimore, in 1906 showing the Scarecrow and the Tin Woodman in the "Hurrah for Baffin's Bay" number, which had recently been reinserted into the production.

they sought a court injunction to prevent their stars from leaving.[41] The courts eventually ruled in favor of Montgomery and Stone, however, and they played the Tin Woodman and the Scarecrow for the last time on 19 May in Trenton, New Jersey. The following September, they opened successfully in Victor Herbert's new musical *The Red Mill,* playing two wiseacre American tourists, Kid Conner and Con Kidder, on a tour of Europe. The second company of *The Wizard of Oz,* meanwhile, had been permanently disbanded at the end of February 1906.[42]

The comedy team of Montgomery and Stone continued to be extremely popular with audiences until Montgomery's untimely death in 1917, but their characterizations in *The Wizard of Oz* always remained their benchmark performance. The stars themselves seem to have been aware of this fact. As Punks and Spooks in *The Lady of the Slipper* (1912), a musical based on the Cinderella story, for example, their costuming and makeup resembled that of the Tin Woodman and the Scarecrow. After his partner's death, Stone continued to enjoy success, but he would never escape the pull of *The Wizard of Oz.* He donned his Scarecrow attire and re-created scenes from the show as late as 1936, when he celebrated his fifty-third year in the theater.[43]

Gray and Mitchell, for their part, had an uphill battle attempting to send *The Wizard of Oz* out for another season without their two star comedians. When Gray began to set up bookings for the fall of 1906, he met with resistance from many theater managers. They resented being forced to take the show on the same financial terms as in years when it had been at its peak. In July 1906, for example, Bert Whitney, the manager of the Detroit Opera House, wrote a letter of complaint to the New York firm of Klaw and Erlanger, Gray's booking agent, stating, "I do not think it advisable for . . . the attraction to play in Detroit without Montgomery and Stone. It has played three weeks in the last three seasons and [during] the last engagement business dropped . . . below the previous one. I do not think this attraction is entitled to the same terms without Montgomery and Stone. In fact, I would rather not play it."[44] Through Klaw and Erlanger, Gray obliged Whitney and canceled the three-night engagement scheduled for Detroit in the fall.

An even bigger protest was registered by Sherman Brown, the manager of the Davidson Theatre in Milwaukee. Klaw and Erlanger had sent him a contract booking the musical into his theater in November. The terms were 70 percent for the producers and 30 percent for the Davidson. On 22 August 1906 Brown sent the contract back to the firm with a note of complaint: "I do not care for the attraction even if the terms were made 60% and 40%, as this attraction, I believe, has quite outlived its usefulness, so far as this city is concerned. Please be so kind as to cancel same."[45] In a letter dated the following day he complained further, "We have played this attraction several times recently with the No. 2, and starved to death (excepting the holiday) and the newspapers roasted us unmercifully."[46]

When Klaw and Erlanger pressured him to accept the booking, Brown wrote once again on 28 August. "Occasionally there are local reasons why a booking is not desirable in a certain city," he explained, emphasizing that he would like to have the attraction canceled. But he knew he was at a disadvantage with Klaw and Erlanger, which was an extremely powerful company. Sensing that he would be forced to accept the booking despite his protestations, he tried to argue for better financial terms and berated the producers for asking "the same percentage as for the big company during its one-time splendid vogue."[47]

In a letter to Klaw and Erlanger dated 1 September, Gray expressed his thoughts about the matter:

> Referring to letter of Mr. Brown in reference to "The Wizard of Oz" Company will say, that the company we have engaged for this season is on a par with the companies which we have played in the number one "Wizard" in former seasons. In many respects it is the best organization that we have ever put on the road. Many new features have been added to the entertainment and a great deal of money expended on the production which looks as bright and fresh to-day as it did the first season. We have always endeavored to keep this attraction right up to the mark. The characters of the 'Scarecrow' and the 'Tinman' are played equally as well as formerly and our expenses are equal to former seasons. If conditions are not found to be exactly as I represent them, I am willing to concede to Mr. Brown the five Per Cent concession he requests, but otherwise I think that it is only justice that we should get terms that will allow us to exist.[48]

But Brown would not concede, and Gray finally agreed to change the terms of the contract to 65 percent and 35 percent.[49]

Recalcitrant theater managers were not Gray's only problem. In what was probably a calculated move, Gray had replaced Fred Stone with an actor named George A. Stone, who had been a member of the comedy team of Gaston and Stone. Fred was less than pleased at this attempt to capitalize on his popularity, and he protested. One newspaper reported that Gray responded by changing George Stone's name to George Rock until the actor complained and his real name was restored.[50]

Beleaguered as it was, *The Wizard of Oz* nevertheless began a new season at the end of August. Fred Nie played the Tin Woodman; Anna Wilks, Dorothy;

and Ethel Green and Rosa Gore, Dashemoff and Cynthia. Some new songs were added, but in other respects the musical remained basically unchanged. One reviewer noted that it was "as bright and beautiful to the eye as ever, scenery and costumes are as gorgeous and the chorus is as big numerically and vocally, but much of the singular, individual charm of the original version has been effaced by the interpolation of meaningless, tawdry special numbers and the weakening of the cast."[51]

Fred Hamlin's heirs had long before decided not to invest in new theatrical productions, and now they were faced with dwindling profits from *The Wizard of Oz* and their other touring shows, all of which were past their prime. The decrease in profits, along with a desire to wind up the Hamlin estate once and for all, led them to the decision to close *The Wizard of Oz* by early November and put the production up for sale. All remaining tour dates, including those that had been arranged with Sherman Brown, were canceled.[52]

On 20 November 1906 Baum's musical gained something of a new lease on life when the theatrical firm of Hurtig and Seamon acquired all rights to the show.[53] Hurtig and Seamon was involved in many theatrical enterprises, from cut-rate producing to theater management. By the end of November *The Wizard of Oz* was once again on the road.[54] Billed as "Hamlin and Mitchell's Original Production," the show was little changed in the way of physical production. George Stone and Joseph Schrode, who had been playing Imogene since 1903, remained with the show throughout the season. Other key players, at least for much of the season, included Minerva Coverdale as Dorothy and Irving Christian as the Tin Woodman. Several new songs were added, but most of the old standards, such as "Alas for the Man without Brains," "When You Love, Love, Love," "Sammy," "Football," and "The Traveller and the Pie," were retained.[55] Photographs and artwork from the original Montgomery and Stone production were sometimes used in advertisements for the show.

Hurtig and Seamon evidently was successful with *The Wizard of Oz*. The extravaganza returned to New York City for almost the whole month of December, played return engagements in Philadelphia, Jersey City, Brooklyn, Providence, and Boston, and was back again in New York in February. It played Chicago in May. Not only did the musical finish out the 1906–7 season but it was on the road during the following two seasons as well. George Stone and Joseph Schrode remained with the show throughout, and during the 1908–9 season James Wesley, who had played the Wizard with Montgomery and Stone, once again took on that role.[56] As before, new songs were added each season to freshen up the musical.

Although business had been good, Hurtig and Seamon decided not to put

The act 3 finale as presented by Hurtig and Seamon,
c. 1907. The set is basically the same as it had been in the
Hamlin production, but it is less opulently trimmed and
appears a little worse for wear. There are fewer people in
the cast as well.

The Wizard of Oz out for the 1909–10 season. Perhaps it was that the original agreement with the Hamlin estate had expired, or perhaps the death in February 1909 of Ben Hurtig, one of the major players in the firm, was a factor. By 1911 the musical had been released for stock and amateur production, which meant that for the first time theatrical companies around the country could lease the rights to *The Wizard of Oz*. The first significant production to come out of stock was the one put on by John Craig's Castle Square Company in Boston in 1911.

Craig, who had begun his career as an actor, had taken over the management of the Castle Square Theatre in 1908.[57] The playhouse, which had been in operation since 1897, seated about eighteen hundred people and sold tickets at popular prices, with the scale ranging from $.15 to $.75. The theater blossomed under Craig's influence and achieved a high degree of respectability. Craig believed in taking chances, and in addition to presenting plays that had been made available to stock companies, he took great pride in presenting new works. He is also credited as being the first manager to introduce musical plays into the repertoire of a dramatic stock company when in 1908 he presented *The Circus Girl*. The production was a huge hit with audiences, and the performance of musicals became an annual holiday event for the company from that time forward.

In the fall of 1911 Craig announced that the Castle Square's holiday musical for that season would be *The Wizard of Oz*, which would begin performances on 22 December 1911. Aside from the high regard in which Craig's work was held, what made his mounting of Baum's extravaganza significant was its link to the original Hamlin production. Arthur Hill agreed once again to take on the role of the Cowardly Lion, and his wife Alice "Stubby" Ainscoe, who had played several roles in *The Wizard of Oz* chorus from 1902 to 1905, was hired on as codirector with a man named William Parke.

Preparations for the elaborate show began during the latter half of November. The entire stock company was to appear in it, and others were to be hired for chorus roles. Advance promotional literature boasted that the cast would number almost one hundred.[58] Mary Young, Craig's wife and the company's ingenue, was to play Dorothy. She was popular with audiences and had successfully tackled the Castle Square's previous forays into musical comedy. George Hassell and Donald Meek, who later would win success as a motion-picture actor, were to assume the roles of the Scarecrow and the Tin Woodman, while Walter Walker, Morgan Wallace, Mabel Montgomery, and Mabel Colcord would play the Wizard, Pastoria, Tryxie, and Cynthia. Breaking with tradition, a man, Carney Christie, would take the role of Dashemoff Daily.

Alice "Stubby" Ainscoe, codirector of the Castle Square
Theatre (Boston, Mass.) production, as photographed
c. 1905, when she was a member of *The Wizard of Oz*
chorus. Ainscoe was the wife of Arthur Hill, who
originated the role of the Cowardly Lion in 1902 and
reprised his role at the Castle Square Theatre in 1911.

Programs and reviews indicate that the basic Hamlin and Mitchell concept was followed.[59] The synopsis of scenes remained the same for act 1. Act 2 was now set in "The Emerald City, Land of Oz," and act 3 simply in "The Land of Oz." Many of the songs from the earlier production were retained. A few notable changes were made to the show, however. In act 1, "Carrie Barry," originally sung by Dorothy, was given to Dashemoff, which makes sense narratively since the number is a song that the poet has written for Dorothy. In addition, act 2 seems to have been restructured quite a bit. "Niccolo's Piccolo," which Cynthia sang in act 1, was moved to the beginning of this act—and inexplicably assigned to Dorothy. Apparently, Mabel Colcord, as Cynthia, was not a singer, because her character's second-act number also was deleted. The Scarecrow's "Sitting Bull" appears to have been all that remained of the Dance of All Nations suite, and "Sammy," which followed it, was now sung by Dorothy instead of Tryxie. Finally, Sir Wiley Gyle, played by Leslie Palmer, was given a number of his own—probably for the first time in the show's history. Labeled in the program simply "Song," the piece may have varied from week to week; one review gave the title of Gyle's song as "Jack's the Lad."[60] As for act 3, its structure seems to have remained basically unchanged. Dorothy sang a song entitled "Fraidy Cat" (James A. Brennan), which, although its lyrics are addressed to a boy, may have involved the Cowardly Lion.

The production was well received by both critics and audiences. Mary Young, George Hassell, and Donald Meek were all praised. One reviewer who was obviously familiar with the show from its heyday found Hassell "excellent," though he noted that the actor "couldn't tumble about so irresponsibly as Mr. Stone." The same critic found much unintentional humor in Carney Christie's performance as Dashemoff. Remembering that the role always had been played *en travestie,* he commented that "the poor 'juvenile' was having a desperate lot of trouble trying to look like a girl playing a boy."[61] Regarding the music, another reviewer claimed, "The music was better played by the orchestra than one often hears it done in houses that confine themselves to musical comedy."[62] As for the overall quality of singing voices, Craig himself pointed out that he always selected his company members for their ability to tackle both drama and musical comedy.[63]

The cyclone and the Poppy transformation were staged much as they had been in the original production, relying on a gauze curtain. The scenes must have been especially effective, for they were repeatedly singled out for praise. One observer marveled that "the audience itself seemed to be in the midst of the storm, and more than one person instinctively shivered."[64]

Audiences flocked to the Castle Square. During Christmas week, two

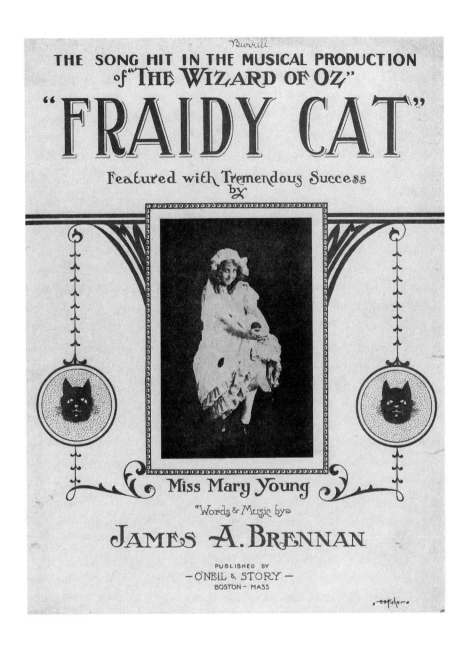

The Castle Square Theatre in Boston mounted the first stock production of *The Wizard of Oz* in December 1911. This sheet music cover shows Mary Young, as Dorothy, who sang one of a few new musical interpolations. She was the wife of John Craig, manager of the Castle Square Theatre.

performances were given each day, at two o'clock in the afternoon and eight in the evening. The theater's *Program Magazine* for 1 January 1912 noted that "the demand for seats has been unprecedented, and never before has our box office staff been kept so steadily on the jump from the first thing in the morning till the latest hour of the evening. Our previous holiday productions have succeeded, but their success is as nothing to the huge triumph of *The Wizard of Oz*."[65] And as was always the case, the musical seemed to be equally popular with children and adults. The show closed on 20 January 1912 after a run of four weeks.

It is likely that numerous productions of *The Wizard of Oz* were staged by other stock companies. In July 1913, for example, the Bainbridge Musical Stock Company presented its version of Baum's show at the Metropolitan Opera House in Minneapolis. The reviewer for the *Minneapolis Morning Tribune* found the performance "excellent enough to be enjoyed even by those who were fortunate enough to see it presented by the company headed by Montgomery and Stone."[66] But it was not only in the memory of audiences that the original production lived on. In 1918 Joseph Schrode, who had played Imogene both with Montgomery and Stone and in the subsequent Hurtig and Seamon productions, reprised the part when the Poli Musical Comedy Players produced their version of *The Wizard of Oz* at Poli's Theatre in Washington, D.C.[67]

Exactly why the stage version of *The Wizard of Oz* so thoroughly captured the imagination of the theatergoing public during the first years of the twentieth century is difficult to say. Certainly much of the complexity and meaning of Baum's original tale were lost in Julian Mitchell's elaborate reworking of the text. And there was little in the way of intellectual content. It was fun, it was glitzy, it was appropriate for families, and at least while Montgomery and Stone were with it, it offered some show-stopping performances. Perhaps these things were enough to attract crowds. Or perhaps audiences were familiar enough with the book that they were able to fill in parts of the story that had become hidden among all the various subplots of the musical. Then, too, perhaps the fact that the uniquely American character of Baum's tale had been retained appealed to people. In addition to the Scarecrow, such characters as Dorothy the farm girl, Tryxie the waitress, and the Wizard, a crooked politician, were distinctly recognizable types in the American landscape.

For whatever reasons, however, the show did not lose its hold on the American public. Aside from the productions that continued to crop up here and there, *The Wizard of Oz* also lived on in its theatrical legacy. Its success had led to a vogue for musical comedies with fairy-tale plots, and shows of this type proliferated both on Broadway and in regional theaters during the first decade of the twentieth century. At least one of them, *Babes in Toyland,* Hamlin and Mitchell's successor to Baum's extravaganza, also became a favorite of stock companies.

Baum himself would try to score again with other musicals based on his Oz books. Ever mindful of the tremendous success of *The Wizard of Oz* on stage, in 1905 he wrote an extravaganza with composer Frederic Chapin called *The Woggle-Bug,* based on *The Marvelous Land of Oz,* his 1904 follow-up to his first Oz tale.[68] The Scarecrow, the Tin Woodman, and Glinda reappeared in *The Marvelous Land of Oz,* even though the other principal characters in the book were all new. In writing the script for *The Woggle-Bug,* however, Baum tried to minimize all references to *The Wizard of Oz* on stage, even going so far as to eliminate those characters that had appeared in his first story.

After a tryout in Milwaukee, *The Woggle-Bug* opened at the Garrick Theatre in Chicago on 18 June 1905, but it was not well received. Despite the author's efforts, critics still found the show to be too derivative of its predecessor. The comic team of Jack Pumpkinhead and the Woggle-Bug, for example, had the same dynamic as the Scarecrow and the Tin Woodman, and a chorus of Chrysanthemums now substituted for the Poppies. In addition, the musical lacked any talent of the magnitude of Julian Mitchell, Fred Stone, or Dave Montgomery. Its producer, Henry Raeder, was no Fred Hamlin, and according to Chapin, the show was badly mismanaged.[69] After being lambasted by critics and ignored by audiences, it closed after less than a month's run.

Baum was extremely disheartened by the failure of *The Woggle-Bug.* Still hoping to duplicate the glory of *The Wizard of Oz* on stage, however, he turned to musical theater once again with a show called *The Tik-Tok Man of Oz.* At its core was the third of the author's Oz books, *Ozma of Oz,* which was published in 1907. By the time the show was produced in 1913, however, it had acquired elements from Baum's fourth and fifth Oz books, *Dorothy and the Wizard in Oz* (1908) and *The Road to Oz* (1909). Collaborating with composer Louis F. Gottschalk and producer Oliver Morosco, Baum this time did achieve a modicum of success. Although the musical also had similarities to *The Wizard of Oz,* it included much that was new and original. On 31 March 1913 *The Tik-Tok Man of Oz* opened in Los Angeles, where it had a five-week run at the Majestic Theatre. It then played engagements in San Francisco and Chicago, but in the end, Morosco was preoccupied with other productions and decided not to take it to Broadway.[70] Baum would continue to dabble in live theater, mostly on an amateur basis, until his death in 1919.

The legacy of the musical *The Wizard of Oz* was felt in other fields as well. The success of the stage play fueled interest in Baum's Oz books, and in fact he dedicated *The Marvelous Land of Oz* to Montgomery and Stone. And the cinema was not immune to the lure of the stage show. In fact, filmmakers were soon to find inspiration in the musical, as well as in Baum's original book. If the tale could attract both theatergoers and readers across America, then why would it not appeal to cinema audiences too? In fact, it was not long before filmmakers would attempt to capture the Wizard of Oz story on film.

PART 2

The Silent Films, 1908–1925

Chapter 6

"A Novel Entertainment"

Fairylogue and Radio-Plays (1908)

ONSIDERING L. FRANK BAUM's broad and forward-looking interests, it should come as no surprise that the first films based on the novel *The Wonderful Wizard of Oz* were initiated by the author himself. Filmed for Baum by the Selig Polyscope Company, these brief motion pictures appeared in his *Fairylogue and Radio-Plays,* a multimedia show that he toured in 1908. They were a prime example of a genre of early motion pictures known as the fairy-tale film, which featured fantastic stories and trick effects. The foremost producer of these films was the pioneer filmmaker Georges Méliès, of France, whose work, dating from 1896 to 1912, was exported to America. But American filmmakers, among them Edwin S. Porter, produced their own films in this genre. Fairy-tale films were extremely popular with audiences during the early part of the twentieth century, and Baum hoped to capitalize on their appeal.

Fairylogue and Radio-Plays epitomized both Baum's endless creativity and his lack of financial acumen. The structure of his entertainment was unusual but clearly inspired by the illustrated lecture format.[1] Baum functioned as the onstage narrator, presenting a travelogue of some of the fairy lands—hence the term *fairylogue*—that he had created in his books. Like many other lecturers of the time, he illustrated his talk with both films and slides. The twenty-three films in the show all had been shot in the Chicago studio of the Selig Polyscope Company and then sent to Paris, where they were hand-colored by Duval Frères. There is no clear explanation for the term *radio-play.* It is likely just another example of Baum's whimsy—using the word *radio,* which connotes something transmitted by radiant energy, to refer to his fairy films so as to make them seem exotic and technologically modern.[2] The motion pictures have not survived, but fortunately the script of Baum's accompanying narration gives us some idea of their content.[3]

Although the films were the show's primary attraction, the projectors of the time, including the Selig Polyscope machine Baum used, produced shaky images. For this reason, slides were interspersed with the films in order to provide some relief to the audience's eyes. A total of 113 hand-colored slides, all of which survive, were included in the entertainment.[4] Most of them were painted by E. Pollock based on illustrations appearing in Baum's books. A few slides presented photographs of the costumed actors in the radio-plays. As a further accompaniment to Baum's talk, a live orchestra (members of the Theodore Thomas Orchestra) performed twenty-seven instrumental numbers composed by Nathaniel D. Mann, who had also written music for the 1902 *Wizard of Oz* play.

The evening's program was divided into two distinct sections. The first, lasting about seventy minutes, was called "The Land of Oz" and was based on three of Baum's books, *The Wonderful Wizard of Oz, The Marvelous Land of Oz* (1904), and *Ozma of Oz* (1907). The second, lasting approximately forty minutes, concerned the author's non-Oz book *John Dough and the Cherub* (1906). During the fifteen-minute intermission that separated the two parts, Baum screened slides promoting his latest book, *Dorothy and the Wizard of Oz.* Following the show, his published works were for sale in the lobby.

Fairylogue and Radio-Plays played a tryout engagement in Grand Rapids, Michigan, from 24 to 26 September 1908 before premiering at Chicago's Orchestra Hall on 1 October. Baum gave a total of one matinee and three evening performances in his hometown, with ticket prices ranging from $.25 to $1.00. He then toured fairly continuously until the end of the year, visiting St. Louis (5–7 October), Milwaukee (8–10 October), St. Paul (12–14 October), Minneapolis (15–17 October), Chicago, for a return engagement (24 October–6 November), Rockford, Illinois (10 November), Rock Island, Illinois (11 November), Burlington, Iowa (12 November), Peoria, Illinois (13 November), Syracuse, New York (2–3 December), Auburn, New York (4 December), and, finally, New York City (14–31 December).[5]

ON THE STAGE
Dorothy and the Wizard in Oz
In PARISIAN COLOR-PHOTOGRAPHY and
WONDERFULLY LIFE-LIKE!

DOROTHY AND THE WIZARD IN OZ
THE LAND OF OZ
JOHN DOUGH AND THE CHERUB

all three by

L. FRANK BAUM

form the basis for the merry, whimsical, and distinctly original

Fairylogue and Radio-Plays

Advertisement for *Fairylogue and Radio-Plays* showing
Dorothy with a Mifket, a character in *John Dough and the
Cherub* (*Publishers' Weekly,* 26 September 1908). Most of
the show's publicity emphasized the lifelike qualities of
the motion pictures' colors.

Except in the initial Chicago engagement, evening shows were the exception rather than the rule. Matinees allowed Baum to cater better to a juvenile audience. In Syracuse, for example, he went so far as to schedule school-day matinees at four o'clock so that children could attend more easily.[6] On 29 October, during his return engagement in Chicago, he held a special "Dorothy Matinee," at which he asked Romola Remus, who played Dorothy in the radio-plays, to attend in her costume. She was introduced to the audience and later went out to the lobby to sell books.[7] At certain performances the author himself also autographed books, to much fanfare.

As the script indicates, the first part of *Fairylogue*'s "Land of Oz" section comprised three film segments and six slides and dealt largely with *The Wonderful Wizard of Oz.* At the outset of the show, Baum appeared onstage wearing a white frock coat and matching trousers. In a brief prologue he discussed the phenomenon of fairies. A fairy, he explained, had once whisked him away to the Land of Oz, where he had lived for a time and learned about its inhabitants' history. The fairies had given him permission to write about them when he returned home. Through his books, he said, he hoped to inspire a love for Oz. Announcing that he would now introduce the principal characters, Baum stepped into the wings as a curtain was drawn to reveal a square screen measuring eight or ten feet across, framed in scarlet velvet.[8]

As Baum continued his narration from the wings, his son Frank Joslyn, in charge of projection, showed the first film. A large closed book was seen on the screen. A pageboy swung it open to reveal a black-and-white image of Dorothy. Baum, attired in the same outfit that he was wearing onstage, appeared in the film next to the book and beckoned to his heroine. She stepped out of the volume, coming to life in full color. The book was closed and then reopened to reveal another of Baum's characters, the Scarecrow, who also stepped down from the pages of the book and came to life. This was repeated until, one by one, other characters were introduced, including, from *The Wonderful Wizard of Oz,* the Tin Woodman, the Cowardly Lion, and Glinda. Baum and his creations on film bowed to the camera as this first motion picture segment ended.

Baum now came out from the wings and began narrating an abbreviated version of *The Wonderful Wizard of Oz.* To the accompaniment of slides, he told how Dorothy and Toto were blown to Oz in a cyclone and how they then set off on the yellow brick road to find the Wizard. At this point another film was screened. In it, Dorothy and Toto are seen coming upon a cornfield where the Scarecrow is attached to a pole. After sitting down, Dorothy sees the Scarecrow move and beckon to her. This frightens her, and she starts to run away. The Scarecrow calls her back. She helps him down from the pole, but since his legs are not stable, he stumbles as he walks and finally falls over a fence into the road. After helping him up, Dorothy continues to assist him. There is a comic moment as she tries to hold the Scarecrow while picking up her basket. Finally, she leads him in the direction of the Emerald City.

Showing a slide, Baum now discussed the next occurrence in the story, when Dorothy and the Scarecrow stop by the roadside and Dorothy eats the lunch in her basket. Next, another film was introduced. Dorothy and the Scarecrow are seen in a dark forest, and the Scarecrow slips and has to be helped to his feet again. The two come upon the Tin Woodman and oil his joints. Then the Lion arrives on the scene and knocks down the Scarecrow and the Tin Woodman. Dorothy scolds the Lion, causing him to cry. The Scarecrow and the Tin Woodman shake hands with the Cowardly Lion, and the group, now friends, are ready to continue the journey to the Wizard.

Baum then completed the story through slides. He told his audience how the Wizard, a humbug who does not actually have any magical powers, helps fill the needs of Dorothy's companions. A balloon meant to carry Dorothy back to Kansas, however, escapes holding only the Wizard. Finally, Dorothy seeks out Glinda, who sends her home by means of the silver shoes. During the remainder of the show, Baum, using additional films and slides, related a similarly summarized version of *The Marvelous Land of Oz,* followed by more complete treatments of *Ozma of Oz* and *John Dough and the Cherub.*

In creating the introductory Wizard of Oz section of *Fairylogue and Radio-Plays,* Baum specifically chose to film scenes from the 1900 novel that had served to introduce Dorothy, the Scarecrow, the Tin Woodman, and the Cowardly Lion. Not only were these favorite characters from the book but they would play major roles in the other Oz stories that made up *Fairylogue.*

As presented, the Wizard of Oz story was fairly faithful to the novel. *Fairylogue* was, after all, a promotion for Baum's books, which were sold in the lobby. In fact, his publisher at the time, the Reilly and Britton Company, took out advertisements for the entertainment.[9] Nevertheless, some changes were made to the narrative, and important elements were removed for the sake of abbreviation. Most notably, as in the 1902 musical, there was no Wicked Witch of the West, and her absence here undoubtedly weakened the dramatic tension.

The musical was still touring during the 1908–9 season, so it is not surprising that it exerted an influence on this section of *Fairylogue.* In fact, Baum's narration contained puns that came straight from the stage production. After coming down from the pole, for example, the Scarecrow remarks that he feels better in his "polar regions." Also, he turns down the lunch that Dorothy offers him, claiming that he is already "stuffed full." Since these jokes had been used

Two versions of Dorothy, Toto, and the Scarecrow taking a break from their journey: *right,* W. W. Denslow's illustration for Baum's book; *below,* E. Pollock's lantern slide for *Fairylogue and Radio-Plays.* Pollock used Denslow's basic layout of the scene but rendered Dorothy and the Scarecrow in the style of John R. Neill, who had illustrated Baum's sequels to *The Wonderful Wizard of Oz.*

in the play, Baum could be sure of their success with audiences. In addition, the portrayal of the Scarecrow here owed much to Fred Stone's stage performance. Stone gave his character unsteady, wobbly legs, an inspired piece of business that had not appeared in the novel.

The script suggests that other changes made to the narrative when it was filmed were due to the very nature of silent film. Because there was no dialogue, broad physical pantomime was used to display thoughts and emotions. The Scarecrow and the Tin Woodman, for example, shake hands with the Lion to show that they have become friends. Also, instead of expressing curiosity as she does in the book, Dorothy runs away frightened when the Scarecrow comes to life.

The Selig Polyscope Company of Chicago was a pioneer motion-picture company established by "Colonel" William Nicholas Selig. In 1896 Selig constructed a film camera and a projector based on the Lumière Cinematographe.[10] Soon he was shooting films. In September 1907 he had finished construction on an immense new filmmaking plant in Chicago. At the time of its opening it was billed as the largest such plant in the United States, covering a full city block. The loft of one building held an extensive property room. Also, at the plant's south end was a giant studio constructed of glass reinforced by strips of steel. Although the glass allowed ample sunlight to enter, supplemental lighting was provided by overhead lamps installed in groups, or batteries, to light the stage. Several dynamos supplied electric light and power. Under the studio were dressing rooms.

Selig employed a large number of people to work on his films. A contingent of stage carpenters worked under the property loft. E. Pollock was the chief scenic artist and superintendent of the studio. A company of actors were also on the payroll. Otis Turner, a veteran stage director, served as the studio's chief director, while another former stage director, Francis Boggs, also on the staff, was often sent on the road to film on location.

Boggs was in Chicago at the time the motion pictures for *Fairylogue and Radio-Plays* were made and was responsible for directing the "Land of Oz" segment. Turner directed the "John Dough and the Cherub" portion. According to the reminiscences of Romola Remus, however, it was Baum who "superintended everything." He "went from one set to another to give directions to everyone—but always in a calm voice . . . not aggressive, very calm. But when he gave an order, they respected it."[11] Neither scripts nor sides were used. Rather, the director first read the story to the actors and then they rehearsed their parts to his commands before the actual film was shot.

As designed and painted by Pollock, the sets for the Wizard of Oz scenes

Francis Boggs, director of the motion pictures for the
"Land of Oz" segment of *Fairylogue and Radio-Plays.*
Formerly a stage director, Boggs supervised many of the
Selig studio's location shoots.

showed "A Cornfield in Oz" and "The Black Forest." The costumes, done by Fritz Schultz and the Chicago Costuming Company, can be seen in surviving *Fairylogue* slides. Dorothy wears a white polka-dot dress with white socks and a necklace. In her hair, which is short, she wears a bow. A minimum of makeup was used on the little girl's face.[12] Dorothy's appearance was patterned after John R. Neill's drawings for *Ozma of Oz* rather than William Wallace Denslow's original drawings for *The Wonderful Wizard of Oz*. Neill had replaced Denslow as the illustrator for Baum's books following the publication of the original Oz tale of 1900.

The Scarecrow looks much as he did in the illustrations by both Denslow and Neill and in the 1902 play. His gloves, however, are even more oversized, and this adds to his comic appearance. The Tin Woodman's costume was clearly based on Montgomery's costume in the musical. He sports the same biblike collar and large round joint pieces. The black dot on the tip of his nose, however, harkens back not to Montgomery's makeup but to Denslow's illustrations, in which the Tin Woodman's nose consists of a metal cone with an opening at the end. As for the Cowardly Lion, his costume is strikingly similar to the one in the musical. It is even possible that it was borrowed from the stage production.

It is difficult to judge the quality of the actors' performances in the film. Amy Leslie, the chief dramatic critic for the *Chicago Daily News,* noted that "the people who had posed for the pantomimic representation treated the characters aptly and well."[13] Romola Remus, a Chicago girl, was paid five dollars a day for taking the part of Dorothy in front of Selig's camera.[14] Leslie, pointing out that the actress's name was "a tremendous thing," judged her "especially pretty and graceful."[15] Frank Burns, who may have been a Selig stock player, played the Scarecrow; the critic for the *Chicago Record Herald* noted that he gave "a faithful imitation of Fred Stone."[16] George E. Wilson, perhaps another stock player, assumed the role of the Tin Woodman, and Joseph Schrode, who played Imogene in the musical and in fact was still in that show in 1908, took the part of the Cowardly Lion. A real dog was used for the role of Toto.

Like many short films of the time, the three opening *Fairylogue* films were probably shot with a stationary camera positioned, as if in the audience of a show, directly in front of the action. But the first film, in which the characters came to life from the pages of Baum's book, involved a special effect later described by Baum in an interview: Each of the actors representing a character stood motionless within a groove cut into the large replica of a book and then stepped down from it when Baum beckoned. The camera was stopped after each character was introduced to allow the next one to take his or her position in the book.[17]

The Duval Frères coloring process supposedly gave the films an especially delicate and lifelike look. Burns Mantle, of the *Chicago Tribune,* found them to be "motion pictures of rare beauty."[18] And the critic for the *Chicago Record Herald* called them "surprisingly fine," noting that "a striking novelty is the fact that they are beautifully colored." The same critic even went so far as to say that the films carried "the record of illusion in the moving picture field as far as it would seem possible to go."[19]

Fairylogue and Radio-Plays as a whole garnered favorable reviews. Baum's performance especially was highly regarded. Burns Mantle noted that the author "reveals himself as a trained public speaker of abilities unusual in a writer. His enunciation is clear and incisive," and he is able "to hold a large audience's attention."[20] The *Chicago Record Herald* noted that "those who have read Mr. Baum's books or seen the extravaganza made from them will find this entertainment very much to their liking."[21]

In most locations attendance was good. Children made up a large part of the show's audience. The program for the Syracuse engagement, in fact, boasted that *Fairylogue and Radio-Plays* was "endorsed by Educators, Parents and the Clergy everywhere as an ideal entertainment for children."[22] And O. L. Hall, writing in the *Chicago Journal,* felt that "this entertainment ought to prove one of the finest things ever devised for children."[23] Those children lucky enough to attend evidently enjoyed themselves thoroughly, for the *Chicago Record Herald* reported that "the children squealed with delight."[24]

If the show was geared toward a juvenile audience, many adults also found much to like in it, and parents were encouraged to attend with their children. Louise Brand, of the *Milwaukee Sentinel,* judged *Fairylogue and Radio-Plays* to be "fascinating alike to old and young." And the *St. Paul Pioneer Press* recommended that "the best thing to do is to take the whole family, from baby to grandma."[25]

Fairylogue and Radio-Plays, however, was extremely costly to produce, and it looked it. This "novel entertainment [is] so admirably worked out in all its details," reported one newspaper, "that manifestly it has cost a great deal of money."[26] The slides and especially the films were a large expense. Then, too, Baum had to pay for theater rentals, the live orchestra that accompanied him, and the show's transportation. In addition, he had to provide his own projection equipment and, in accordance with fire laws, a steel projection booth. At the end of December 1908 the author, in difficult financial straits, gave up hope of touring the show further and abandoned the project.

Baum had borrowed money to produce *Fairylogue and Radio-Plays,* and even then he was not able to pay many of his bills in full. To the Selig Polyscope

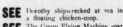
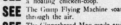

This advertising leaflet from 1908 features many of the characters that appeared in *Fairylogue and Radio-Plays* (*Baum Bugle*, August 1961). They appear much as they were drawn by John R. Neill in Baum's published books. The whimsical rhymes beneath the figures may have been authored by Baum himself.

Company, in particular, he had signed notes totaling $3,000, an amount he was unable to repay.[27] Apparently to help ease this debt, he gave the firm the rights to make new and more extensive motion pictures based on three of his books—*The Wonderful Wizard of Oz*, *The Marvelous Land of Oz*, and *John Dough and the Cherub*. The resulting film of *The Wonderful Wizard of Oz* would be the first substantial adaptation of the novel for the screen.

Chapter 7

A One-Reel Spectacle

The Wonderful Wizard of Oz (1910)

THER THAN GIVING the Selig Polyscope Company of Chicago the rights to film his novel, L. Frank Baum apparently was not directly involved in making that company's 1910 version of *The Wonderful Wizard of Oz*. Even without Baum's involvement, however, Selig, in pre-release publicity for the film, felt free to quote from the author's introduction to the novel, in which he said his story was a modern fairy tale with new kinds of characters.[1] Clearly, Selig wished to promote the film in the context of the fairy-tale genre of motion picture, but with an up-to-date slant.

In late December 1909 the Selig company commissioned the printing of four-color lithographic posters to be used to advertise its upcoming film version of *The Wonderful Wizard of Oz*.[2] It was probably about this same time that production on the film began. Filming, it seems, took place on the West Coast, although this is open to debate. In any case, in August 1909 Selig had begun construction of what would be the first permanent film studio in California, at Edendale, a suburb of Los Angeles. The studio was in use by the end of that year.[3] Francis Boggs, who had worked on *Fairylogue and Radio-Plays*, was in charge of directing productions there. However, the credits for Selig's finished Wizard of Oz film, as published in the standard reference work *American Film-Index, 1908–1915,* list Otis Turner as the director of the film.[4] Turner, who had also worked on *Fairylogue,* was based at the Selig studio in Chicago in 1909–10.

Assuming the published credits are correct, it is likely that Turner made a trip west to shoot *The Wonderful Wizard of Oz.* Indeed, the credits also include at least two performers who surely would have been in Los Angeles at the time, Bebe Daniels and Hobart Bosworth. Daniels, who was only eight or nine at the time of filming, must have played Dorothy, and it is unlikely that a girl so young and relatively unknown as an actress would have been asked to journey to Chicago to appear in this film. As for Hobart Bosworth, he had settled in California by 1909, seeking a warm climate to alleviate the symptoms of his tuberculosis. His condition would have kept him from going to Chicago in the winter, when the film was likely made. In fact, according to his later autobiographical statements, once he settled in California, he did not travel out of the state until the 1920s.[5]

Turner certainly was a good choice to direct *The Wonderful Wizard of Oz.* Having embarked on a stage career as a young man, about 1880, he won fame as a stage director working for producers such as Henry W. Savage and Charles

Otis Turner, director of the Selig studio's *The Wonderful Wizard of Oz* in 1910. A former stage director, Turner was Selig's chief director. He was no stranger to the works of L. Frank Baum, having worked on *Fairylogue and Radio-Plays* in 1908.

Frohman before turning to film work about 1907.[6] The directors of Selig motion pictures usually wrote their own scenarios, and in fact, the published credits for *The Wonderful Wizard of Oz* attribute the scenario to Turner, based on the story by Baum. The scenario, which survives, shows, however, that the film was made from only a rough list of scenes.[7]

When it was finished, Selig's *The Wonderful Wizard of Oz* was a one-reel motion picture of a thousand feet. Intended as a wholesome family entertainment, it was issued as an Easter release on 24 March 1910. In the decades following its release, the picture was believed lost until a copy fortuitously surfaced in 1983.[8]

It is likely that Baum gave the Selig Polyscope Company the rights only to the novel and not to the musical. In pre-release publicity the film was called *The Wizard of Oz*, the same title as that of the 1902 play. Selig, however, must have soon realized that this title was inappropriate. About the time that the film was released, the company announced that its correct title was *The Wonderful Wizard of Oz*, that of the original novel.[9]

In many ways the film went directly back to the novel for its inspiration and bypassed the narrative changes made for the 1902 stage adaptation. Still, the influence of the 1902 show could not be escaped. By the time Selig's film was issued, the musical had wrapped up almost eight years of continuous touring. Audiences across America were more than familiar with the show and must have expected to see it reflected in the film. The filmmakers obliged by borrowing some specific elements from it, but since they apparently did not have the rights, they veered away from copying it in too much detail. Nonetheless, the Selig film manages to capture much of the flavor of the musical. In fact, the film looked enough like the 1902 play to cause one reviewer to comment, "The Selig Co. has surely given us an elaborately spectacular film in this picture reproduction of the famous stage success. We miss the music and the lines, but all the rest is there."[10] Selig's motion picture, however, also introduces many original plot elements, elements not seen in previous versions of the story.

The film opens with a scene at Dorothy's farmhouse in Kansas. A farmer and his wife, two farm hands, and Dorothy are involved in some high jinks with a mule that is running loose. The mule, followed by the farm hands, chases the farmer's wife to the house. It then jumps repeatedly at her and the farmer. When one of the farm hands turns to speak to the other, the mule kicks him and then chases him toward the rear of the house.

The title "Meets the Wonderful Scarecrow" heralds the next scene, set in a Kansas cornfield, where a strong wind is blowing. In front of a scarecrow on a pole are steps and a turnstile. Dorothy is seated on the top step, and the mule

FOLK lore, legends, myths and fairy tales have followed childhood through the ages, for every healthy youngster has a wholesome and instinctive love for stories fantastic, marvelous and manifestly unreal. The winged fairies of Grimm and Andersen have brought more happiness to childish hearts than all other human creations.

Yet the old-time fairy tale, having served for generations, may now be classed as "historical" in the children's library, for the time has come for a series of newer "wonder tales" in which the stereotyped genie, dwarf and fairy are eliminated, together with all the horrible and blood-curdling incidents devised by their authors to point a fearsome moral to each tale. Modern education includes morality; therefore the modern child seeks only entertainment in its wonder tales and gladly dispenses with all disagreeable incident.

"Wizard of Oz" will be without doubt the crowning success of the season and must be seen to be appreciated.

Length, 1000 Feet   Released March 24th   Code Word, Oz

This promotional announcement for Selig's *The Wonderful Wizard of Oz* includes text taken from Baum's own introduction to his *Wonderful Wizard of Oz* novel (*Selig Polyscope News,* 15 March 1910). The illustration shows Dorothy's first encounter with the Cowardly Lion, though not as it appears in the film itself.

and a cow are on either side of her. An opened umbrella can be seen off to the side. Dorothy tosses a ball for Toto, a cairn terrier, to chase. She then approaches the scarecrow. It begins to speak to her, and startled by this, she jumps back. Quickly losing her fear, she unties the Scarecrow from the pole. Having unsteady legs, he now falls on top of the turnstile, causing Dorothy to laugh and the mule and the cow to run off. He then tumbles to the ground, and Dorothy comes to his assistance. She points offscreen toward the approaching cyclone, and the Scarecrow picks up the umbrella, which is blown out of his hands. They both flee.

A cut takes us to a field with a large haystack, on either side of which are the mule and the cow. Dorothy and the Scarecrow enter as the wind blows fiercely and bits of hay fly through the air. The Scarecrow helps Dorothy and the two animals seek refuge under and around the haystack and then fetches Toto before joining the others. All shake in fear as the wind increases.

A title announces, "The Cyclone." We see another field, this one with ominous clouds moving in the sky. Hay and debris blow by. Then, with Dorothy and her friends clinging to it, the haystack from the previous scene appears and whirls across the field. As it passes, it breaks a piece of fence in the foreground. Later a large tree carried by the cyclone collides with the remaining fence and smashes it.

The next scene is titled "Blown into the Land of Oz." The haystack, now in Oz, is surrounded by tropical foliage. Dorothy and the cow tumble off it. Carried by the wind, the Scarecrow flies in. All three scamper off, and the mule jumps out of the hay and follows them.

After the title "Momba the Witch Asserts Her Power over the Wizard of Oz," we are in the palace of the Wizard of Oz. The Wizard, on his throne, is reading aloud a proclamation. Next to him sits his aid. Guards hold watch over the scene. Female courtiers enter and perform a dance with kicks. They then file out as the Wizard gets up from his throne to hand his aid the proclamation, whose text is shown in a shot insert:

> I will give my crown to anybody that releases me from the Power of Momba the Witch—so I can go back to Omaha. *On the level,* as a Wizard I'm a humbug and tired of this King business—
> N.B.—Wishing to keep this secret I have issued this proclamation.
> The Wizard of Oz
King

After sending his aid off to post the proclamation, the Wizard falls to the ground. He rises to see Momba the witch flying in on a broomstick. The guards

Like both Baum's novel and the 1902 *Wizard of Oz* musical, the Selig film begins with a scene on the Kansas farm. But here an element of slapstick comedy is added when the mule rears up and kicks the Kansas farm hands. Aunt Em stands at the right.

Momba the witch threatens the Wizard in his throne room.

scamper in fright, while Momba, now on foot, chases the Wizard. She conjures up a demon, who prevents him from running away. The courtiers return, but the demon chases them away. With her broom Momba then beats the Wizard back onto his throne, apparently so that she can keep him there as a puppet monarch. Momba and the demon exit, but more confusion follows. The courtiers return, only to be frightened by Momba, who flies in again. The Wizard sends the courtiers away as his guards reenter.

The next scene, "Glinda the Good Changes Toto into a Real Protector," is set in the Oz countryside, where we see the yellow brick road and the Fighting Trees. On one of the trees is posted the Wizard's proclamation. Dorothy is playing ball with Toto. The Cowardly Lion slowly sneaks up behind her. At this point Glinda rises in the background and casts a spell with her wand that causes Toto to change into a bulldog in order to protect Dorothy from the Lion. After the bulldog and the Lion chase each other in circles, the Scarecrow enters and the Lion starts to cry. Dorothy then fusses over the dog as the Scarecrow slaps the Lion's head. The cow, the mule, and a cat now run in from the rear. Glinda slowly rises up toward the sky and disappears. The Scarecrow notices the proclamation, and we are again shown its text. The Lion and the dog embrace, and the other animals dance. Dorothy takes the Lion and the dog in arm, and they dance off. The mule follows. The Scarecrow, laughing, grabs the cow's tail, stumbles, and then rises, and the pair exit.

A new scene is announced with the title "The Rusty Tin Woodman after Being Oiled Proves Grateful." Dorothy and the Scarecrow, followed by their animal companions, enter a forest setting, where they find the immobile Tin Woodman holding an axe. After Dorothy and the Scarecrow oil him, the Tin Woodman begins to move. He marches in place a couple of times and takes out a piccolo. At the Scarecrow's request, he plays a tune on it. The Scarecrow and the various animals dance to the music, while Dorothy stays in the background. When the Tin Woodman stops playing, the dancers separate to make way for Dorothy, who performs a solo skipping dance. Finally, the characters file off in pairs, the last being the Tin Woodman escorting Dorothy.

A title reading "Our Friends Encounter Momba the Witch" introduces the next scene. We see Momba's thatched hut, in front of which are large toadstools. A giant winged frog stands guard and patrols the grounds. Hearing Dorothy and her friends approaching, he jumps to the roof of the hut and opens a window, from which Momba suddenly appears. He tells her about the approaching intruders, and she then goes back inside the hut. Dorothy and her companions now come running excitedly into the scene. Brandishing her broom, Momba again appears at the opening in the roof. She flies to the ground

Dorothy, the Scarecrow, the Cowardly Lion, the Mule,
Toto (as a Bulldog), and a cat listen as the Tin Woodman
plays his piccolo.

After Momba melts, Dorothy picks up the witch's magic
cap as the Scarecrow *(left)* and the Tin Woodman *(right)*
release their friends from the prison cells.

and grabs Dorothy. At the same time, Momba's entourage—male guards, horned demons, and a giant spider—emerge from the house. They torment and seize Dorothy's friends. As the scene ends, Momba flies above the struggle.

A title now announces, "Dorothy Learns That Water Is Fatal to a Witch." The action shifts to Momba's prison. At the rear is the gateway entrance to the prison, flanked on either side by cells holding Dorothy's companions. Two of the witch's attendants—a horned demon and an owl—stand behind the gateway while Momba pushes Dorothy through it. Forced to be the witch's slave, Dorothy is carrying a bucket of water to clean the floor. Apparently in anger, she suddenly throws the water at the witch. Drenched, Momba fades away, leaving her hat on the floor. Her two attendants flee. The Tin Woodman now emerges from his cell and goes to Dorothy. The witch's guards enter, ready for a fight, but are repulsed by the Tin Woodman with his axe. He picks up Momba's key and releases the prisoners from the cells. Dorothy takes the witch's hat to prove to the Wizard that she is dead, and the Scarecrow reminds everyone about the Wizard's proclamation by unrolling it in front of them.

"Dorothy Reaches Emerald City to Claim Crown" is the next title. The location is the gates of the Emerald City, where a female guardian of the gate, male guards, and female courtiers stand. Dorothy and her companions enter the scene. After seeing Momba's hat, the guardian of the gate allows them to enter the city escorted by guards.

With the title "The Wizard Free, The Scarecrow Made King," the action returns to the Wizard's throne room. Female courtiers stand behind the Wizard, who is seated on his throne. The guards enter, followed by the guardian of the gate, who ushers in Dorothy and her friends. At first the potentate is afraid of the Lion and the bulldog, and there are some comic antics when he encounters them. Dorothy then shows him Momba's hat. In response, the Wizard tries to give Dorothy his crown, but she tells him to crown the Scarecrow instead, which he does. All cheer as the Scarecrow ascends the throne. The Wizard now dances and performs a feat of magic—waving his wand, he disappears and then reappears at the back of the scene. Afterward, he takes Dorothy's arm and exits, and the animals follow. The Scarecrow and the Tin Woodman stay behind, as the new king clowns around on the throne and then falls down on the steps in front of it.

The next scene, "The Wizard Prepares for Flight," takes place in a palace workshop. At the center of the scene is a large clock that reads 11:58. King Scarecrow, the Tin Woodman, and the Wizard oversee women factory workers who are seated at sewing machines constructing a balloon. As they toil excitedly and the clock ticks, the Wizard exhorts them to hurry. One worker then

Dorothy approaches the gates of the Emerald City, where she is greeted by the Guardian of the Gate.

The Scarecrow and the Tin Woodman dance during the film's finale. This scene well captures the essence of the pair's antics in the 1902 musical.

displays a sign that reads, "Union Rules: No Work after 12." As the clock strikes twelve, the women put on their hats, do a dance, and exit. The Wizard, distraught, falls to the ground. Dorothy enters and is shown the sign. She and both the Scarecrow and the Tin Woodman laugh.

After the title "The Wizard Bids Good Bye to Oz," we are taken to the courtyard at the palace. The Wizard is in the basket of the balloon, and a crowd is gathered to watch the ascent. The Wizard entertains the onlookers by pulling first a rabbit and then some birds out of a hat. Next, he empties one of the balloon's sandbags, and the craft starts to rise. The Lion and the bulldog, followed by the cat, run under the rising balloon and dance around playfully. Confetti falls on the crowd. The Scarecrow and the Tin Woodman attempt to lift Dorothy so that she can board the balloon, but it is too late. The scene now shifts to the Wizard in the balloon's basket. He is throwing a seemingly endless supply of confetti from his hat.

We return to the courtyard, where the crowd is still gathered. Men wearing exotic costumes ride by on horseback, followed by black slaves on foot, who lead camels bearing harem women. As the procession passes, the Scarecrow and the Tin Woodman, at the rear, are shaking hands. Once it has passed, they run forward to execute a dance as a duo. The Scarecrow mugs as he dances, opening and closing his mouth. Dorothy and her animal friends move animatedly to the music. The film ends as the Scarecrow and Tin Woodman continue to dance.

Key elements from Baum's original novel can be found in the Selig film. Many of the characters are here. As in the book, Dorothy is a young preadolescent girl, not old enough to be involved in a romantic relationship. In the course of her adventures she meets the Scarecrow, the Tin Woodman, the Cowardly Lion, the Wizard, and Glinda. In addition, Toto and the Wicked Witch of the West figure prominently in the action, although the latter is given the name Momba, a variation of Mombi, the sorceress in Baum's *The Marvelous Land of Oz*. The various demons, guards, and sinister animals under the witch's command are reminiscent of those in the novel. Her giant spider brings to mind the spiderlike monster that the Lion kills in the book. The major premise of the Kansas girl's being carried to Oz by a cyclone is here too, but so are more specific incidents from the book. For example, the witch enslaves Dorothy but is finally melted when the girl throws a bucket of water on her. Also, Dorothy is not able to accompany the Wizard in his balloon because she does not board in time, and the Scarecrow is made king in place of the Wizard.

In condensing the plot for the motion picture, however, some important narrative components were removed. There is no Good Witch of the North, nor do the Munchkins appear. Furthermore, Dorothy does not obtain magical shoes or encounter a deadly poppy field. What is most important, the film does not express the idea that Dorothy, the Scarecrow, the Tin Woodman, and the Cowardly Lion journey to the Wizard to find home, brains, a heart, and courage. There is no real sense of a quest here.

Elements from the 1902 play are also apparent. For one thing, Kansas is presented in a playful way, much like in the musical, rather than as the bleak place it is in the novel. The farm too is complete with farm hands and a frisky cow that is reminiscent of Imogene. When the Scarecrow comes to life, he is unsteady on his feet, just as Fred Stone had been on the stage. In addition, the Tin Woodman plays a piccolo, his trademark in the musical. As a pair, the Scarecrow and the Tin Woodman clearly harken back to Stone and Montgomery. They act like a vaudeville team, singing, dancing, and clowning around together. This is no more apparent than in the scene where the Scarecrow is crowned king and in the film's final frames, when the pair executes a lively dance.

The film's portrayal of both the Cowardly Lion and the Wizard also brings to mind the play. As in the stage version, the Lion does not speak and has no significant role in the action. Here too he is introduced before the Tin Woodman. For his part, the Wizard performs common vaudeville-style magic tricks, as in the musical, rather than the marvels described in the novel. In addition, in both the film and the play he issues a proclamation—here, to be saved from Momba; in the musical, for the arrest of Pastoria. In some ways, the Wizard takes on the traits of Pastoria in the musical. After all, Pastoria issued a proclamation of his own. Furthermore, the Wizard's fear at first meeting the Lion and the bulldog brings to mind Pastoria's initial meeting with the Lion.

The marching guards and dancing courtiers of the Wizard's court almost seem to duplicate the choruses that surrounded the Wizard in the 1902 play. And it is hard not to see a parallel between the female factory workers who make the Wizard's balloon in the film and the chorus of working-class women in the third act of the New York version of the play. Also, the way Momba imprisons Dorothy's friends recalls Pastoria's imprisonment of his enemies, including Dorothy and her companions.

Much of the comic slapstick tone of the motion picture is similar to that of play, although most specific comic elements are new to the film. The animal characters clown around, for example, and the Scarecrow and the Tin Woodman cavort on the throne. The Selig film also includes a number of dances, much as the musical did, but there is no evidence they were directly patterned after any from the musical. Significant too is the sense of spectacle, so important to the musical, that this essentially small film tries to convey. The crowd scene at the balloon ascension must have been inspired by the 1902 play. Here, though, the exotic procession in that scene adds an extra marvel that was not in the musical.

Missing from the film are the major characters introduced by Julian Mitchell—Cynthia Cynch, Pastoria, Tryxie Tryfle, Dashemoff Daily, and Wiley Gyle. Furthermore, the film stays away from the themes of politics and romance, which had been central to the stage production.

There is also much that is novel in the Selig film. Several new animal characters played by costumed humans are added—the mule, the bulldog, and the cat join Dorothy's entourage; and the frog and the owl, the witch's. These creatures are in keeping with the spirit of Baum's original book, which also was filled with animals. But whereas the beasts in the novel often speak, these are mute, in line with theatrical pantomime tradition. They add a sense of spectacle to the film. Furthermore, in that Dorothy, who previously had only a dog or cow to accompany her, is now surrounded by an entire coterie of friendly animals, she clearly stands in contrast to the witch with her group of sinister creatures.

In the film, the Scarecrow, surprisingly, is first introduced in Kansas, and he is alive almost from the moment we meet him. This is an odd change to have made to the narrative since it affords Kansas a magical quality and detracts from the magic of Oz. The distinction between Kansas and Oz thus becomes blurred. In addition, far from being bumbling and brainless, the Scarecrow manages to save Dorothy and the animals from the cyclone by making them take refuge in the haystack. Evidently, the filmmakers thought that the Scarecrow was such a key character that he needed to be introduced at the earliest possible moment, even if this meant involving him in the action in Kansas.

In the motion picture it is a haystack, and not Dorothy's farmhouse, that is blown to Oz. This makes for a dramatic scene as the haystack whirls by. The fact that Dorothy, the Scarecrow, Toto, the mule, and the cow are all carried with it to Oz, however, significantly alters the tenor of the story. It is no longer a self-reliant Dorothy, accompanied only by Toto, who is seen discovering and experiencing Oz. Instead she has company from home to provide support and to keep her from feeling too homesick.

Unlike in the earlier incarnations of the story, here the Wizard is eager to relinquish his throne. Continually besieged by the witch, he will give his crown to anyone who frees him from her power. He also declares himself a humbug at the outset, but he is really not so much a humbug as a helpless pawn. As for

Glinda, her role is much diminished in the film, but the idea that she is watching over Dorothy is conveyed by her act of transforming Toto into a bulldog, another Selig innovation.

The depiction of the melting of the witch is novel as well. In the book, she dissolves, clothes and all, leaving behind only a brown puddle. In the film, after she melts, Momba's magic cap remains on the floor—perhaps a more effective visual image. Dorothy then takes the hat to prove that the witch is dead. Finally, at the end of the film Dorothy's plight has not been resolved. The audience is left to wonder about the little girl's future in Oz and whether she will return to Kansas. Unless footage is missing from the end of the motion picture as it survives, Selig must have expected to continue her story in a later film.

Taken on its own, Selig's *The Wonderful Wizard of Oz* lacks many of the deep resonances of Baum's original tale. To create the film, the story was drastically condensed, leaving little room for character development. As a result, many of the psychological, mythological, and other interpretations that have been applied to the novel do not pertain here. Dorothy, for example, is a cipher about whom little is known. Since Aunt Em and Uncle Henry are never formally identified, it is not even entirely clear whether the child is an orphan, which is of course important to understanding her psychology. Dorothy's motivations are also vague. Her adventures seem to lack an underlying, well-defined purpose; nowhere are we told that her goal, once in Oz, is to return home. She is far less independent and determined than in Baum's novel. Furthermore, the idea that the little girl learns from her adventures in Oz is absent, and she does not readily fit the role of the mythological hero who overcomes hardships on the path to self-knowledge. The fact that Dorothy's three companions—the Scarecrow, the Tin Woodman, and the Cowardly Lion—also lack clear goals further serves to dilute the impact of the story.

This is not to say that the tale has been rendered meaningless. It still lends itself to various interpretations. From a folkloric perspective, for example, the Scarecrow's coming to life in Kansas can be taken to indicate that the magical is present in everyday life. And from a modern psychological viewpoint, Dorothy's encounter with Momba can be seen as a conflict with the domineering mother, and her relationship with the Wizard as an attempt to reach the passive father.

But it is important to keep in mind that most of the audience for Selig's *The Wonderful Wizard of Oz* would not have taken the film purely on its own terms. Instead, they would likely have come to it with a knowledge of the book or the musical and would, in their minds, have filled in gaps in the narrative and supplied nuances that were not presented on the screen. The filmmakers probably counted on this while also relying on the motion picture's playful mood and ample spectacle to compensate for the simplified narrative.

The sets in the film are very theatrical, with abundant set pieces and painted backdrops. There are no exterior shots; instead, all the scenes were created on an indoor stage. Several are particularly noteworthy. When we first meet the Scarecrow, for example, he is on a raised platform with steps leading up to it. He is mounted on a post, with his arms held by a slanted crossbeam. At one side, on the platform, is a turnstile. Cornstalks surround the platform. A painted backdrop shows fields and a farmhouse in the distance. Much of this set was essentially a duplication of the "Scarecrow" set in the New York version of the musical.[11]

At the start of the cyclone scene we see a ramshackle fence in the foreground and a painted flat showing a field at middle ground. At the very rear is a moving panorama depicting the storm clouds passing by. Then, mounted on a rotating platform, the haystack whirls by with Dorothy and her companions clinging to it. Considering the rather primitive technology available to the filmmakers at the time, the moving panorama and the rotating platform were particularly creative ways to enhance the scene.

For the Wizard's throne room, an ornate painted backdrop was devised that included classical and Orientalist elements in the form of columns, temples, sculptured animal figures, domes, and spires. Undoubtedly, the Orientalist theme was influenced by the same motif in "The Courtyard of the Wizard's Palace" scene in the 1902 musical, although that in turn had been inspired by William Wallace Denslow's depictions of the Emerald City in Baum's novel.

The scene in which Glinda appears is set against a backdrop showing the Oz countryside with a winding road, which the film's scenario indicates is meant to be the yellow brick road. Also depicted are several of the Fighting Trees from Baum's novel, presented much as they were drawn by Denslow.[12] They are large, gnarled trees on whose trunks are deeply furrowed faces with big bulging eyes, round gaping mouths, and bulbous noses. Interestingly, neither the yellow brick road nor the Fighting Trees play any role in the film.

Also distinctive is the scene showing the thatched hut belonging to Momba. The dwelling has oversized windows at ground level, from which the witch's cohorts enter and exit. There are also large toadstools in the foreground. Momba's prison is no less interesting. On the right and left we see set pieces depicting jail cells. At the center rear is a gateway through which can be seen a painted backdrop showing a gargoyle statue and, in the distance, the countryside. It would appear from this vantage point that the witch's house is high on a mountain top.

When Dorothy, having killed Momba, reaches the Emerald City, we see a drop showing the gates of the city. In the center of a wall with buttresses is a doorway decorated with an oversized face. The face on the doorway was inspired by a similar face in Denslow's drawing of the gates in the novel.[13] The final scene of the film takes place in the courtyard of the Wizard's palace, where a set of steps flanks the rear of the set. A backdrop shows an archway surrounded by lush vegetation, and in the distance is the horizon.

The film also has noteworthy costumes, many of which borrow freely from the Oz books and the 1902 musical. Dorothy wears a dotted country dress with an apron and bonnet patterned after her outfit in act 1 of the musical. The Scarecrow's costume and makeup are similar to those worn in the play by Fred Stone, which, in turn, were based on Denslow's illustrations for the novel. As for the Tin Woodman, his appearance is close to that of Dave Montgomery, except that he has a long nose harkening directly back to Denslow's drawings. The Wizard wears a long dark coat, light-colored pants, and a high hat. Like Bobby Gaylor in the musical, he has bushy eyebrows and the top of his head is bald. When we first see Momba outside her house, she wears a typical witch's outfit—a long cape with a ruffled collar and a pointed hat. In the scene in her prison she wears a robe decorated with strange symbols and designs, like the one seen in a Denslow drawing of the Wicked Witch of the West.[14]

The costumes of the Wizard's guards and courtiers are playful and visually appealing. Male palace guards sport long jackets and tall hats. White bands decorate their clothing. They have extremely long beards, and their appearance was based on Denslow's drawings of the Soldier with the Green Whiskers in the original novel.[15] The female guardian of the gate wears a light-colored jacket and tunic with a bow at the neck and has a pointed hat with balls hanging from the brim. Her appearance is patterned after that of Denslow's Munchkins. The female courtiers wear short jackets with ruffled collars and small hats. They also sport leotards with one light leg, adorned with a black garter, and one dark leg, with a light garter, a concept that probably was influenced by the harlequin outfit worn by Dorothy and the chorus in the Ball of All Nations suite in the 1902 musical. The union workers who toil on the Wizard's balloon wear dark dresses with full skirts and a crossband on their upper torso. Their costumes strongly resemble those of Glinda's soldiers as depicted by Denslow.

The costumes of the animals played by humans—the mule, the cow, the lion, the bulldog, the cat, the frog, the spider, and the owl—were probably stock animal costumes for the most part. The Cowardly Lion's costume is similar to the one in the 1902 musical, but the cow's is lighter and furrier than

The gates of the Emerald City as depicted by William
Wallace Denslow for Baum's *The Wonderful Wizard of Oz*.
This drawing served as the basis for the design of the
gates in the Selig film.

Glinda's soldiers as portrayed by Denslow—the basis for
the costuming of the female factory workers in the film.

Denslow's drawing
of the Soldier with
the Green Whiskers,
which inspired the
appearance of the
Wizard's guards in
the film.

Imogene's outfit. Finally, the procession in the concluding scene of the film features men wearing ornate, exotic costumes with fezzes, women in harem dresses, and slaves in loin cloths. These costumes continue the Orientalist motif seen in the design of the Wizard's throne room.

The published credits for the film list the performers as Hobart Bosworth, Eugenie Besserer, Robert Leonard, Bebe Daniels, Winifred Greenwood, Lillian Leighton, and Olive Cox. Daniels, Bosworth, and Leonard are known to have been members of the Selig stock company at the time. It is likely that the other actors were in the stock company as well. Unfortunately, the cast list does not indicate who played what role. We can surmise the parts Daniels, Bosworth, and Leonard had, however.

Bebe Daniels, born Phyllis Daniels, a girl of eight or nine when the film was made, must have played Dorothy. Her father had a stock company in which her mother was the leading woman. At the age of ten weeks Bebe first appeared in one of that company's productions, and at three she had her first speaking role. She moved to Los Angeles when she was five to join the Burbank stock company, managed by producer Oliver Morosco. After her final stage appearance at the age of eight in *The Squawman,* she joined the Selig company in Edendale to play child parts in motion pictures. Daniels went on to become a major star in both silent and sound films.[16]

Hobart Bosworth probably took the part of the Scarecrow. Since he was the Selig company's major actor of the time, it would have been fitting for him to play that role, arguably the lead in the film. Beyond that, he was forty-two when the film was made, and the performer in the part of the Scarecrow could well be of that age. Acting since the age of fifteen, Bosworth was a Broadway star by the time he was thirty. It was in 1903, while starring in the Broadway production of *Marta of the Lowlands,* that the actor developed tuberculosis. Because of the illness, he eventually moved to California for the climate. After directing at the Belasco Theatre in Los Angeles, he established a dramatic school in partnership with Oliver Morosco, but the school was a failure. In 1909 he went to work for the West Coast studio of the Selig company. A theatrical celebrity, he was given lead roles in Selig films.[17]

Robert Leonard, the only other male cast member credited, probably took the part of the Tin Woodman, the second most important male character in the film. Leonard was only twenty or twenty-one at the time, and the performer in the part does seem fairly young. He had been with Selig since 1907.[18]

Many real animals were used in the film. These included a cairn terrier in the part of Toto, birds and a rabbit in the Wizard's magic trick, and the horses and camels in the exotic procession. Selig kept zoos, which were quite famous, at both the Chicago and Edendale film studios, and the animals must have come from one of these.

As might be expected in an early silent film, the performances in *The Wonderful Wizard of Oz* are exaggerated and very physical. Dorothy, for example, bends back in laughter when the Scarecrow tumbles over the turnstile, and the cow shakes violently in fear as it clings to the haystack. The director, Otis Turner, believed that film actors needed to display constant and rapid movement. "To get an effect with moving pictures there has to be plenty of action," Turner said in a 1909 interview. For a stage actor, "repose is one of the strongest methods of obtaining an effect, but it's exactly the opposite here. The gestures have to come quick, and the expression of the features has to change rapidly to convey the idea we wish to."[19] The acting in *The Wonderful Wizard of Oz* received a favorable review from the *New York Dramatic Mirror:* "The parts are taken by people apparently up in their parts, for everything moves on oiled wheels."[20]

In terms of filmmaking technique, *The Wonderful Wizard of Oz* is fairly primitive. Scenes were shot with a stationary camera positioned frontally, as if viewing action on a stage. Cinematography was, of course, done in black and white, but the film may have been available in a tinted version as well. In simple black and white the film must have been quite a disappointment to those familiar with either the colorful book or the musical. The editing is very simple and basically serves to move the action from one scene to the next. The most elaborate editing occurs when, during the scene showing the crowd watching the balloon ascension, there is a cutaway to the Wizard in his balloon in the clouds.

As was typical for fairy-tale films of the time, the motion picture featured special effects. Achieved through relatively simple means, they were sometimes quite effective: wires were used to make Momba and Glinda fly; a trap door or perhaps stop-motion filmmaking was used to make Momba's demons appear; and a dissolve showed the witch melting away.

When *The Wonderful Wizard of Oz* was released, film criticism was not yet a regular feature in newspapers. As a result, only a few reviews of the picture exist. The critic for the *New York Dramatic Mirror* concluded that it "should prove in strong demand."[21] And *Moving Picture World* gave it a positive review: "The reproduction of a story of this character in motion pictures is an achievement of sufficient importance to attract more than the usual degree of interest. That it has been successfully accomplished needs hardly to be said. The reputation of this house for producing striking and unusual films is too well established to require further description. It is an excellent film, well acted and clearly photographed."[22]

Although Selig telescoped Baum's tale and omitted much, the 1910 *Wonderful Wizard of Oz* film has a fairly clear progression from beginning to end and manages to convey some of Baum's sense of otherworldliness. In addition, it nicely captures the playful quality of both the original novel and the stage version. Its eclectic theatricality—including magic tricks, vaudeville clowning, pantomime animals, and choral dancing—also reflects the popular appeal of the Julian Mitchell musical.

Later in 1910, following *The Wonderful Wizard of Oz,* the Selig company completed three additional films based on the Baum books to which it had rights. Each was a thousand feet. Unfortunately, none is known to survive. The first of these, *Dorothy and the Scarecrow in Oz,* also directed by Otis Turner, was released on 14 April. According to its scenario, the film incorporated narrative elements from two of Baum's novels—*The Wonderful Wizard of Oz* and *The Marvelous Land of Oz.* Derived from *The Wonderful Wizard of Oz* were scenes showing Dorothy and her friends being put to sleep by a field of poppies, a giant spider being killed, and Dorothy being sent back to Kansas by Glinda.[23] The next film to be released, on 19 May, was *The Land of Oz,* which was based on *The Marvelous Land of Oz. John Dough and the Cherub,* depicting the tale of the same name, came out on 19 December.

None of these films seems to have made a substantial profit, at least not enough to offset Baum's debt of $3,000 to Selig for making the motion pictures for *Fairylogue and Radio-Plays.* Baum filed for bankruptcy in June 1911, at which time he still owed Selig $1,500 for the *Fairylogue* work.[24]

It is quite possible that Selig's *The Wonderful Wizard of Oz* suffered at the box office because it was identified with a work of children's literature at a time when children were not a significant part of the motion-picture audience. In his stage version Julian Mitchell certainly had recognized the story's appeal to children, but many of his alterations had been aimed toward making the show appeal to adults as well. The Selig film, however, made no such concessions, and motion-picture exhibitors may have found that it had limited interest.

⌒ Although the Selig films of 1908 and 1910 did not achieve as much success as had been hoped, Baum, still excited by the relatively new medium of the motion picture, was driven to produce additional films based on his works. In 1914 he played a central role in founding the Oz Film Manufacturing Company in Hollywood.[25] His backers in the enterprise were members of two social clubs, the Uplifters, which Baum helped establish, and the Los Angeles Athletic Club, which provided space in its headquarters for the Uplifters' meetings.

Baum was nothing if not ambitious. The new company's plans, as delineated

The Oz Film Manufacturing Company studio in
Hollywood, California. Built on a site of seven acres,
the facility included an enclosed stage, 65 ft. × 100 ft.,
that Baum himself designed.

in *Moving Picture World* in April 1914, entailed filming first all of Baum's fairy-
tale novels and then his plays, including *The Wizard of Oz*.[26] Even though this
goal was never realized, the company began working toward it in the following
months. Three feature-length films, each five reels in length, were quickly produced in 1914. Baum supervised and wrote the scenarios, and J. Farrell Mac-
Donald directed. Prints of all three films survive. The first, *The Patchwork Girl
of Oz*, was based on Baum's 1913 book of the same name. This was followed
by *The Magic Cloak of Oz*, derived from his *Queen Zixi of Ix*.

The third, *His Majesty, the Scarecrow of Oz*, was the most ambitious and
costly. It contained much new material, supplemented by plot elements from
the books *The Wonderful Wizard of Oz*, *The Marvelous Land of Oz*, *The Road
to Oz*, and *The Patchwork Girl of Oz*. The story of the film centered around
Princess Gloria, daughter of King Krewl of Oz, and her love for Pon, the gar-
dener's boy. Disapproving of his daughter's love, Krewl has the witch Mombi
freeze her heart. Through a series of adventures, Gloria's heart is restored and
the lovers are reunited.

For our purposes, *His Majesty, the Scarecrow of Oz* is important only in
that some of the secondary action of the story was derived from the book *The
Wonderful Wizard of Oz*. Dorothy, a Kansas girl enslaved by Mombi, for ex-

ample, comes upon the Scarecrow and lets him down from his pole. In another scene, Dorothy and the Scarecrow discover the Tin Woodman, who stands rusted outside of his tin castle. Later, when Dorothy, the Scarecrow, and the Tin Woodman are pursued by Mombi, they escape on a raft. The Scarecrow guides the raft with a pole, which becomes stuck in the river's bottom. The raft continues on without him as he hangs from the pole in the middle of the river. He is eventually rescued by a bird, which carries him ashore. Soon after this, the travelers meet the Wizard of Oz and the Cowardly Lion, who assist in the effort to reunite Gloria and Pon. In the course of the action the Scarecrow is also proclaimed king.

The Oz Film Manufacturing Company produced its first three films at a rapid pace, but it found that it was not so easy to distribute them. As a new, independent company, it had a hard time convincing national distributors to handle its product. After much negotiation, however, Paramount Pictures Corporation agreed to distribute *The Patchwork Girl of Oz,* opening it in September 1914. The film had a terrible fate at the box office. Audiences were now tired of the fairy-tale theme, which had defined a prevalent genre of early film. But more important, they thought the film was geared too much toward children. Baum had, in fact, given the film a romantic subplot not present in the original novel, but this was apparently too small a concession to adult taste. Paramount, burned by its experience with *The Patchwork Girl of Oz,* refused to handle *The Magic Cloak of Oz,* and other distributors followed its example. The Oz Film Manufacturing Company resorted to editing that motion picture down to two two-reel shorts and marketing them as fillers. In fact, it was not until 1917 that the film, purchased by the National Film Corporation, was released in its entirety.

His Majesty, the Scarecrow of Oz also proved to be a difficult sell, although it boasted a large budget and many nice special effects. Even the extremely positive reviews that followed the film's preview showing on 5 October 1914 did not help. To increase the marketability of the film, the Oz Film Manufacturing Company began issuing publicity materials linking it to the popular *Wizard of Oz* stage musical. A company circular produced about the end of October noted, "The thousands—yes millions—of people who saw and enjoyed the famous 'Wizard of Oz' during the eight years it ran on the legitimate stage will be delighted to know that all their old favorites may be seen once more in motion pictures." The circular went on to say that *His Majesty, the Scarecrow of Oz* "is practically a photo-visualization of this popular extravaganza. Here we see again the Scarecrow as loveable and wobbly as when Fred Stone tumbled

Advertisement for *The New Wizard of Oz,* formerly known
as *His Majesty, the Scarecrow of Oz* (*Motion Picture News,*
6 February 1915). Although the plot of this Oz Film
Manufacturing Company film had little to do with Baum's
original novel or the 1902 stage musical, publicity for the
movie strongly implied its link to the latter.

around the stage—the Tin Woodman—the Wizard of Oz—Dorothy the little Kansas Girl—the Wicked Witch, and others."[27]

Toward the end of 1914 the company, still without a national distributor for *His Majesty, the Scarecrow of Oz,* was selling territorial distribution rights. Increasingly desperate to market the film, the firm was becoming even more brazen in its promotional literature. A circular of the time referred to the film only as *The Wizard of Oz* and noted that the company had "put into motion pictures that well-beloved musical comedy, 'The Wizard of Oz,' so that its millions of friends from the days of its stage success can once again enjoy the story and action that has delighted them so thoroughly in the past."[28]

This sales approach did not involve a complete lie, since, after all, *His Majesty, the Scarecrow of Oz* did contain plot elements from Baum's first Oz tale. But it was close to pure fabrication, for those elements had been inspired by the novel rather than by the subsequent musical. In any case, it would appear that for Baum and his associates honesty was not always the best policy. By January 1915 Baum's son Frank Joslyn, now business manager for the company, secured a contract with Alliance Films Corporation to release the motion picture in the United States. National distribution began in February or March. The picture, however, was now officially retitled *The New Wizard of Oz.* In the end, it mattered little what the film was called, as it achieved only limited success at the box office.

The end of the Oz Film Manufacturing Company was not long in coming. After its initial three films, it changed its course and produced two purely adult melodramas, reserving the fairy-tale theme only for some shorts. But as a small independent company with a record of past failure, it could not get its pictures shown. Its name was too much associated with films for children.

The Oz Film Manufacturing Company ceased to exist late in the summer of 1915. Baum regained the motion-picture rights to all of his books, but the company's output in 1914–15 would be his last foray into the world of the cinema. After his death in 1919, his son Frank Joslyn, who had been involved with both the *Fairylogue* project and the Oz Film Manufacturing Company, was to pursue again his father's vision of bringing Oz to the screen.

Chapter 8

Hollywood High Jinks

The Wizard of Oz (1925), I

AFTER THE DEATH of L. Frank Baum in 1919, his publisher, the Reilly and Lee Company (formerly the Reilly and Britton Company), was far from anxious to give up a good thing. Baum's Oz series continued to sell well, and Reilly and Lee arranged with Maud Baum, the author's widow, to hire a new writer to continue it. The firm selected Ruth Plumly Thomson, an up-and-coming children's author, as the new Royal Historian of Oz. Her first Oz book came out in 1921.

Apparently, however, Frank Joslyn Baum, who was abroad serving in the military when Thomson was chosen, had literary aspirations of his own. He was none too pleased that he had been overlooked as a possible successor to his father, and as compensation, his mother gave him permission to sell film and other rights to the original Oz stories. After making sure that these rights had all reverted to his father's estate, he began approaching film companies, which were still producing silents. The first property he tried to sell them was, not surprisingly, the ever-popular Wizard of Oz story.[1]

In 1924 the Metro-Goldwyn studio expressed some interest in filming *The Wonderful Wizard of Oz*, but a deal was not settled.[2] Later that year, however,

Baum concluded an agreement to sell the film rights to the tale to Chadwick Pictures Corporation, an independent producer. The Chadwick company was a relatively small player in the film industry, but it had large ambitions. Founded by Isaac E. Chadwick by 1920, the New York firm at first acted on the independent market as a distributor of films produced by other companies. By 1924, though, it had become an active producer on its own, contracting with such important stars as Lionel Barrymore and Madge Bellamy.

In the mid-twenties, independent film companies such as Chadwick were struggling to survive in the face of mammoth competition from a few monopolistic corporations, the most notable being Paramount Pictures Corporation, Metro-Goldwyn (with its parent company, Loew's, Incorporated), and First National Exhibitors Circuit. These large organizations not only made movies but also owned theaters to show them. As producers, distributors, and exhibitors, they were self-sufficient entities, effectively controlling all aspects of the film business. Their power grew enormously as they acquired or built more and more theaters around the country and forced independent exhibitors to book their films.[3]

Besides running his own film company, I. E. Chadwick was president of the Independent Motion Picture Producers and Distributors Association, which was formed to give a greater voice to the many independents working outside the big corporations. Chadwick and his colleagues across the country believed that both the public and the industry would suffer if the powerful combines were given totally free reign. "The artistic advance of the motion picture lies in the open market," he told the association of independents on 30 October 1924, "and if these doors are shut, artistic progress cannot develop to its highest extent."[4]

In standing up to the big companies, the independents were fighting a difficult battle that was not to be settled until 1948, when the court ruled that film producers could not own theaters.[5] Nevertheless, Chadwick forged ahead with his efforts to make and support independent productions. In fact, he thought that the greatest weapon in the battle against the large corporations was the films themselves. If Chadwick Pictures Corporation and other independent producers could turn out high-quality films that were in great demand, they would be well on their way to victory.

With the phrase "Each Production an Achievement" as his company's slogan, Chadwick sought to ensure that his films would be successful by developing screenplays based on noted books and plays, selecting directors and producers with established reputations, and hiring famous actors.[6] His stable of talent included the comedian Larry Semon, who, as head of one of the company's production units, was to make a series of films, one of which was to be *The Wizard of Oz*. Chadwick must have considered it a coup to obtain the services of Semon, whose popularity at the time, though not up to that of Charlie Chaplin and Buster Keaton, was quite high. Experienced as a writer, director, and actor for the screen, Semon filled all three of these roles in *The Wizard of Oz*.

Born in West Point, Mississippi, in 1889, Semon was raised in a show-business family.[7] His father was a magician, known professionally as Zera the Great, who was assisted in his act by his wife. Larry accompanied his parents on the road, along with a vaudeville company that was part of Zera's show. Larry himself often performed, and he developed a variety of skills, including acrobatics, dancing, singing, magic, and hypnotism. He also had a talent for drawing, which he pursued by attending art school in Savannah and then finding employment as a cartoonist for New York newspapers, among them the *Evening Sun* and the *Evening Telegram*.

Soon Semon transferred his creative skills to the making of motion pictures for Vitagraph, the New York film company. In the early part of 1916 he was writing and directing one-reel comedies for that company, and later in that year he began acting in them as well. Growing ever more popular, he graduated to producing two-reelers for Vitagraph in 1918. But despite his popularity with audiences, in the early 1920s Semon lost favor with the executives of Vitagraph. His production costs were too high. In 1922 a deal was worked out whereby Semon could continue to make shorts at the Vitagraph studios but he had to cover the expenses of his staff. Within two years, however, the company ended its association with the star.

In his Vitagraph shorts Semon took the role of a comic simpleton, wearing white facial makeup, a bowler hat, and high-waisted baggy pants that were too short for him. The films had minimal plot but lots of action in the form of sight gags, slapstick, and chases. The physical comedy included difficult and elaborate stunts, which Semon and his fellow actors often performed themselves. He also encouraged his actors to improvise and did not hesitate to use old gags as long as they were done in a new way. Much of the humor was directed at children because, Semon reasoned, they constituted a large part of the matinee audiences, which were important to a film's success.

In the early twenties, major comedians such as Charlie Chaplin, Buster Keaton, and Harold Lloyd were moving into the production of features, and Semon was eager to keep pace with his colleagues. The opportunity arose in May 1924, when Chadwick Pictures Corporation gave him a contract to make a series of full-length comedies. Semon was appointed the head of a Chadwick production unit based on the West Coast.[8] On 15 May he began work on *The Girl in the Limousine.* In keeping with the Chadwick philosophy of making movies from successful stories, this was based on Avery Hopwood's 1919 hit play of the same title. Semon starred in the film and codirected it with Noel Smith. When the film was released in July, it received mixed reviews.[9]

By the end of the summer of 1924 it had been determined that Semon's next Chadwick feature would be based on the Wizard of Oz fantasy.[10] The comedian, with his appeal to children, had long wanted to make a film version of the tale, and Chadwick, who preferred to adapt well-known stories to the screen, was happy to accommodate him.[11] From Frank J. Baum, Chadwick apparently acquired the film rights to both Baum's novel and the 1902 play based on it.[12] In turning over the rights, Baum's son, who was eager to have creative input, must have requested that he have a hand in writing the screenplay. In the final film, in fact, the screenplay is credited to him, along with Semon and Leon Lee, who was also responsible for the intertitles.[13]

Preproduction on Semon's *The Wizard of Oz* was under way by October. Although some of the planning and organization for the film took place at the New York offices of Chadwick Pictures Corporation, the actual production work was based in Hollywood at the lot of the Film Booking Office, an important supplier of studio space to independents. There Semon oversaw the selection of the cast, the making of the costumes, and the building of the sets.[14] Planning to direct the film and assume the role of the Scarecrow, he saw it as a "monumental" work for the screen.[15] And *monumental* might also be the word to describe the sets for the picture, which were said to be among the largest ever erected on the Film Booking Office lot.[16]

Meanwhile, eager to create an air of excitement, Chadwick Pictures Corporation released the information that both Semon and the company were receiving letters and wires daily from fans, exhibitors, and prominent people praising them for their decision to film the Wizard of Oz story.[17] The company also reported that Frank J. Baum had approached Semon about staging a revival of the Wizard of Oz play following the completion of the film. Fred Stone supposedly had been contacted to reprise his role as the Scarecrow but had refused because he could no longer dance as limberly as he once had. Semon, therefore, would also take the part of the Scarecrow on stage.[18] In any case, whether these plans had any basis in reality or were merely concocted by the Chadwick publicity department to remind people of the popularity of the 1902 play, Semon would never stage a revival.

At the end of October, I. E. Chadwick announced bold plans for the film's release. As part of an intensive selling campaign, he hoped to arrange for first-run exhibitions of *The Wizard of Oz* during the holiday season. He also promised extensive advertising and promotional tie-ins. *Exhibitors Trade Review* went so far as to say that his efforts would "overshadow in magnitude anything hitherto attempted on a motion picture production."[19]

Chadwick himself was in Hollywood in early December to witness the closing shots of Semon's film, and he reported that what he saw exceeded all his expectations.[20] About the same time, production stills were reaching the New York headquarters of the Chadwick company. "The stills," commented *Exhibitors Trade Review* in another piece full of hype, "are of rare beauty showing that the production has been mounted with excellent taste and in frequent cases, genius. The costuming of the cast is as extraordinary an achievement as the production itself." The paper concluded by calling *The Wizard of Oz* "one of the most eagerly anticipated pictures in recent times."[21] By 20 December the first print had been received in New York.[22]

Chadwick and Semon realized from the outset that *The Wizard of Oz,* a wholesome family film, would be an ideal Christmas release. But Semon, who had established a reputation for long shooting periods while still at Vitagraph, finished the film too close to Christmas to allow enough time for booking it into theaters. As a result, distribution was delayed until the following year.[23] Chadwick was probably happy to postpone the release to avoid competition from Paramount Picture Corporation's *Peter Pan,* a big-budget production that was being heavily promoted and was scheduled for theaters in late December. No doubt this film and *The Wizard of Oz,* both fantasies, would have fought for the same audience. And there is also no question that with its money and clout, Paramount would have made sure its film emerged the victor.

At the end of December, Semon arrived in New York to meet with Chadwick about *The Wizard of Oz* and his future film projects, as well as to play two weeks in vaudeville beginning on 19 January 1925.[24] A particularly notable event occurred on the fourth day of Semon's vaudeville engagement. Dorothy Dwan, the actress who played Dorothy in Semon's *The Wizard of Oz,* arrived in New York, and on the afternoon of that same day, she and Semon were married, providing added publicity for their upcoming motion picture. As a wedding present Dwan reportedly received part interest in the film.[25]

During the month of January, Chadwick Pictures Corporation began arranging for initial showcase exhibitions of *The Wizard of Oz.*[26] The grandiose plans are clear evidence that I. E. Chadwick had confidence in the film and in his company's ability to surmount the booking problems facing the independents. A special pre-release engagement was scheduled at the Forum Theatre in Los Angeles in February, and efforts were under way to book a Broadway house for the subsequent official premiere. In effect, the film would have two major openings, one on each coast.

Then the film was to go out as a road show, complete with a special prologue staged by Ned Wayburn, famed dance director of the *Ziegfeld Follies.* The road-show release pattern was generally reserved for special big-budget motion pictures. It involved presenting a film at a series of large first-class theaters in key cities for unlimited runs. Seats were reserved, and ticket prices were high. If successful, the road show not only made money for the producer and the exhibitors but also, through publicity and word of mouth, helped create a demand for the picture in its eventual general release. Apparently, however, the Chadwick company was not able to find exhibitors who shared its confidence in *The Wizard of Oz,* for the film seems never to have been presented in this way.

Also in January, a special department was formed at the Chadwick offices devoted solely to the promotion and exploitation of the Semon fairy-tale film. Advertisements, tie-ins, feature stories, photoplay books, press kits, and exploitation events were all in the works.[27] A full-page advertisement in the 14 January 1925 issue of *Variety* illustrates the level at which the motion picture was to be promoted. Calling the film "The Greatest Sensation Among Screen Classics Since 'The Birth of a Nation,'" it claimed that "over $300,000 was spent in the production of this stupendous masterpiece!" The advertisement also reminded potential exhibitors that the motion picture had "the largest ready-made aggregate public in the world, consisting of the millions who saw the original play, and the millions who have read the famous Oz books!"[28]

Momentum was building for the film's debut at the Forum Theatre in Los Angeles. But on 2 February, less than a week before the opening, William LaPlante, president of National Film Corporation, stepped forward to claim that he owned the film rights to the Wizard of Oz tale. Apparently LaPlante believed he had a stake in the title because in 1917 his company had acquired the rights to distribute the Oz Film Manufacturing Company's *The Magic Cloak of Oz.* He threatened the management of the Forum with legal action if it went ahead with its plans to screen the Semon picture. The Chadwick corporation, in turn, threatened a countersuit against National.[29] In the end, the Chadwick company must have succeeded in defending its rights, because *The Wizard of Oz* made its debut as planned at the Forum and nothing ever came of National's claim.

The Forum Theatre, which seated eighteen hundred people, was relatively new, having opened in May 1924 with the prestigious D. W. Griffith film *America.* It was a handsome house with a Roman architectural theme. The original plan for the theater entailed booking special films for long runs at higher than usual admission prices. But the Forum suffered because of its out-of-the-way location—at the extreme end of West Pico Street—which made it more of a neighborhood house than a "downtown" theater. As a result, it began to experience financial difficulties within a month of its opening. By the time *The Wizard of Oz* was booked there, the theater had revised its policy, lowering ticket prices and vowing to limit runs to no more than four weeks.[30] Although the theater was certainly respectable, it had limited potential for profit and must have given the Chadwick company a favorable rate.

Larry Semon, his new wife, and I. E. Chadwick attended the Los Angeles opening on 7 February. Semon was reportedly infuriated to find that his name was not included in billboard copy for the film; apparently Julius K. Johnson, the managing director of the Forum, had felt that the title of the motion picture alone was a sufficient selling point. Perhaps because his role in the film had not been promoted beforehand, Semon received only a lukewarm reception when he appeared onstage at the debut.[31]

For opening night, seats were reserved and priced at $1.10. Later showings were unreserved, with tickets for adults selling for $.65 in the evening and $.35

Program for the world-premiere engagement of the Larry Semon film at the Forum Theatre in Los Angeles, 7 February 1925.

for the matinee and tickets for children, $.15 at all times.[32] During its first week at the Forum, the Semon film grossed about $8,000, a good profit that justified a total run of three weeks. For the second week the names of both Semon and his wife were included on the billboards, but the gross dropped to $6,400. And then in the third week the film grossed only $4,800. Despite the declining profits, *The Wizard of Oz* had done better than had any of the Forum's previous films in a comparable week.[33] *Variety,* in fact, noted that it was "rather remarkable for a picture to hold up three weeks in this neighborhood house." The paper also observed, "Had it had a downtown play this picture no doubt would have played to double the business that it did here for the length of time."[34]

Throughout its run at the Forum the film was presented with a prologue. Often consisting of a series of variety acts, prologues were common in first-run movie theaters at the time. The prologue in this case began with a performance by the Forum Symphony Players, conducted by Harry H. Silverman. This was followed first by a newsreel compilation and then by a musical selection by Julius K. Johnson, the theater's director, on the house organ. A short travel film entitled *Little Journey into Lands Afar* was next on the program.

Then the audience was entertained with *An Adventure in the Land of Oz,* a "Spectacular Musical Fantasy" created and mounted by the Forum's resident production manager, Norman K. Whisler. In twelve scenes, this stage show used song and dance to present a story with an Oz theme. Unfortunately, however, except for a cast and scene list in the printed program, no information about the mini-musical is available.[35] The action, according to the program, begins on a Kansas farm, where the characters Dorothy, Hiram, and Cyrus are introduced. Then, the second and third scenes—titled, respectively, "The Journey over To-Morrow Land" and "The People in the Wizard's Book"—move the action to the Land of Oz. There are found the Scarecrow Man, the Tin-Man, the Wizard of Oz, Prince Kynd, and the Queen of Song and Flowers. Two choruses of women represent various flowers, perhaps a nod to the Poppy Chorus of the 1902 musical version of Baum's story.

The scenes situated in the Land of Oz have no clear relation to the familiar Wizard of Oz tale. Scene 6, for example, has the enigmatic title "Childhood's Love As Seen through a Leaky Moon." As in the 1902 musical, however, several of the scenes and songs have ethnic themes. Scene 8, for example, features the Spanish song "Me Neenyah," and scene 9, the Irish song "The Wearing of the Green." The show culminates in a finale entitled "The Queen's Flower Ball," centered around a ballet performed by the flower choruses.

In this prologue musical, Dorothy was played by Andree Bayley, the Scarecrow by Harry L. Wagner, the Tin-Man by Roy Sager, and the Wizard by

Josef Johnson. None of the performers in the live show also appeared in the Chadwick film, but the costumes for the Scarecrow and the Tin-Man were credited to the Larry Semon Studios, so it is likely that the costumes at least were the same as those used in the motion picture. Finally, following the stage musical was the projection of the feature, *The Wizard of Oz*. To accompany it, the house orchestra played selections from standard compositions that were cued to the action in the film.[36]

The Los Angeles premiere gave the Chadwick company a chance to test the waters and try to interest California distributors in the film. In fact, the West Coast Theatres chain picked up the film and gave it brief runs in some of its Los Angeles–area venues beginning in March.[37] The Forum premiere also had a ceremonial function since the picture had been filmed in Los Angeles. As far as the business side of the film industry was concerned, however, the New York City debut would be the film's real test. In fact, the major trade papers, most of which were based in New York, did not review the film during its run at the Forum.

Although a New York booking was a given from the start, a theater for the premiere there did not become final until March. Chadwick Pictures Corporation had been holding out for a major Broadway venue, and it got one in B. S. Moss's Colony Theatre, a new, 1,980-seat house that had opened for the first time the previous Christmas Day. A large and elaborate movie palace, it specialized in first-run showings prior to general releases. It had been successful in booking prominent pictures because its standard contract had terms favorable to producers and distributors; that is, the theater gave them a percentage of the gross above house expenses, with a guarantee that they would receive a minimum of $25,000 for the entire run.[38]

The Wizard of Oz opened at the Colony on 12 April, Easter Sunday. As had the Selig company in 1910, the Chadwick company felt that a film based on Baum's tale was an appropriately wholesome release for Easter. Larry Semon, of course, traveled to New York for the opening. During the first week of the film's run admission to matinee shows was $.35 to $.50, and to evening shows, $.60 to $.85.[39] Attendance for the week was good, but the bulk of the patronage was at matinees, which were popular with children. Because evenings, with their higher ticket prices, were not as well attended as they might be, the total gross for the week amounted to only $14,000, less than half of the theater's potential take.[40] Evidently Semon's hope that children would boost his box office backfired in this case.

Despite this disappointing box-office performance, the film was held over for a second week, as there was no other picture available for the Colony. This reportedly made *The Wizard of Oz* the first independent motion picture to play more than a week on Broadway.[41] To attract audiences, the admission for the evenings was now dropped to a single flat rate of sixty cents.[42] The second week actually worked out relatively well since the film grossed $13,600. Considering that most films experience drops in attendance after their premiere week, this was a respectable showing. *Variety* attributed it to the "wide exploitation" of *The Wizard of Oz* by publicists.[43] Still, the film was not held over for a third week. In fact, given the Colony's contract with the Chadwick company, it is likely that the theater made little, if any, profit on the booking.

The Chadwick Pictures Corporation had worked hard to advertise and exploit *The Wizard of Oz* during its New York engagement.[44] Poster and billboard advertising ranging from half-sheets to twenty-four sheets was posted throughout metropolitan New York. And advertisements, often including whimsical drawings of the film's characters, were carried in all the major dailies. A full-page advertisement, fairly unusual at the time, appeared in the *Bulletin* on the film's opening day.[45] Aside from emphasizing the film's humor, many advertisements also made sure to mention its connection both to Baum's book and to the legendary stage musical. A notice in the 21 April *Daily News,* for example, boasted that the Wizard of Oz "has been running for 25 years and is still going with the speed of a cyclone! He ran for four years without stop in one theatre with Montgomery and Stone. He is now . . . at the Colony."[46]

Among the Chadwick-organized promotions and tie-ins was a special "photoplay" edition of Baum's book. Published by the Bobbs-Merrill Company, it featured scenes from the motion picture. Book stores and department stores throughout the city displayed the volume. In addition, Scarecrow and Tin Woodman dolls, which had been manufactured since 1924 by the Oz Doll and Toy Manufacturing Company, founded by Frank J. Baum, were used to advertise the film.[47] Baum had arranged for window displays featuring the dolls, along with stills from the movie.

On 16 April, as a promotion for the film, the world-famous Roseland Ballroom held a "Wizard of Oz" night with a prize waltz contest. Radio spots advertised the event, as well as the film itself. Also, two weeks in advance of the dance both the interior and exterior of the ballroom were decorated with characters from the Baum story. The most noticeable decoration was an eighteen-foot cutout of Larry Semon as the Scarecrow mounted on the marquee.[48]

Two major New York newspapers ran special contests for the Chadwick film. The *Daily News* asked children to write letters explaining why they deserved to be the newspaper's guest at a screening of *The Wizard of Oz* on 18 April. The two hundred children who submitted the best letters were invited

Proof for the dust jacket of the Larry Semon Photoplay
Edition of *The Wizard of Oz*, published by Bobbs-Merrill
in 1925. This book was one of several promotional tie-ins
for Semon's film.

to attend. Of these, the fifty whose letters were judged the *very* best were to receive, in addition, a doll made by the Oz Doll and Toy Manufacturing Company.[49] The *Daily Mirror* ran a cartoon of Larry Semon as the Scarecrow that children were asked to color and mail in. The contest, with a deadline of 25 April, offered a total of 353 prizes.[50]

To introduce the film, the management of the Colony produced a new multipart prologue.[51] As presented during opening week, the prologue began with the Colony Orchestra playing a selection of music called *Symphonajazz,* a unique blending of classical and modern popular music. Next followed a newsreel presentation. Then Dan Casler, a pianist, and Eva Clark, one of Arthur Hammerstein's musical-comedy stars, performed several selections. After *The Struggle for Existence,* a short nature film, was screened, the Twenty Albertina Rasch Girls appeared in the *Pastelle Ballet,* which the program described as "An Exquisite and Popular Ballet Arrangement of Light, Color, and

The marquee of the Roseland Ballroom, New York City, heralding the Wizard of Oz dance contest held there in association with the Semon film (*Motion Picture News,* 2 May 1925).

Contrast Created to the Popular Tunes of the Day."[52] Finally, Dan Marble executed a *Scarecrow Dance* to introduce the film. The curtains opened to reveal a scarecrow mounted on a pole, seen through a scrim hung at the front of the stage. After climbing off his pole, he executed a dance. Then, as the dance was finishing, there was a smooth transition to the presentation of the feature film: The lights began to dim, and the main titles of the motion picture appeared on the scrim. When the lights went out completely, the scrim was removed, the screen appeared, and the film itself was projected.

Reviewing the entire program, *Variety* called it "about the snappiest of shows that has been seen along the street for some time in a picture house."[53] To attract repeat audiences, however, changes were made for the second week. The show still began with the Colony Orchestra playing *Symphonajazz* and included a newsreel presentation. But now the other acts in the prologue were the tenor Frederick Brindley performing a song; *A Bouquet of Melodies,* a piano and dance recital featuring the Colony Ballet; *Aloha Land,* a travel film; and the team of Fowler and Tamara presenting South American dances.[54]

The main feature, of course, was still Chadwick's *The Wizard of Oz,* which consisted of 6,300 feet in seven reels. In the opening scene of the film, prints of which survive, Larry Semon appears as an elderly toymaker in his shop.[55] He places a Scarecrow doll on a table alongside dolls of Dorothy and the Tin Woodman. A little girl, his granddaughter, enters carrying the Baum book. The toymaker places her on his lap and opens the book to reveal the film's credits.

The ensuing story begins in the palace throne room in the Land of Oz. The people, led by their spokesman Prince Kynd, have gathered to confront the treacherous Prime Minister Kruel, who appointed himself their ruler, and his associates, Lady Vishuss and Ambassador Wikked. The people are angry because the princess of Oz vanished as a baby and now the kingdom has no rightful queen. Assuring the crowd that the Wizard of Oz can find their queen, Kruel summons the Wizard, his yes-man, who is nothing but a medicine showman. He instructs the Wizard to distract the crowd while he contemplates a plan to deal with them. The Wizard performs a magic trick, making the so-called Phantom of the Basket appear out of an empty basket. The Phantom entertains everyone with a dance.

Back in the toymaker's shop, the little girl asks to hear about Dorothy, the Tin Woodman, and the Scarecrow. When the old man turns the page of the book, the film takes us to a Kansas farm. Here we are introduced to Dorothy, a girl about to celebrate her eighteenth birthday. She is compared to a rose and is, in fact, first seen carrying roses and wearing a hat of the same shape. Her guardians are her loving Aunt Em and her abusive Uncle Henry. Also on the

The Wizard entertains the crowd
by performing his "Phantom of
the Basket" illusion. This scene
is reminiscent of act 2 of the 1902
musical, in which the Wizard
also staged a basket trick. Here
the Phantom is played by the
female impersonator Frederick
Ko Vert.

farm are three farm hands. One is a black man named Snowball, who is always quaking in fear. The other two, whose names are not given, are played by Larry Semon and Oliver Hardy. The Semon and Hardy characters are rivals for the affection of Dorothy. The former has a lengthy series of comic encounters with farm animals—a chicken lays an egg on him, a donkey kicks him into a cactus patch, a duck vomits on him, and a swarm of bees attacks him.

Not only is Henry abusive toward Dorothy but he is always angry at the farm hands, especially when they shirk their work. He reprimands Snowball for eating melon in the melon patch, for example, and the farm hand played by Semon for sleeping during the daytime. But at times Henry gets his due. At one point Dorothy is swinging very high on a swing when it breaks and sends her flying into the air. She falls on lumber that extends under two barrels of paint, and the barrels are thrown onto Henry, covering him with paint.

When Dorothy complains to her aunt about her uncle's cruel behavior, Em tells her that she is not really their niece. A flashback reveals that Dorothy was left on Em and Henry's doorstep as an infant, along with a sealed envelope that she was to open in eighteen years.

The scene shifts once again to the toymaker reading to his granddaughter and then back again to the throne room in Oz. To preserve his power, Kruel wants to keep from Dorothy that she is the queen of Oz. He sends Wikked to Kansas to destroy the envelope that she is about to open. Wikked departs in an airplane, and then we return once again to the toymaker and the little girl, who demands to hear more about Dorothy. Her grandfather obliges.

Back in Kansas, Dorothy is celebrating her eighteenth birthday and expecting to learn the contents of the envelope. Suddenly Wikked and his assistants arrive and demand the letter from Uncle Henry, who chases them away. Dorothy then promises the farm hand played by Semon that he will be the first to see the letter after she reads it. Jealous, the farm hand played by Hardy chases him away and proposes marriage to Dorothy. She refuses and walks away. Wikked now approaches the Hardy character and offers him both wealth and Dorothy if he can get the letter. Next, Henry retrieves the letter from its hiding place but quickly hides it again elsewhere when he sees Wikked advancing with a gun.

Increasingly desperate, Wikked and his men now grab Dorothy and dangle her from a tower. They light a fire under the rope that supports her and threaten to let her fall unless the letter is surrendered. The Hardy farm hand meanwhile finds the letter and is about to give it to Wikked, when the Semon character grabs it and runs. In the ensuing chase Semon climbs to the top of a pair of silos and dives off, and Hardy follows in pursuit. Semon escapes and manages

Dorothy, a young woman of eighteen, is threatened by
Uncle Henry as Aunt Em and the farm hand played by
Oliver Hardy look on. This film places much greater
emphasis upon life on the Kansas farm than did any
previous incarnation of the Wizard of Oz tale.

The farm hands played by Oliver Hardy *(kneeling)* and
Larry Semon *(right)* compete for Dorothy's affections.

to break Dorothy's fall. As Wikked and his men advance again, a cyclone strikes, with bolts of lightning, and everybody runs for cover.

Dorothy, Henry, and the Semon and Hardy characters retreat to a shack, only to find Wikked already there. The farm hand played by Hardy knocks Wikked unconscious. The cyclone then destroys the farm and lifts the shack off its foundations. The building, a fence, and a tree are seen flying through the sky. Lightning also lifts the terrified Snowball off the ground and deposits him in the house in midair.

The shack eventually crashes down in the Land of Oz. Dorothy, her uncle, and the farm hands emerge from the ruins of the building relatively unharmed. They see that they are just outside the city gates, where soldiers are performing a drill. At this point the Semon character remembers the letter in his pocket and hands it to Dorothy. It says that Dorothy is the rightful ruler of Oz and will ascend to the throne on her eighteenth birthday. Wikked, who revives as Dorothy is reading the letter, runs off to alert Kruel, who is approaching with other representatives from Oz.

Arriving on the scene, Kruel is clearly upset that the queen has been found. He asks the Wizard to work his magic and transform the three farm hands into anything he chooses. The Wizard confides to the farm hands that he has no real powers but must try to fake something. Seeing themselves in a bad situation, the Wizard and the farm hands flee. The Semon character runs into a cornfield, where he decides to assume the disguise of a scarecrow, while the Hardy character hides in a junk pile and disguises himself as a tin man. The Wizard and Snowball, however, are detained. The Wizard then tells Kruel that he has transformed the farm hand played by Semon into a scarecrow. Coming down from his pole, the Scarecrow flops around on unsteady legs. Similarly, the Wizard lays claim to transforming the farm hand played by Hardy into the Tin Woodman. The prime minister takes the three farm hands prisoner.

The scene changes to the throne room, where Dorothy is being honored as queen and the three prisoners are to be thrown into the dungeon on the trumped-up charge that they kept Dorothy from the throne. The Tin Woodman proclaims his innocence to Prince Kynd and is pardoned, but the Scarecrow and Snowball are deposited in the dungeon. At Wikked's suggestion, Kruel plots to marry Dorothy. The Hardy character is then made the Knight of the Garter, and the overweight Henry is made the Prince of Whales.

Piratelike dungeon masters threaten the Scarecrow and Snowball, when the Wizard appears and surreptitiously gives Snowball a lion's costume to wear as a joke on his captors. Donning the costume, Snowball becomes the figure of the Cowardly Lion. In this guise he pounces on the dungeon masters, who

Prime Minister Kruel threatens (*from left to right*)
Snowball, the Hardy farm hand in his disguise as the Tin
Woodman, the Wizard, and the Semon farm hand in his
disguise as the Scarecrow.

run away in fright. The Scarecrow now escapes from the dungeon and warns
Dorothy about Kruel and his associates. The Knight of the Garter, however,
catches the Scarecrow in the palace and chases him back into the dungeon.
The Scarecrow evades the Knight by hiding in one crate after another. The
chase ends when both the Scarecrow and the Cowardly Lion are locked in a
cage within the dungeon that holds real lions. Comedy results as the two try
to escape the beasts. At one point the Scarecrow is horrified to realize that the
lion beside him is genuine and not, as he had thought, his friend in disguise.
The Cowardly Lion finally escapes by jumping out of an opening in the walls
of the dungeon and somersaulting away. As for the Scarecrow, the Wizard leads
him out of the prison.

In the palace, meanwhile, the prime minister tries to kiss Dorothy but is interrupted by the prince. Kruel and Kynd have a sword fight. Just as Kynd is cornered, the Scarecrow appears on a balustrade above and drops a vase onto Kruel's head. The prime minister, begging for mercy, explains that he was the one who had taken the future queen to Kansas. He had done this to save her from a hostile faction. Kruel is now taken prisoner. After this, the Scarecrow wipes off his makeup, and Dorothy gives him a "thank-you" kiss. But then, spurning him, she turns and exits with Kynd in a romantic embrace.

Suddenly the Knight and Wikked enter and begin chasing the Semon character. He flees to the top of a guard tower, but when Wikked fires a canon at it, he swings on a rope over to another tower. An airplane bearing Snowball comes to the rescue. The Semon character grabs hold of a ladder hanging from

Snowball and the Scarecrow are menaced in the dungeon by a group of dungeon masters dressed like pirates.

Prime Minister Kruel is taken prisoner after his plan to usurp the throne of Oz is exposed. The Scarecrow, who has saved the day, looks on.

the plane and starts climbing. The ladder breaks, however, and he falls through the air.

The scene shifts to reveal the toymaker's Scarecrow doll tumbling to the floor. The next shot shows the little girl, who has been asleep nearby, awaking with a start. Apparently, some, if not all, of the preceding story was merely her dream. The girl rises, picks up the Scarecrow doll, and takes the two other Oz dolls in her arms as well. She goes over to her grandfather and then leaves his shop with the dolls. The toymaker takes Baum's novel from his table and opens it to reveal text stating that Dorothy and her prince lived happily ever after.

And so the film ended as it began, with the pretense that the story as screened could be found in Baum's book, here given the shortened title *The Wizard of Oz*. Yet nowhere is it more apparent than in the final scene just how far Semon strayed from the text of the novel. The stereotypical romantic fairy-tale ending, involving a prince and princess who live happily ever after, was light years away from Baum's original conception. But whether Semon and his film would meet a similarly happy ending at the hands of the New York filmgoing public still remained to be seen.

Chapter 9

A Slapstick Scarecrow

The Wizard of Oz (1925), II

T FIRST GLANCE Larry Semon's *The Wizard of Oz* seems to have little to do with either Baum's original book or the later dramatic adaptations of the tale. Close scrutiny of the film, however, finds many familiar elements, although Semon reinterpreted them or placed them in a new context.

Retained from the original book, for example, is the concept of two separate worlds, Kansas and Oz, but their use in the film is very different. Following the introductory scene in the toymaker's shop, we are taken not to Kansas, as we might expect based on Baum's version of the story, but rather to Oz. In fact, the structure of the tale is reversed in that Oz, not Kansas, is Dorothy's true home.

This is still ostensibly Dorothy's story, even though other figures, particularly the Scarecrow, often overshadow her in importance. Dorothy's personality, background, and station in life are also very different here. Baum presented her as a plain, no-nonsense farm girl, independent in spirit and not easily intimidated. Throughout the film, however, her heavy makeup, frilly clothes, and flirtatious behavior show her to be far from plain and straightforward. In addition, she is anything but independent. She takes no initiative; rather, she is led from one situation to another by the men in her life. Furthermore, as in Baum's book, it is uncertain here whether Dorothy is an orphan. But we do learn that she is utterly different from her counterpart in the novel in that she is of royal blood. Revealed to be a queen, she rises high above the role of farm girl.

At the tale's outset Dorothy is still under the care of Aunt Em and Uncle Henry, but here these two are not related to her, as they are in Baum's original version of the story. Em's motherliness is compatible with Baum's description of her. But whereas in the novel Dorothy's longing to return home is centered around Em, in the film Dorothy quickly forgets about her once in Oz. Uncle Henry, for his part, is portrayed here as abusive and blustery instead of merely industrious. As for the many animals on the Kansas farm, these recall the numerous creatures that appear in the pages of Baum's book, but here they are all ordinary and never personified.

The cyclone that carries Dorothy to Oz is present in the Semon film as well, but rather than occurring soon after the tale begins, it takes place about halfway through the movie. It does not set the story in motion, and its role is to bring Dorothy home instead of carrying her away. In addition, it serves as a deus ex machina, saving the girl and her companions in Kansas from Ambassador Wikked and his associates. Once Dorothy arrives in Oz, the settings of the city gates and the throne room figure prominently, as in the novel, but the action that takes place there is very different.

The Scarecrow, the Tin Woodman, and the Cowardly Lion also appear in the film, of course, but this time just as disguises for three Kansas farm hands. And unlike Baum's original conception of them, the Scarecrow and the Tin Woodman are rivals and adversaries rather than friends. The Wizard of Oz also plays a part, but here he has no political power whatsoever. From the outset he is nothing more than a ruler's yes-man.

An obvious parallel to the novel occurs in the film's final scene in Oz. The airplane carrying Snowball brings to mind the balloon that carries the Wizard away in the book. And just as the Semon character is unable to climb into the airplane, so Baum's Dorothy does not succeed in boarding the balloon.

To be sure, Chadwick's *The Wizard of Oz* did exclude several key features of the original novel. Perhaps Semon took his cue from the 1902 stage adaptation in deciding not to include Toto, the Wicked Witch of the West, and the yellow brick road. But he went even further, eliminating many of the book's supernatural and spiritual elements that had been retained in the play. In general, there are no magical poppies, witches, or other extraordinary beings or animals; even the Scarecrow, the Tin Woodman, and the Cowardly Lion are nothing but ordinary farm hands. In addition, Dorothy and her three traveling companions no longer undertake the quasi-spiritual journey to find home, brains, a heart, and courage that leads to the discovery of powers within themselves. Apparently, Semon aimed to emphasize farce and slapstick humor and felt that too much fantasy and reflection would detract from these. He was also likely aware that old-fashioned fairy-tale films, with their supernatural elements, had limited appeal in the jazz-age 1920s.

Actually, it is to those audiences who were most familiar with the 1902 stage version of Baum's book that Semon's film adaptation probably would have made the most sense. To a great extent, in fact, the screenplay was inspired by the musical, which had been on the boards continuously for almost ten years before becoming a staple for stock companies throughout the country. By the time Semon's movie was released, the play was probably still being revived here and there, and a large segment of the film's adult viewers would have seen the old standard in one form or another. Indeed, much of the movie's advance publicity, as well as many of its subsequent reviews, described it as an adaptation of the stage play.[1]

It is not surprising, then, that many of the film's plot elements can be traced to the 1902 musical. As in the play, the Kansas farm is here picturesque and thriving instead of bleak and barren, as Baum presented it in his original book. Also in both adaptations Dorothy is old enough to be courted and, in fact, has several suitors. Thus, the theme of romance is apparent in both the film and the play. In addition, the farm hands, who are central to the film's story, were first introduced in the musical, although as minor figures. The depiction of the cyclone, too, is similar in both versions: in both the play and the film we see a person as well as various objects flying through the air.

On the stage, Fred Stone gave the Scarecrow his famous wobbly legs, and the character in the film is unsteady on his feet when he comes down from his pole. Also, as in the play, the Cowardly Lion is a minor character who figures little in the action, serving primarily as a source of physical comedy. In fact, the film's toymaker does not even have a doll for the character. The Wizard of Oz too is similar in both the film and the musical. In both he is depicted as a comic figure, far less dignified than in Baum's novel. Furthermore, as in the musical, the Wizard performs a basket trick to entertain the crowd.

Political intrigue and conspiracy, revolving around the right to the throne, are central to both the Semon film and the earlier play. Power mad, Prime Minister Kruel parallels Pastoria, although the latter has a genuine claim to rule, whereas Kruel does not. Each man is so fearful of being usurped that he imprisons innocent people, including the Scarecrow. Kruel's cohorts, Ambassador Wikked and Lady Vishuss, correspond to General Riskitt and Tryxie

Tryfle, Pastoria's associates in the musical. Unlike their predecessors, however, Wikked and Vishuss are clearly malevolent.

Even minor characters are similar in both the film and the play. The guards who perform a drill in front of the city gates in Oz, for example, are borrowed from the musical. In addition, the motion picture, like the play before it, features women in the role of palace courtiers.

The comic tone of the film recalls the humor of the play. In both versions much of the comedy arises from slapstick gags. Puns too are important to both. In this regard, the names of Prime Minister Kruel, Lady Vishuss, Ambassador Wikked, and Prince Kynd rank with Wiley Gyle, General Riskitt, Dashemoff Daily, and other comedy characters in the musical. And when Snowball is shown eating watermelon, an intertitle describes him as "melon-cholic."

Finally, like the musical, Chadwick's *The Wizard of Oz* was designed to appeal to both adults and children. The romantic and political motifs carried over from the play were directed at adults, while the fairy-tale elements were primarily for children. As with his Vitagraph films, though, Semon always made sure, even when presenting adult themes, to maintain the interest of children, toning down the romantic and political elements so that a child could understand them. In the first Kansas sequence, for example, when the farm hand played by Semon longs for Dorothy, the sexual content of the scene is undermined with a comic intertitle reading, "In the spring a young man's fancy turns to thoughts of—lollypops." Furthermore, Semon avoided much of the adult humor relating to politics and current events that had been featured in the musical.

In a few small ways the Chadwick motion picture may also have been inspired by the Oz films of 1908, 1910, and 1914. The idea of having someone, in this case the toymaker, introduce the story by turning the pages of a book was taken directly from *Fairylogue and Radio-Plays,* of 1908. Frank J. Baum, who was the projectionist for *Fairylogue,* was probably behind this concept as a way to acknowledge and promote his father's book, especially the photoplay edition that the Bobbs-Merrill Company was issuing in conjunction with the Semon film.

In both the Chadwick film and the Selig Polyscope Company's *The Wonderful Wizard of Oz* of 1910, Dorothy is accompanied by an entire entourage on her journey from Kansas to Oz, unlike in Baum's novel, where her only companion is Toto. In both films we also find the Wizard revealing himself to be a humbug early on in the story. And it is hard not to assume some relationship between the name of King Krewl in *His Majesty, the Scarecrow of Oz* and Prime Minister Kruel in the Chadwick film. After all, if Semon was not familiar with the 1914 film by the Oz Film Manufacturing Company, Frank J. Baum certainly was.

But if much of the new Wizard of Oz film can be traced to the story's various past incarnations, it also contained a great deal of original material. As already mentioned, Semon retained elements of Baum's original novel but reinterpreted them or set them in a new context. The comedian also introduced several new characters not seen in previous adaptations of Baum's tale. The toymaker was evidently added as a chance for Semon to play a straight part in addition to his comic role as the farm hand and Scarecrow. Also, the inclusion of the toymaker and his dolls was no doubt a marketing ploy to promote the dolls made by the Oz Doll and Toy Manufacturing Company. As for the toymaker's granddaughter, she brought a child's perspective to the story, in which Dorothy herself was now portrayed as an adult. Through the little girl, Semon was assuring children that the film was for them as well as for adults.

Although Prime Minister Kruel, Ambassador Wikked, and Lady Vishuss have their counterparts in the 1902 play, they contribute much that is new to the narrative in terms of their schemes to hold power. Prince Kynd, for his part, is a fully original addition to the story. He was obviously added to be a royal suitor for Dorothy's hand. Other new characters, although minor, appear in Oz. The Phantom of the Basket is a particularly interesting example. Conjured up from the Wizard's basket, the Phantom, played by a female impersonator, performs a dance wearing an elaborate and exotic costume. Clearly, the Phantom's number was a vaudeville-type act incorporated into the film because of its audience appeal. Also new are the dungeon masters, who, dressed like pirates, add to the escapades in the prison.

In addition, the Semon film includes a major character who is black, the Kansas farm hand Snowball. Much of the humor revolving around Snowball was, unfortunately, based on the negative stereotypes of blacks that were often perpetuated in film, vaudeville, minstrelsy, and other forms of popular culture at the time. He was portrayed as stupid and fearful: When the cyclone strikes, for example, he is hit in the head by several lightning bolts but seems oblivious to them. Then, a bolt hits the ground and he becomes frightened and flees, only to have the lightning lift him and pursue him through the air as he runs in utter terror. Because of his fearful nature, Snowball, of course, makes a fitting Cowardly Lion. In fact, after he puts on the lion's costume, he has plenty of opportunity to act afraid. At one point he becomes so terrified of a real lion in the dungeon that his feet remain glued to the floor when he tries to flee.

Although the 1902 play laid the groundwork for including slapstick elements in the Wizard of Oz tale, Semon went much further in reworking the story to feature this kind of humor. His previous films, of course, had featured slapstick at the expense of the plot. Indeed, his comic approach so dominated *The Wiz-*

ard of Oz that one reviewer felt the story had been "moulded into a typical Larry Semon vehicle."[2]

The Kansas scenes, which constitute a substantial part of the picture, for example, seem to exist primarily as a backdrop for a series of slapstick sketches. At one point a duck steals a lollipop from the farm hand played by Semon and takes a bite from it. Then, with the farm hand in pursuit, the animal manages to evade capture behind a fence. It keeps sticking its head through holes in the fence to jeer at the farm hand, who tries to hit it with a board. Before its final escape, the duck sends a long volley of vomit into the man's face. Grimacing, he turns to the camera and slowly wipes away the mess. At another point a donkey kicks the same farm hand in the backside and sends him flying through the air into a cactus bed. The farm hand pulls pieces of the sharp plants from his rear and throws them over a fence. We see them land on a bench, where Uncle Henry accidentally sits on them, and then he immediately jumps up in pain.

Other Semon trademarks, in line with his slapstick sensibility, were elaborate chases and stunts, and there is no shortage of these in *The Wizard of Oz*. The major chases feature the Hardy character pursuing the Semon character. In Kansas, for instance, trying to get the secret letter, he follows him to the top of the silos. Later, in Oz, he attempts to catch him as he hides under a series of crates and again as he climbs to the top of towers. The stunts include Dorothy swinging very high on the swing, the farm hands played by Semon and Hardy diving off the silos, and Snowball as the Cowardly Lion somersaulting away from the dungeon. As in his Vitagraph films, Semon encouraged his actors to do their own stunts, and all except Dorothy Dwan, who played Dorothy, apparently avoided using doubles.

Also included in Semon's adaptation of the Wizard of Oz story are elements borrowed from standard action films. The airplanes, for example, bring both excitement and modernism to the story. And with their flowing black capes, Ambassador Wikked and the associates who accompany him to Kansas look like typical screen villains. The sequence in which they string Dorothy up to a tower is standard damsel-in-distress material. In addition, the lions'-den scene is straight from adventure films, while the dungeon masters seem to have walked out of pirate sagas.

Chadwick's *The Wizard of Oz* is not without its subtleties, however, and it plays with visual motifs and correspondences. When we first meet the farm hand played by Semon in Kansas, for example, he is sleeping in some straw. With his arms spread wide, one leg stretched straight out in front of him, and the other bent at the knee, his posture suggests a scarecrow—a visual preview of things to come. Another subtle touch is the parallelism between the chase up the pair of silos in Kansas and the similar chase up the two guard towers in Oz.

Perhaps the most sophisticated aspect of the film is the idea that its version of the Wizard of Oz story is at least in part merely a child's dream. With its loose structure and topsy-turvy logic, the story certainly makes most sense as a dream. As presented, the tale raises many unanswered questions: Why, for instance, was not Prince Kynd ruling Oz in Dorothy's absence? Is Prince Kynd related to Princess Dorothy, and if so, is their courtship incestuous? Why does not Dorothy, now queen of Oz, prevent the Scarecrow and Snowball from being thrown into the dungeon? How is it that Uncle Henry escapes imprisonment altogether? Aside from rendering these and other questions less bothersome, the device of the dream also helps to justify the film's deviation from Baum's original book. And furthermore, through the final scene, in which the little girl wakes up, it allows an otherwise hectic movie to close with a nice bit of quiet whimsy.

Ultimately, there were several reasons why Semon made so many alterations to the Wizard of Oz story, the foremost being that he wanted to transform the tale into a vehicle that would highlight the kind of thing he did best—broad, slapstick comedy. But he probably also felt that his audiences wanted something new. As a result, rather than give them the story told in the same old way, he updated it with a fast and energetic jazz-age approach. Then, too, Frank J. Baum, anxious to show the world that he could pen an original Oz story, must have had a hand in taking the tale in new directions.

Although it is not possible to view Semon's innovative version of the Wizard of Oz tale along the same symbolic lines as Baum's original novel, nonetheless the adaptation does have some meaningful resonances. No longer a child, Dorothy is now a young woman whose experiences represent her sexual coming-of-age. Her four suitors may be said to represent different aspects of an amorous relationship: the Hardy farm hand, immature and opportunistic love; the Semon farm hand, pure and innocent love; Prime Minister Kruel, forced love; and Prince Kynd, mature romantic love, which finally wins out over all the others.

Furthermore, no longer an ordinary girl who journeys to a magical kingdom and then returns home, Dorothy now follows a reverse pattern: she begins as a royal figure, is placed in hiding in common surroundings, and then returns to her elevated position. Whereas the former pattern gave Dorothy the qualities of a mythic hero who undergoes a quest, the new pattern, itself a standard folkloric formula, lends itself to new interpretations. There is an underlying message that the precious can be found hiding in the mundane. Furthermore, Dorothy's restoration to power conveys an optimistic message that the true order of the world can be set right.

Not surprisingly, however, it is Semon's character, and not Dorothy, who is the real focus of the film. In the final analysis, Dorothy's character is ill defined, psychologically undeveloped, and emotionally unchanged from beginning to end. Her transformation into a queen is merely superficial. The character played by Semon, on the other hand, evolves from being a lazy country bumpkin to a hero who saves a kingdom through guile and determination.

Like the Wizard of Oz in Baum's original novel, Semon's character also has the attributes of a benevolent trickster, a mythological figure. He is cunning and prankish in the way he evades his pursuers and outsmarts the villains. He is also able to change his appearance by transforming himself into a scarecrow. And all the while, he fights for good and against evil. But despite his heroism and his comic antics, he is ultimately a pitiful figure, patterned, no doubt, after the tragic clown of the French pantomime tradition. In the end, his love is spurned and he looks on painfully as Dorothy walks off with Prince Kynd. Furthermore, he is chased out of the kingdom he helped to save, and in our last sight of him, he falls from a flying airplane, possibly plunging to his death.

Of course, the narrative took shape through the sets, costumes, acting, and filmmaking techniques. Designed by art director Robert Stevens, the film's sets were, as at least one newspaper critic noted, more elaborate than those seen in typical slapstick comedies.[3] In fact, they reflected Semon's penchant for expensively produced films.

The set for the toymaker's shop features a large staircase framed by a decorative arched doorway. Toys are arranged on shelves, and the toymaker's worktable is cluttered with tools and toys. A realistic farmyard forms the setting for the Kansas sequences, many of which take place outdoors. Most impressive are the huge silos and the tower from which Dorothy dangles high above the ground.

Countering the realism of the Kansas scenes is the artificial nature of many of the Oz environments. Apparently inspired by William Wallace Denslow's illustrations for Baum's book, as well as the sets of the 1902 play, Oz is depicted in an Orientalist style. The Oz skyline includes fanciful interpretations of Islamic minarets, towers, and domes. It is represented by miniatures when Ambassador Wikked's airplane departs for Kansas; by a painted drop when guards perform a drill at the city gates; and by outdoor set constructions when the Semon character flees to the top of the towers. The interior of the palace has Moorish windows and doorways to carry through the Orientalist theme. Otherwise, however, it has traditional European furnishings set in modern, stream-lined room configurations. The palace's dungeon is cavelike, its walls made of plaster and papier-mâché rocks. As for the Scarecrow's cornfield, it is a small set clearly constructed inside a studio.

The film features a wildly eclectic variety of costumes. The white-haired toymaker wears a full-length apron over work clothes, while his granddaughter is dressed in a frilly white dress and has a bow in her hair. Most of the outfits in the Kansas sequences are ordinary farm clothing, with the exception of those worn by Dorothy and the farm hand played by Semon. When we first see Dorothy, her country dress is accompanied by an oversized artificial rose in her hair. The flower calls to mind the Poppy headdresses of the 1902 musical and may be a reference to that show. For her birthday celebration she wears a fancier dress trimmed with small dark ribbons and decorated with large hori-zontal stripes at its base. In her hair she wears a small bow. In both the Kansas scenes and the later ones in Oz, Dorothy is costumed in styles fashionable for the 1920s; in fact, she resembles nothing less than a flapper, with her bobbed hair, eyeliner, and painted Kewpie-doll lips.

As a farm hand, Semon wears striped overalls that are too short, white socks, black shoes, a white dress shirt with a cravat around his neck, and heavy white makeup. This was obviously not the outfit of the average farm hand of the day; rather, it was a modified and toned-down version of the clown costume that Semon had worn in his Vitagraph films.

The common people of Oz resemble Dutch peasants. The women, in partic-ular, wear traditional Dutch hats with upturned wings. The male members of the ruling class, on the other hand, wear clothing in the style of Middle Euro-pean royalty with some militaristic elements. They seem to have stepped out of the Graustarkian operettas of the 1910s and 1920s. Prince Kynd, for example, wears a military uniform decorated with medals, a sword at the waist, an er-mine-trimmed cape over one shoulder, and a plumed hat. Prime Minister Kruel wears a decorative jacket over a shirt with a ruffled collar and sleeves. A large sash is draped across one shoulder, and he too carries a sword. When he leaves the palace, he wears a feathered admiral's hat. The Wizard, however, does not fit this pattern. Befitting his role as a medicine showman, he wears the garb of a nineteenth-century doctor—top hat, tails, and pince-nez.

As for the women of the court, Lady Vishuss and Queen Dorothy both wear long beaded gowns of a 1920s style. Lady Vishuss has a jeweled cap, while Dorothy wears a beaded headband. Needless to say, Lady Vishuss wears the darker outfit. There is also some exoticism in the costumes of the court. Black pageboys wearing baggy pants and turbans continue the Orientalist motif of

The throne room of the palace in Oz. Prince Kynd and Dorothy are at the rear; the Wizard and Uncle Henry, as the Prince of Whales, are at the center. The decor is a mixture of art deco and Orientalist elements.

The introductory shot of Dorothy. Aside from emphasizing the young woman's feminine allure, her roselike hat and her placement among the rose bushes bring to mind the Poppy scene of the 1902 stage musical.

the Oz settings. And the Phantom of the Basket is adorned with the most spectacular costume in the film—a sequined and bejeweled bodysuit and skirt and an enormous and elaborate peacock headdress.

Finally, there are the costumes of the Scarecrow, the Tin Woodman, and the Cowardly Lion. Like Fred Stone before him, Semon as the Scarecrow wears a tattered and patched shirt and pants, oversized white gloves, and a rope around his waist, and bits of straw protrude from his garb. But in some other respects Semon's Scarecrow outfit differs from that of his predecessor. Semon's shirt has a ruffled collar, and once again in keeping with his trademark clownish character, his pants are too short and he wears white socks with black shoes. In terms of his makeup, Semon wears whiteface to correspond to the pink greasepaint on Stone. Like Stone, he has a dark triangle painted over his nose, but whereas Stone had a circle around one eye that was larger than that around the other, Semon's are both the same size. He also wears his hair slicked back, unlike Stone's messy top.

Hardy as the Tin Woodman wears a suit of metal and a funnel as a hat, but stylistically his costume differs substantially from that worn by Dave Montgomery in the part. The suit's metal sections, made of cardboard painted to simulate tin, are bulky. At the hips, strips of tin form a skirt. The outfit is also covered with numerous large dots meant to represent rivets. His facial makeup, which includes painted studs and squares around the eyes, is also unique. The Lion's costume, however, seems virtually identical to the one worn in previous stage and screen versions of the Wizard of Oz story.

The performance style of the actors is almost uniformly broad. Dorothy Dwan, in the part of Dorothy, is not called upon to do much except look pretty and act coquettish. Critics generally commented on her pleasant appearance—and little else. Dwan's first film had been the Vitagraph short *The Sawmill* (1922), which Semon had codirected and in which he had starred. In 1924 she had appeared opposite Semon in two shorts produced by Chadwick Pictures Corporation, but *The Wizard of Oz* marked her debut as a leading lady in a feature.[4]

Mary Carr, well known in the film industry for her mother roles, plays Aunt Em as sweet and sympathetic. As the critic for *Variety* commented, "Of course, nothing need be said regarding Mary Carr, for she is cast as a mother, and no one could ask for more."[5] Frank "Fatty" Alexander, a large man, had appeared in Semon's Vitagraph films. As Uncle Henry he blusters, rages, and literally throws his weight around.

Oliver Hardy, who would soon go on with Stan Laurel to become a Hollywood legend, also had acted with Semon previously, often taking the part of Semon's adversary. As the farm hand after Dorothy's affections, he is once again the rival of the Semon character. His acting is full of comic gesture, but he is able to show tender moments with Dorothy as well.

G. Howe Black plays Snowball with all the obvious stereotyping that his role requires. When fearful, he does a double take, opens his eyes wide, and trembles. His performance is athletic and well timed, and critics often singled it out. *Variety* even went so far as to deem him "almost as funny as Semon."[6]

Among the major characters in the court of Oz is Josef Swickard, a famous character actor and longtime vaudeville comedian, who does his best to look sinister and threatening as Prime Minister Kruel.[7] His shifty eyes and scowling face are reciprocated by Otto Lederer in the part of Ambassador Wikked. Virginia Pearson's role as Lady Vishuss amounts to little more than a cameo. But to audiences familiar with the actress's previous performances as a vamp, rivaling those of Theda Bara, one brief appearance was all that was needed to convey her character's wantonness.[8]

Bryant Washburn, whose early career included many comic roles, here plays it straight as Prince Kynd.[9] He has little to do except look suave and dashing.

With a playful pomposity, Charles Murray takes the role of the Wizard. His extensive experience as a comedian on the stage and in Mack Sennett films is evident in his broad clowning and constant mugging for the camera. The actor had long been an inspiration to Semon, who had previously borrowed some of his gags to use in his own shorts. In addition, Murray had been featured in Semon's *The Girl in the Limousine.*[10] In passing, it might also be mentioned that the role of the Phantom of the Basket was credited to female impersonator Frederick Ko Vert. Ko Vert's work extended to making the chorus costumes and choreographing the ballet seen in *An Adventure in the Land of Oz,* the stage musical that preceded the Los Angeles premier of the film.[11]

In the end, few would deny that *The Wizard of Oz* centers around Semon's performance. As the toymaker who introduces the story he is a believable old man. He moves slowly, his back slightly hunched over. He looks at the little girl with an expression of warmth and amusement. His acting style as the farm hand and the Scarecrow, however, is radically different. In both the Kansas and the Oz sequences, he is energetic and frisky, at times appearing almost childlike. As a comic actor Semon was prone to exaggerated movements and facial expressions. He milked his comic antics for all they were worth. In the lions' den, for example, he prolongs the humor by delaying his realization that he is in danger. In general, although Semon's performance is fairly obvious and heavy-handed, it is extremely spirited and gives the film a lively center. *Exhibitors Trade Review* was even inspired to say that he played the Scarecrow in "brilliant style" and with "wondrous agility."[12]

Shot by H. F. Koenenkamp, Frank Good, and Leonard Smith, the film has relatively simple camera work; there is very little camera movement, and most scenes were photographed from a direct, straight perspective. The editing, done by Sam Zimbalist, is also fairly basic. Simple crosscutting takes us back and forth between the toymaker scenes and the Wizard of Oz story. Standard editing is also used to introduce new sequences. In the opening scene in Oz, for example, a long shot establishes the throne-room setting, and then a series of close-ups and medium shots focus on individual characters. There is also rapid cutting during action sequences, which helps to move the scenes along swiftly and to compensate for the lack of camera movement.

The film's special effects are particularly noteworthy.[13] Stop-motion photography, for example, was used to conjure up the Phantom of the Basket. Filming was stopped after the basket was brought before the people of Oz. The Phantom then took her place in it before the camera rolled again. In the film she seems to appear suddenly, in a puff of smoke, as if by magic. The same technique was also employed in other sequences, including the one in which the

Publicity shot of Dorothy with the Scarecrow and the
Tin Woodman. In the film itself Dorothy never appears
in the same scene with the two disguised farm hands.

farm hand played by Hardy leaps from the silo. The camera first filmed Hardy initiating the jump. Then it changed angle to shoot a dummy completing the fall. At the moment the dummy hit the ground, the camera was stopped to allow Hardy to take its place. When filming started again, the actor, appearing dazed, got up from the dirt.

Reverse projection was used in the sequence in which a donkey seems to back up deliberately just to kick the farm hand played by Semon in the rear. The animal was filmed walking away from the actor, and the resulting footage was shown in reverse to achieve the desired effect. Also projected in reverse was a subsequent scene in which cactus pads appear to fall on a bench just before Uncle Henry sits on it. During the original shooting, the pads, tied to an invisible string, were actually pulled away from the bench.

An animation technique involving drawing directly on the film stock was evidently employed to create the volley of vomit the duck directs at the Semon farm hand and also the swarm of bees that attacks him. During the cyclone sequence, the lightning is created using the same technique.

The cyclone sequence, in fact, was so remarkable that Mildred Spain, the critic for the *New York Daily News,* called it "one of the best photographic tricks" that she had ever seen.[14] The destruction of the Kansas farmyard was achieved by means of a wind machine directed toward miniatures representing the setting. A matte shot also came into play to create the effect of the shack's flying through the air and Snowball's running after it in the clouds. A later sequence in which Snowball, now in a lion costume, escapes from the lions' den by somersaulting down a hill is also significant for its use of a special effect. His tumble was shot with a wide-angle lens, which distorted the field of vision, making it seem as if he were covering a longer distance.

Taken overall, Chadwick's *The Wizard of Oz,* the critics reported, was generally liked by the audiences that saw it during its premiere run in New York City. As Semon had hoped, children, in the majority at many of the screenings, responded particularly well to the film. Adults, however, also seemed to like it. "It was obvious that the youngsters enjoyed every moment of this picture," noted Mordaunt Hall, of the *New York Times,* "and as critics of such a production they excel. At the same time there was a constant outburst of parental mirth elicited by the humorous antics of the shadow players and the witty subtitles."

Hall went on to report that the film's viewers "not only laughed till the tears came but they roared until they coughed." Calling the film "the type of rough and tumble farce that sends bright faces from the theatre," he also noted how exiting audiences were "still smiling as they walked forth on sunny Broadway." One boy, he reported, had been so transported by the picture that he "stood on the sidewalk immediately after seeing the show and shouted jubilantly: 'And here we are back in New York!'"[15]

In addition to Hall, other New York critics responded favorably to the film. "There's a bona fide laugh in nearly every scene," said George Gerhard, of the *Evening World,* "and most of them are of the howl variety."[16] And according to Dorothy Herzog, of the *Daily Mirror,* "Larry Semon has made a highly entertaining picture. It's loaded with excitement and thrills and fun and even a faint splash of romance." Herzog, who "enjoyed this picture and then some," concluded her review by calling it "clean cut, novel, splendid entertainment."[17]

This is not to say, however, that reviewers had nothing but praise for the picture. Several New York critics were disappointed that the film bore so little resemblance to Baum's original story. Calling the film "a good picture" that is "screamingly" funny, Mildred Spain, of the *Daily News,* nevertheless found it difficult to "take so kindly to a story that only suggests the beloved original."[18] And the *Evening Post* wrote that "we rather expected a fantasy as fascinating as the book and, of course, we did not find it," although, as the newspaper further noted, "probably the slapstick is above average slapstick."[19]

Some critics also faulted the structure of Chadwick's *The Wizard of Oz.* While recommending the film, *Variety* thought that its narrative should have been presented in a straightforward sequence; and for Laurence Reid, of *Motion Picture News,* the story was too "episodic."[20] The *Evening Post* also pointed out that the Kansas scenes were too long in relation to the rest of the film.[21] The slapstick too was sometimes criticized. Although the film's gags, according to Reid, were generally "well timed," some were "old and feeble."[22] And *Variety* found too much repetition in the shenanigans involving the crates and the lions in the dungeon scenes.[23]

Although Chadwick Pictures Corporation could take some consolation in the fact that *The Wizard of Oz* was reportedly the first independent motion picture to play more than a week on Broadway, it must have been somewhat disappointed by the film's relatively lackluster box-office performance in New York. Still the company persevered with its selling campaign. The 2 May issue of *Motion Picture News,* for example, contained a two-page illustrated advertisement that quoted excerpts from six favorable New York newspaper reviews and claimed that the film was "the biggest Independent production of the year."[24]

The studio also had the trade papers' forecasts to bolster its confidence in the film's potential marketability. *Moving Picture World* predicted that it would "prove an excellent box-office attraction" that would "certainly go over big with all of the Semon fans and patrons who enjoy slapstick, and it should prove a regular riot with the kiddies."[25] With much advertising and support, according to *Motion Picture News,* the picture could play the larger first-run houses, but it was particularly well suited for theaters of average size.[26] Likewise, *Variety* speculated "that in the small towns and smaller cities the picture should mop up." "The exhibitor," the paper continued, "can count pretty much on getting money with it, especially if the kids bring their elders in the towns where it plays the same as they do on Broadway."[27] *Exhibitors Trade Review,* a bit more reserved in its enthusiasm, felt that the film "should record satisfactory box-office results, especially if the exhibitor booking it makes a direct play for the juvenile trade." Nevertheless, the paper added, the theater owner should also assure patrons that "the older folks will find lots to laugh at."[28]

After New York, *The Wizard of Oz* did play several engagements, including one in Chicago, prior to its general release.[29] A four-week London engagement at the new Rialto Theatre was also announced.[30] Meanwhile, Chadwick Pictures Corporation was setting up the film's general release, scheduled for 1 August 1925. It was hoping to lure a national distributor for this release. A national distributor was never found, however, apparently because the film did not have stellar box-office receipts in New York. And in any case, national distributors usually handled only the work of the major studios. As a result, the company had to rely on the usual route for independent films—the states-rights system of distribution. In this approach, the studio contracted with a series of small distributors, each of which booked theaters in a particular geographical region. Only with the cooperation of many such distributors could the film reach all the major markets in the country. This states-rights system was, of course, more labor intensive and less consistent and reliable than obtaining the services of a national distributor. But it was Chadwick's only option.

In April, Independent Films of Boston, which handled the New England territory, contracted to distribute *The Wizard of Oz.*[31] Soon other states-rights distributors were signing on, so that by the first of August Chadwick had lined up distribution for the film in much of the United States.[32] Presumably because the states-rights agents booked the film primarily in small and medium-sized houses with limited grosses, the general release received little coverage in the trade papers.

A few theater owners, however, reported their experiences showing the film during the 1925–26 season. An exhibitor in a large Missouri town with a population of 324,410, for example, declared that the film played to a "mixed" class of patronage and provided "good" box-office value. Another exhibitor, in a small Oklahoma town with 300 inhabitants, called the film "a very good comedy" that was wholesome enough for Sunday screenings.[33] The owner of a theater in Olney, Texas, had harsh words for the movie. "Listen, fellow exhibitors," he warned, "lay off this piece of cheese. It's the biggest bunch of bunk I ever ran. I was told, of course, that it was a great picture. This was done in order to sell it."[34] But another exhibitor, this one in Mt. Pleasant, Texas, responded, "I note some exhibitor knocking this production. My patrons complimented this and we found it so much different from the rest, we will report it extra good." And one from Ovalo, Texas, added, "This is a dandy good picture if your folks like slapstick comedy. My folks enjoyed it for a change and the kids were wild about it. They sure did raise the roof off the house."[35]

Figures disclosing the final domestic grosses of *The Wizard of Oz* have not survived. The film was included in the *Exhibitors Herald*'s list of the most lucrative motion pictures of 1925, but barely so. The list included 692 films named by one or more of the exhibitors who responded to the survey as among their ten biggest moneymakers during the year ending on 15 November 1925. Only three exhibitors named *The Wizard of Oz*. A similar list for the following year included the film among 685 top productions, but on the basis of the recommendation of only one exhibitor.[36]

The movie also had distribution overseas. The foreign department of First National Exhibitors Circuit, for example, booked it in Australian theaters, while Exhibitors Films of Britain handled the United Kingdom.[37] European audiences were very receptive to the motion picture. In fact, Semon enjoyed great popularity in countries like France, where he was called Zigoto; Italy, where he was known as Ridolini; and Spain, where he was called Romasin.[38] In publicity for the film, one French magazine remarked that Semon was "without doubt the American artist who is most similar to French clowns," singling out especially the comedian's "fantasy and grace" and his "sense of tragedy."[39]

In 1925 Semon appeared in *The Perfect Clown,* another Chadwick feature, and also founded his own production company. That company created two more Semon features, *Stop, Look, and Listen* and *Spuds,* but they were not commercial successes.[40] Soon thereafter, in 1928, Semon came to a sad end. Within the course of that single year, he declared bankruptcy, suffered a nervous breakdown, and died from pneumonia. He lived to be only thirty-nine years old.[41] Chadwick Pictures Corporation temporarily ceased production in the same year, and by that time *The Wizard of Oz* was all but forgotten.[42] Interestingly, a revival of the film took place in 1931, when it was aired on television station W2XCD, owned by the DeForest Radio Company. This early television broadcaster, based in Passaic, New Jersey, serialized the film over the course of three nights, 8, 9, and 10 June.[43]

In the end, there is no easy answer to why Semon's *The Wizard of Oz* did not have more lasting success. Certainly, today's audiences generally find it dated, especially in its humor. The film, however, is a decent example of a genre of comedy that was popular in the mid-1920s, and viewers of the time apparently found much to like. Perhaps its being produced independently was a strike against it. Had it been made by one of the larger studios, it might have reached a bigger audience and made a more lasting impression. Semon's untimely death at a time when his career was at its nadir also could not have helped the film's reputation. Then, too, as slapstick comedies became a thing of the past, the film was evaluated more as an interpretation of Baum's original story than as a comedy on its own terms. Perhaps one New York critic writing in 1925 was speaking for future audiences when he mused, "Why the bouncing Mr. Semon bought 'The Wizard of Oz' and then neglected its chief charms must be added to the rapidly increasing list of unsolved mysteries of the Times Square district."[44]

But Frank J. Baum was not yet ready to give up on the motion-picture industry. After sound came to the movies in 1927, he was still trying to sell film rights to the Oz stories. Although several studios expressed interest, nothing concrete materialized until 1931, when United Productions made a short called *The Scarecrow of Oz*. Featuring the Ethel Meglin Kiddies, a children's performance group from California, the film was not based specifically on the Wizard of Oz tale.[45]

Then, in 1933, Baum granted Canadian animator Ted Eshbaugh the rights to produce a short cartoon entitled *The Wizard of Oz*. Frank J. Baum wrote the scenario, which, again, wandered far from his father's original narrative. The motion picture, filmed in Technicolor, was never released because Eshbaugh encountered legal problems with the Technicolor Corporation.[46] In that same year, however, Baum also began negotiations for a feature-length musical film version of *The Wizard of Oz*. It was a project that would change Oz history forever.

Epilogue

The Wizard of Oz (1939)

Its Roots and Repercussions

I N 1924, just before Chadwick Pictures Corporation acquired the film rights to Baum's book *The Wonderful Wizard of Oz*, the Metro-Goldwyn studio had expressed interest in the property but had been unable to arrange a deal with Baum's son Frank Joslyn. In 1933, now officially known as Metro-Goldwyn-Mayer (MGM), the company again approached Frank J. Baum, in the hope of producing a series of animations based on the Oz books. But again negotiations were not successful.

The following year, though, brought a deal between Baum and the independent producer Samuel Goldwyn, who was not affiliated with MGM, having resigned from his company Goldwyn Pictures Corporation before it became part of the MGM conglomerate. Goldwyn purchased the film rights to Baum's first Oz book for forty thousand dollars. He hoped to turn the work into a Technicolor musical comedy starring Eddie Cantor as the Scarecrow, W. C. Fields as the Wizard, and either Helen Hayes or Mary Pickford as Dorothy. His plans were never realized, however, primarily because Eddie Cantor was no longer the hot property he had been a few years earlier.

In 1937 a series of circumstances converged to make MGM more eager than ever to obtain the rights to film *The Wonderful Wizard of Oz*. Previously, Louis B. Mayer, who ran the studio's operations, had relied heavily on the creative genius and business acumen of producer Irving G. Thalberg. But Thalberg died in 1936, and Mayer was in need of a replacement. He pinned his hopes on Mervyn LeRoy, a director at Warner Brothers. In the fall of 1937, before being hired as a producer at MGM, LeRoy told Mayer that he was particularly interested in producing a film based on the Wizard of Oz story—as a boy he had enjoyed both the book and the 1902 musical.

At the same time, Arthur Freed, a composer at MGM, was eager to move into producing, and Thalberg's death gave him an opportunity to advance. He worked well with Mayer and had convinced the studio chief to allow him to try to put together a project for Judy Garland, a young MGM singer in whom he saw great potential. He thought a film of the Wizard of Oz tale could be just the thing he was seeking—he too had enjoyed Baum's book as a child.

Then, when Walt Disney's feature-length animated motion picture *Snow White and the Seven Dwarfs* became a hit of the 1937 holiday season, MGM became even more interested in developing a movie with a fantasy theme. Other studios too began to look at *The Wonderful Wizard of Oz* as a story that might appeal to the same audiences that had been drawn to the Disney picture. Twentieth Century–Fox, for instance, thought that it would be an ideal project for its popular child-star Shirley Temple. But MGM wanted the property the most. Its offer of seventy-five thousand dollars to Samuel Goldwyn ensured that it would obtain the sole rights to make a film of the Baum story. On 3 June 1938, after some legal wrangling, a deal was officially concluded in which MGM was given permission to use not only Baum's original novel but all the commercial dramatic adaptations that had been made of it.

In January 1938, even before the deal with Goldwyn had been completed, MGM had begun preparing the film, planned as a musical.[1] Principal photography started in October and ended in March of the following year, and post-production work took an additional four months. Mayer put LeRoy in charge of the film's production, and Freed was assigned to assist him. A series of four directors worked on the film, although Victor Fleming received the final screen credit.

In addition, fourteen writers were involved in producing treatments and drafts of the script, with the final credit for the screenplay going to Noel Langley, Florence Ryerson, and Edgar Allan Woolf. The lyricist Edgar Yipsel ("Yip") Harburg and the composer Harold Arlen were responsible for the songs. The choreographer Bobby Connolly staged the dances. Many of the cast members, of course, would become well known because of their roles in

Victor Fleming, director of MGM's *The Wizard of Oz,* sets
up a Munchkinland scene.

the film. They include Judy Garland as Dorothy, Ray Bolger as the Scarecrow, Jack Haley as the Tin Woodman, Bert Lahr as the Cowardly Lion, Frank Morgan as the Wizard, Billie Burke as Glinda, and Margaret Hamilton as the Wicked Witch of the West.

From the start, it was decided that this MGM version of the Wizard of Oz story would be a new adaptation of Baum's book. Some people who still remembered the 1902 musical objected to the fact that no songs from that show were being included. In her column of 8 March 1938, Louella Parsons, the famed Hollywood reporter, referred to the MGM project when she asked, "Why do the film companies buy old musical favorites and then disregard the songs that have already proved popular with the public." "The old-time songs," she continued, "are new to the rising generation, and those who loved them in the old days enjoy hearing them again."[2] In reality, however, the stage production of 1902 had yielded no enduring "standards," and in large part its musical numbers had little to do with the story. Arthur Freed wanted the new film to be an integrated musical, with songs that served the plot and the characters.

During the months that MGM was developing *The Wizard of Oz* the film's narrative underwent constant change. And even though this was to be, in general, a new adaptation, many aspects of its preliminary treatments and scripts harkened back not only to the 1902 stage musical but to the various earlier film adaptations as well.

William Cannon, Mervyn LeRoy's assistant, was the first to submit ideas for adapting Baum's story. Because such recent live-action fantasy films as *Alice in Wonderland* and *A Midsummer Night's Dream* had been box-office failures, he recommended that the magical elements be downplayed. Along these same lines, Cannon felt that audiences would not abide the concept of a live Scarecrow and Tin Woodman. He believed that these characters should be human beings who assumed the parts during the course of the story.[3] Cannon's approach, then, was similar to that of Larry Semon in the 1925 film.

Other writers added plot elements many of which seem to have been inspired by previous dramatic adaptations. In one or another of Noel Langley's early drafts of the story, for example, Dorothy, much like her counterpart in the Semon film, has a romantic flirtation with a farm hand who later assumes the role of the Scarecrow in Oz.[4] Langley also added a new character named Lizzie Smithers who works at a soda fountain in Kansas, a character who brings to mind Tryxie Tryfle of the 1902 musical. His Cowardly Lion is a man who was transformed into the beast by the Wicked Witch and who, in order to break the spell, must fight a real lion in the Witch's castle. This recalls how Snowball, in the Semon movie, is "changed into" the Cowardly Lion by the

Wizard and then finds himself face-to-face with real lions. Another of Langley's notions was to reveal the Wizard as a fraud early in the story, as was done in both the 1910 and 1925 films. In addition, he had characters involved in a revolutionary scheme disguise themselves as a traveling circus, a plot element that harkens back to the stage musical.

Florence Ryerson and Edgar Allan Woolf modified the screenplay further. In their adaptation Professor Marvel, the Wizard's Kansas counterpart, is a medicine showman, the profession of Semon's Wizard. And in Oz, when the Wizard is finally exposed as a fraud, it is in front of the citizens of the land, as was the case in the play. In the adaptation too the Wizard performs common magic tricks to appease his subjects, as he does in both the play and the 1925 screen version.[5] Dorothy and her friends are subsequently implicated with the Wizard in political intrigue—another throwback to the plot of the stage musical.

Early drafts of the script, which contained much comic silliness, were also generally closer in mood to both the 1902 and 1925 adaptations than they were to the final film, which aimed for a more dramatic sentimentality.[6] And even some of Harburg's preliminary lyrics for the film's songs included topical humor, of the sort that had been so common in the stage musical. In the end, however, it was decided to discard any references that would date the movie.

In fact, piece by piece, most of the added plot elements, as well as the frivolous comedy, were stripped away, so that much of what remained in the final MGM film closely followed Baum's original novel. Dorothy's trip to Oz via cyclone and her subsequent meeting with the Scarecrow, the Tin Woodman, and the Cowardly Lion, who join her in a journey to see the Wizard, becomes the focus of the film. The quest to obtain from the Wizard qualities or powers that already exist within each individual is also prominent. These themes, so crucial to Baum's narrative, had often been buried, distorted, or entirely overlooked in earlier attempts to dramatize the story.

The portrayal of Kansas as a stark, gray environment is there as well, as are Aunt Em, Uncle Henry, Toto, the good and bad witches, the Munchkins, the magical slippers, the yellow brick road, the Fighting Trees, the poppy field, the Guardian of the Gates, the Emerald City, the Winged Monkeys, the Winkies, and the Wizard's balloon ascension. And among numerous other parallels between the book and the movie, the Scarecrow is dismantled by the Winged Monkeys but later reassembled. In addition, the Wizard first appears as otherworldly and larger than life but then, later, as an ordinary humbug showman. Never before had so many of the key elements of Baum's tale appeared in a single dramatic adaptation.

But even though the final MGM film remained relatively faithful to the 1900 novel, elements from previous stage and screen versions crept in. The influence of the 1902 play could not be escaped: The Kansas farm hands, of course, had originated there, although they later reappeared in the Selig and Chadwick films. In addition, the depiction in the 1939 movie of the cyclone's effects harkens back more to the stage musical than to the novel. In that show, screen projections showed various people, animals, and objects—including cattle, poultry, and pieces of houses—that the storm sent whirling through the air. This effect was imitated cinematically in the 1925 film too. But it found its full expression in the MGM movie, where Dorothy sees flying by her window a similar array, including a chicken coup, a fence, a house, a buggy, an uprooted tree, an old lady in a rocker, a cow, a crate of fowl, two men in a rowboat, and Miss Gulch, who is transformed into the Wicked Witch.

The producers of the MGM motion picture also went back to the 1902 play when deciding how to conclude the poppy scene. That scene, derived from Baum's book, had been a celebrated part of the stage musical but had been eliminated from the subsequent film versions. Now the makers of this movie wanted to restore it to the story, but they needed a viable alternative to the

Aunt Em offers Dorothy and the Kansas farm hands some crullers. The portrayal of Kansas in the MGM musical was influenced by both the Selig and the Semon films.

denouement as it appeared in the book—a rescue involving field mice would have been difficult to film. In the end, they decided to copy the play's solution and have the Good Witch bring about a snowfall to freeze the flowers.[7]

Perhaps the stage production also lay at the root of the scene in the MGM film in which the Scarecrow, the Tin Woodman, and the Cowardly Lion disguise themselves as Winkies in order to enter the castle of the Wicked Witch. A popular feature of the play had been the various costumes and disguises worn by the Scarecrow and the Tin Woodman, and the filmmakers must have realized that audiences would enjoy seeing these same characters, now joined by the Lion, in masquerade.

Although the 1939 motion picture is much more serious in tone than the 1902 musical, it still contains examples of the corny humor that permeated that stage show. Puns and wordplay turn up throughout the film. In fact, Dorothy's surname here, Gale, is a pun copied directly from the stage production; Baum's book does not give the little girl a last name. Also, both the play and this film refer to the Cowardly Lion as a "dandelion." Other jokes, as when the Lion asks the Tin Woodman how long he can stay fresh in his can, although original here, would not have been out of place in the earlier show. And while the stage musical had more than a little vaudeville in it, the MGM film also drew upon this traditional entertainment form. Bolger, Haley, and Lahr, in fact, all had been vaudeville performers themselves, and they brought their old show-business style—including broad clowning, witty exchanges, and well-timed deliveries—to their performances.

Finally, the very fact that the 1939 film was conceived from the outset as a musical probably can be attributed to the success of the 1902 stage adaptation. It is perhaps not surprising, in fact, that several of the musical numbers in the two productions are similar in terms of placement and function within the story. In both the stage musical and the film, for instance, the Scarecrow and the Tin Woodman introduce themselves with songs, accompanied by dancing, lamenting their respective deficiencies. And the song "If I Were King of the Forest," which the Lion sings in the MGM film, brings to mind the musical play's "When We Get What's A'Comin' to Us," performed by Dorothy, the Scarecrow, and the Tin Woodman. Both songs are sung while Dorothy and her friends await an audience with the Wizard, and both reflect how the singers expect the ruler to change their lives.

The motion picture that introduced *Fairylogue and Radio-Plays* was a forerunner to the MGM movie in its use of both black-and-white and color imagery. In the 1908 film Baum's characters were first represented as black-and-white figures in a book; as they stepped off the pages of the volume, however, they

The Tin Woodman, the Cowardly Lion, and the
Scarecrow disguised as Winkies. The 1902 stage
adaptation also had featured the Scarecrow and the
Tin Woodman in disguises.

came to life in color. Likewise, in the 1939 motion picture gray Kansas is depicted in black and white, whereas vibrant, fanciful Oz is full of color. The use of color here similarly symbolizes how Dorothy and her fantasies come to life in this land of dreams.

The Selig Polyscope Company's *The Wonderful Wizard of Oz* may have had some influence on the MGM film as well, especially as far as the Wicked Witch is concerned. In the former film, the witch rides on a broom into the Wizard's palace and sends the terrified palace attendants running in all directions. Similarly, the MGM movie has the Wicked Witch skywriting with her broom as the frightened citizens of the Emerald City look skyward and then flee. Furthermore, the witch's death is portrayed in a comparable way in both productions. In each case, the witch melts away, leaving clothing on the ground. Dorothy then takes with her proof of the witch's demise—in the Selig version, her hat; in the MGM version, her broomstick. In Baum's novel, on the other hand, the Wicked Witch leaves behind only a puddle and Dorothy's silver shoe, and Dorothy takes no evidence of her death.

Some aspects of the MGM film may also be traced to Larry Semon's *The Wizard of Oz* of 1925. It is likely, for example, that Semon's extended Kansas sequences paved the way for the relatively long Kansas preamble in the 1939 film. In both the book and the 1902 play the Kansas prologue is little developed. And even though the farm hands were first introduced in the 1902 play, their developed roles in the Semon film apparently most influenced the 1939 picture. In both movies the farm hands are fond and protective of Dorothy, although in the earlier film there is also a romantic interest. Furthermore, in each film they reappear in Oz as the Scarecrow, the Tin Woodman, and the Cowardly Lion.

Just as Semon envisioned Oz as having contemporary technology in the form of the airplane, so the Emerald City of the MGM film has equipment that appears to be modern—the buffer machine that shines the Tin Woodman and the console that controls the Wizard's manifestations. Another parallel with the 1925 film is the shot of the Cowardly Lion, frightened by the Wizard's roaring command to go kill the Wicked Witch of the West, leaping out of a palace window. This shot recalls how a terrified Snowball, in the costume of the Cowardly Lion, flees the lions' den by diving out of an opening in the wall.

Perhaps most important, in both the MGM picture and the Semon film Dorothy's adventure in Oz is revealed to be a dream. In the 1939 film it is Dorothy who is the dreamer, whereas in the 1925 film it is the toymaker's granddaughter. The Semon film was likely an influence in this regard, even though Noel Langley, who first suggested that Dorothy dream her trip to Oz, claimed

Amidst the round dwellings of Munchkinland, Glinda and the Munchkins welcome Dorothy to Oz. The creators of the 1939 film were more faithful to Baum and Denslow's original conception of Munchkinland than earlier adapters of the tale had been.

that his inspiration had come from a Mary Pickford movie called *The Poor Little Rich Girl.*

Langley agreed with William Cannon that the fantastic characters in Oz had to be introduced first as real people if audiences were to respond well to them. In *The Poor Little Rich Girl,* people in a little girl's real world reappear, in altered form, in her nightmare. Langley used this same concept to introduce ordinary individuals in Kansas, who then, in Dorothy's dream, take on fairy-tale roles in Oz. Semon too had first introduced the Scarecrow, the Tin Woodman, and the Cowardly Lion as farm hands in Kansas. Ultimately, both Semon and Langley were responding in similar ways to the problem of giving Baum's odd characters a basis in reality.

The set designers of the 1939 film occasionally drew on the illustrations and textual descriptions in Baum's original novel, as when they created the Munchkins' round houses. But in general their designs were original, and they seem little influenced by any previous stage or screen adaptation of the book.

The MGM costume designers followed even more closely the original ideas of Baum and his illustrator Denslow. Dorothy's blue gingham dress and the Wizard's striped pants, bow tie, vest, and coat, for example, strongly resemble those in the novel. Even the appearances of the Scarecrow and the Tin Woodman were drawn directly from the book, though Stone and Montgomery had created indelible interpretations of these characters. Perhaps the only nod to Stone was the patches on Ray Bolger's outfit. Not on the clothing of Denslow's Scarecrow, patches first appeared on Stone's costume and were also a feature of the later silent-screen Scarecrows.

At least one actor was strongly influenced by a performer from a previous adaptation of Baum's novel. Ray Bolger, who played the Scarecrow, idolized Fred Stone and considered him the greatest eccentric dancer of his generation.[8] He had first seen him in 1919 or 1920 in the show *Jack O' Lantern.* At one point in that production Stone's character was called upon to save a girl in distress. Bolger remembered that the actor "bounded on a trampoline out of a haystack looking just like a scarecrow, put his hand on his head, and said, 'Just in time!'" "I've never forgotten it," Bolger continued. "That moment opened up a whole new world for me. Up until then, the theater had nothing to do with me."[9] Bolger's performance in the MGM film owed much to that of his predecessor. His wobbly legs and loose-limbed approach to his role were much in keeping with Stone's legendary portrayal.

Although it used material from Baum's book and the subsequent stage and screen adaptations, the MGM film was also innovative in its own right. For example, Dorothy is twelve years old here, making her less innocent than the

Sheet music for the film's most enduring song, "Over the Rainbow." With its lively caricatures drawn by Al Hirschfeld and its photographs of the movie's cast, the cover made a nice souvenir.

five- or six-year-old in Baum's novel but not as sexually mature as the teenager in the 1902 play or the 1925 film. Her story in the MGM film, in fact, represents a coming of age as she approaches young adulthood. Furthermore, her need to get home at all costs is emphasized, and her sentimental attachment to Aunt Em and to Kansas are brought to the fore. Arthur Freed dictated that the movie be "a real assault on our hearts."[10]

The characters of Miss Gulch and Professor Marvel are introduced in Kansas, and they help set the story in motion. And just as Miss Gulch becomes the Wicked Witch of the West and Professor Marvel becomes the Wizard, the parallels between characters and situations in Kansas and those in Oz were developed more fully here than in the Semon film.

The movie also, for the first time in Oz history, specifically situated the fairyland over the rainbow. In addition, Baum's Good Witch of the North and Glinda were conflated into one benign entity, while, more important, the role of the Wicked Witch of the West was magnified. Appearing much earlier in the story, she becomes the primary threat to Dorothy. And the silver shoes of Baum's novel were transformed into the much more photogenic ruby slippers. Finally, seen as Dorothy's dream, the characters and events of Oz function as a psychological signpost to the inner workings of the girl's mind.

Besides these narrative elements, other aspects of the film of course contribute much to the presentation of Baum's story. The sets, including the colorful Munchkinland and the threatening battlements of the Wicked Witch's castle, are often strikingly imaginative. Costumes too are creative and varied. And the casting, needless to say, was often inspired. The 124 little people in the roles of Munchkins, for example, bring Munchkinland to life. The film's lush Technicolor, a type of cinematography that was relatively new at the time, is perfect for displaying the wonders of Oz. The camera work is fluid, and the multiple special effects, such as the cyclone scene and the Witch's skywriting sequence, employed previously untried techniques.

MGM's original plans for releasing *The Wizard of Oz* were similar to Chadwick Pictures Corporation's initial plans for Larry Semon's film. At first, conceived as a wholesome holiday entertainment, the movie was to be ready for Christmas 1938, but this could not be achieved. The studio also considered presenting the film as a road show in its opening engagements, but this too was not to happen. In the end the motion picture appeared in August 1939, opening in many theaters across the country over the course of a few weeks.

To build anticipation, MGM promoted the film heavily before it was officially released. The expensive and carefully conceived publicity campaign then continued during its opening weeks. The studio sought to intensify the public's awareness of the movie, including its stars and production history, and make sure it was not perceived mainly as a fantasy for children. In fact, like the producers of all the previous dramatizations of Baum's story, MGM wanted a broad-based family audience for its film. Advertisements appeared in countless newspapers and magazines, and special postcards, posters, and other publicity materials were issued. Tie-ins—nothing new, of course, to dramatizations of the Wizard of Oz story—included sheet music, dolls, clothing, masks, and toy figures.[11] The Bobbs-Merrill Company also issued an edition of Baum's original book with stills from the new film, just as it had done for Semon's film.

MGM's *The Wizard of Oz* was given its world premiere with a five-day engagement in Oconomowoc, Wisconsin, beginning on 12 August 1939. The town was probably selected as a testing ground for the film's marketability in Middle America. A gala Hollywood premiere at Grauman's Chinese Theatre followed on 15 August. Maud Baum and Fred Stone were among those in attendance. Mrs. Baum had earlier been asked by Mervyn LeRoy what she expected to see in the picture. Knowing only too well what the previous stage

Aunt Em frantically calls for Dorothy as the cyclone approaches.

and screen adaptations of the story had been like, she replied, "Oh, I suppose there'll be a Wizard in it, and a Scarecrow and a Tin Woodman, and maybe a Lion and a character named Dorothy. But that's all I expect, young man. You see, I've lived in Hollywood since 1910."[12] She was, however, pleasantly surprised by the finished product.

In the 1930s, movie screenings, particularly major ones, still often were accompanied by live stage acts. Thus, Judy Garland and Mickey Rooney sang and danced onstage between showings of MGM's *The Wizard of Oz* during the first two weeks of its premiere run in New York City at the Capitol Theatre beginning 17 August. Rooney was teamed with Garland because he was one of MGM's hottest stars and was sure to attract attention. On opening day alone thirty-seven thousand fans saw *The Wizard of Oz*, and hordes were turned away. Public interest in the picture continued into the third and final week of the engagement, when Rooney was replaced on stage by Ray Bolger and Bert Lahr.

Critical and audience response—not only in Hollywood and New York but across America—was generally enthusiastic, and the film was well received abroad. But although *The Wizard of Oz* broke attendance records in many locales and was one of the top-grossing pictures of 1939, it failed to turn a profit during its initial release. Its enormous production cost of $2,777,000, with additional expenses from advertising and distribution, was, of course, an important factor. But in addition, the movie's grosses suffered from the large number of lower-priced children's admissions, a factor that had affected the earnings of Larry Semon's film as well.

The Wizard of Oz was reissued in 1949. Supported by a new publicity campaign, the film did extraordinarily well and finally entered the black. A second reissue in 1955, which took advantage of Judy Garland's success in *A Star Is Born,* was also successful. But if by the middle of the 1950s *The Wizard of Oz* had been seen by millions of people, not until it became a television staple did its audience grow exponentially. The CBS television network broadcast the film for the first time on 3 November 1956. (Semon's motion picture had aired in 1931, so this was not the first time a Wizard of Oz film had been shown on television.) Since its second broadcast in 1959, the MGM film has become an annual television tradition, usually garnering solid ratings. It also has had other movie-theater releases and has been available on home video since 1980.

Many books and articles on the 1939 movie have tried to account for its popularity and its unique position in American culture, citing everything from its deeply felt story to its charismatic stars to its wonderful production values. Jack Haley, the Tin Woodman, attributed the film's success to its repeated

One of a series of MGM publicity shots linking the film to
Baum's book.

airings on television. His assessment downplays the great success the film enjoyed in theaters. "It's like a toy," he remarked. "You get a new generation all the time because of television."[13] Aljean Harmetz, who authored a history of the film, said that it is "almost as accurate to say that the movie is repeated each year *because* it has become part of American culture."[14]

In any case, the overwhelming popularity of the 1939 *Wizard of Oz* has acted as a tidal wave washing over the public's mind and obliterating from it all of the previous stage and screen adaptations of Baum's book. It was not long, in fact, before this film's presence made itself known on stage as well. In 1942 the renowned St. Louis Municipal Opera presented a live theatrical version of *The Wizard of Oz*, for which MGM granted permission to use Harburg and Arlen's songs. An original script by Frank Gabrielson borrowed plot elements, but no actual dialogue, from the MGM film.[15] This show was so popular that the Municipal Opera continued to stage it in later years, and other theatrical companies followed suit. Since the first St. Louis Municipal Opera presentation,

In 1942 the St. Louis Municipal Opera became the first theater company to mount a live stage adaptation of the MGM musical. In this scene in Munchkinland, the Mayor of the Munchkins (Al Downing) dances with Dorothy (Evelyn Wycoff). The St. Louis Municipal Opera has mounted several productions of *The Wizard of Oz* since.

in fact, the majority of the many new stage productions of Baum's tale presented each year throughout the United States have used the 1939 film as their primary point of reference.

One notable exception to this reliance on the MGM movie was *The Wiz,* an all-black musical first presented on Broadway in 1975 and made into a motion picture three years later. For the most part, *The Wiz* returned to Baum's book as its main inspiration even as it transformed the seventy-five-year-old story into an urban fairy tale based on black vernacular culture. It also utilized a completely new set of songs.[16]

In the late 1980s, as the fiftieth anniversary of the MGM film approached, another wave of stage productions based on the movie began to appear. One of these, scripted by John Kane, was initially mounted by London's Royal Shakespeare Company in 1987. With the permission of MGM, it was the first theatrical adaptation to use most of the film's dialogue, along with the songs by Harburg and Arlen. This version has also been produced in the United

The 1992 Paper Mill Playhouse (Millburn, N.J.) production utilized the John Kane version of the MGM motion picture script. The Guard at the Emerald City Gate (Eddie Bracken, who also played the Wizard) greets the Scarecrow (Mark Chmiel), the Tinman (Michael O'Gorman), Dorothy (Kelli Rabke), and the Cowardly Lion (Evan Bell).

States and Canada. In 1992, for example, the Paper Mill Playhouse in Millburn, New Jersey, mounted its own show based on the Kane script. This staging, in turn, was taken over in 1997 by Madison Square Garden Productions and presented in New York City with the popular TV star Roseanne as the Wicked Witch of the West. The Madison Square Garden company then made the show an annual touring event, featuring stars like Eartha Kitt and Mickey Rooney in leading roles.

With its bright colors, elaborate visuals, catchy melodies, and heartfelt sentiments, MGM's *The Wizard of Oz* has influenced much more than stage and screen productions. It has permeated popular culture like few other twentieth-century cultural artifacts have. Imagery from the film is often appropriated by advertising agencies eager to capitalize on what they know will be allusions immediately familiar to vast numbers of people. Take, for example, a 1994 television commercial for Eveready Batteries that presented the Wicked Witch of the West as an adversary of the company's mascot, the Eveready Bunny; or a 1998 print advertisement campaign for Winston cigarettes that showed an older woman smoking a cigarette and wearing Dorothy's ruby slippers. Cartoonists such as Gary Larson, novelists such as Geoff Ryman, and songwriters such as Bernie Taupin and Elton John likewise have relied on the easy recognition of MGM's Oz to underscore their work. References to the film also appear in a wide range of merchandise, including dolls, greeting cards, tee shirts, jewelry, and salt and pepper shakers. The same theme has been featured in ice shows, casinos, shopping malls, circuses, flower shows, theme parks, and department-store displays.

Considering the worldwide iconic status of MGM's *The Wizard of Oz*, it is likely that the film's imagery will continue to be, for most people, the main gateway into L. Frank Baum's fairyland. But the rich world of Oz prior to 1939 ought to be explored as well, if for no other reason than to remind us of the way our past shapes and informs things that we have come to take for granted. We need only to look before the rainbow to find the past in our present.

Notes

INTRODUCTION

1. America is not alone in its esteem for the Wizard of Oz tale. According to Douglas G. Greene, "W. W. Denslow, Illustrator," *Journal of Popular Culture* 7 (summer 1973): 91, Baum's novel has been translated into at least thirty different languages, and countless millions of copies have been sold around the world.

2. Viewer statistics are based on Harry Haun, "Nobody Beats the 'Wizard,'" *New York Daily News*, 15 August 1989.

3. Elizabeth Fuller Goodspeed, *The Wizard of Oz: A Play in Three Acts Dramatized by Elizabeth Fuller Goodspeed from the Story by L. Frank Baum* (New York: Samuel French, 1928).

4. Cornish Players, *The Wizard of Oz*, Savoy Theatre, San Diego, 7 March 1936, program, Billy Rose Theatre Collection, New York Public Library for the Performing Arts; David L. Greene and Dick Martin, *The Oz Scrapbook* (New York: Random House, 1967), 156, 161.

5. Greene and Martin, *Oz Scrapbook*, 161; Marc Lewis, "Oz Films Revisited," *Baum Bugle* 37 (winter 1993): 11.

6. Greene and Martin, *Oz Scrapbook*, 161.

7. Most of the information on Baum's life was drawn from the following sources: Frank Joslyn Baum and Russell P. MacFall, *To Please a Child: A Biography of L. Frank Baum, Royal Historian of Oz* (Chicago:

Reilly & Lee, 1961); Michael Patrick Hearn, introduction, notes, and bibliography to *The Annotated Wizard of Oz: "The Wonderful Wizard of Oz" by L. Frank Baum* (New York: Clarkson N. Potter, 1973); and idem, "L. Frank Baum," in *American Writers for Children, 1900–1960*, ed. John Cech, vol. 22 of *Dictionary of Literary Biography* (Detroit: Gale Research, 1983), 13–36.

8. Information on the life of William Wallace Denslow is drawn primarily from Greene, "W. W. Denslow, Illustrator," 86–96; and Douglas G. Greene and Michael Patrick Hearn, *W. W. Denslow* (Mt. Pleasant: Clarke Historical Library, Central Michigan University, 1976).

9. Baum and MacFall, *To Please a Child*, title page.

10. Roland Baughman, "L. Frank Baum and the 'Oz Books,'" *Columbia Library Columns* 4 (May 1955): 26.

11. L. Frank Baum, *The Wonderful Wizard of Oz* (Chicago: George M. Hill, 1900).

12. Hearn, *Annotated Wizard of Oz*, 100.

13. L. Frank Baum, *The Art of Decorating Dry Goods Windows and Interiors* (Chicago: Show Window, 1900), 87–113, 128–44.

14. Hearn, "L. Frank Baum," 16.

15. Hearn, *Annotated Wizard of Oz*, 31.

16. The following analyses are restricted to those that use Baum's novel, or both the novel and the 1939 MGM film, as the basis for their discussion. There are,

however, many other critiques that focus on the film alone. Paul Nathanson, *Over the Rainbow: "The Wizard of Oz" As a Secular Myth of America* (Albany: State University of New York Press, 1991), for example, is an important work that interprets the 1939 film as a secular myth that expresses "the deepest hopes of the American people" (237).

17. Samuel Schuman, "Out of the Fryeing Pan and into the Pyre: Comedy, Myth and *The Wizard of Oz*," *Journal of Popular Culture* 7 (fall 1973): 302–4.

18. Edward W. Hudlin, "The Mythology of Oz: An Interpretation," *Papers on Language and Literature* 25 (fall 1989): 443–62.

19. Carol Pearson and Katherine Pope, *The Female Hero in American and British Literature* (New York: R. R. Bowker, 1981).

20. Samuel Bousky, *The Wizard of Oz Revealed* (Weed, Calif.: Writers Consortium, 1995).

21. John Algeo, "The Wizard of Oz: The Perilous Journey," *American Theosophist* 74 (fall 1986): 291–97.

22. Carol Billman, "'I've Seen the Movie': Oz Revisited," *Literature Film Quarterly* 9 (1981): 241–50.

23. Madonna Kolbenschlag, *Lost in the Land of Oz: The Search for Identity and Community in American Life* (San Francisco: Harper & Row, 1988).

24. Sheldon Kopp, "The Wizard behind the Couch," *Psychology Today*, March 1970, 72–73.

25. Osmond Beckwith, "The Oddness of Oz," in *"The Wizard of Oz" by L. Frank Baum*, ed. Michael Patrick Hearn (New York: Schocken Books, 1983), 233–47.

26. Jerry Griswold, "There's No Place but Home: *The Wizard of Oz*," *Antioch Review* 45 (1987): 462–75. A slightly modified version of this essay appears in idem, *Audacious Kids: Coming of Age in America's Classic Children's Books* (New York: Oxford University Press, 1992).

27. Henry M. Littlefield, "*The Wizard of Oz*: Parable on Populism," in Hearn, "*The Wizard of Oz*" by *L. Frank Baum*, 221–33. Basically agrarian in spirit, the Populist Party sought economic reforms that would help end the financial plight of American farmers of the time. From 1892 to 1912 it nominated candidates

for president, of whom the best known was William Jennings Bryan, who ran in 1896. Among other things, the Populists advocated a plan to help farmers keep their crops off the market until prices for those crops rose, a graduated income tax, government ownership of the railroads, and the establishment of a bimetallic (silver and gold) standard.

28. Barry Bauska, "The Land of Oz and the American Dream," *Markham Review* 5 (winter 1976): 21–24.

29. Tom St. John, "Lyman Frank Baum: Looking Back to the Promised Land," *Western Humanities Review* 36 (winter 1982): 349–60.

30. For an expanded discussion of the geographical, racial, and monetary symbolism in Baum's tale, see Gretchen Ritter, "Silver Slippers and a Golden Cap: L. Frank Baum's *The Wonderful Wizard of Oz* and Historical Memory in American Politics," *Journal of American Studies* 31 (1997): 171–202.

31. William R. Leach, "*The Wonderful Wizard of Oz*" by *L. Frank Baum* (Belmont, Calif.: Wadsworth, 1991).

32. Stuart Culver, "What Manikins Want: *The Wonderful Wizard of Oz* and *The Art of Decorating Dry Goods Windows*," *Representations* 21 (winter 1978): 97–116.

33. Neil Earle, "*The Wonderful Wizard of Oz*" in *American Popular Culture: Uneasy in Eden* (Lewiston, N.Y.: Edwin Mellen Press, 1993).

34. Ibid., 185.

CHAPTER 1 *Collaboration and Conflict*

1. *Chicago Tribune*, 6 June 1902; "Fairy Tales on the Stage," *Chicago Record Herald*, 18 June 1905; "How 'The Wizard of Oz' Was Written," n.s., ca. 1910. Some newspaper articles relating to the first stage production of Baum's book have been located by searching relevant newspapers. Also consulted were collections of pertinent clippings from such repositories as the Billy Rose Theatre Collection, New York Public Library for the Performing Arts; the Harvard Theatre Collection, Harvard University; the Theatre Collection, Museum of the City of New York; and the Newberry Library, Chicago.

The Billy Rose Theatre Collection has a particularly large collection of clippings (as well as programs, fliers, posters, and other ephemera) dealing with the show. These clippings, many of which are mounted in unpaginated scrapbooks compiled by the show's business manager, Townsend Walsh, and others, are catalogued under the title of the musical and under the names of important individuals connected with it, such as Anna Laughlin, David Montgomery, and Fred Stone. Unfortunately, some of the clippings in this collection have no identification whatsoever; these will be cited here simply as "unidentified." Other clippings are only partly identified. The abbreviation "n.s." indicates that the source, or name of the periodical, is not provided; and "n.d.," that the clipping is not dated.

2. Paul Tietjens, diary, Newberry Library, Chicago. During the early weeks of Tietjens's work with Baum the composer made entries in his diary almost daily. However, the extant diary shows no entries for the period 23 July–7 September 1901. Then, beginning in late September, Tietjens did not write in his diary each day but instead filled in entries from memory, often months later, and because of this the dates are unreliable.

3. Douglas G. Greene and Michael Patrick Hearn, *W. W. Denslow* (Mt. Pleasant: Clarke Historical Library, Central Michigan University, 1976), 104–5.

4. Robert Stanton Baum, "The Autobiography of Robert Stanton Baum," *Baum Bugle* 15 (spring 1971): 5–6.

5. Tietjens, diary, 13 September 1901.

6. Ibid., 22 September 1901.

7. See Brooks McNamara, *Step Right Up* (Garden City, N.Y.: Doubleday, 1976), 64–77, for more on Hamlin's Wizard Oil.

8. Frank Joslyn Baum and Russell P. MacFall, *To Please a Child: A Biography of L. Frank Baum, Royal Historian of Oz* (Chicago: Reilly & Lee, 1961), 10–11.

9. L. Frank Baum's original script, "The Wonderful Wizard of Oz," written in 1901, appears as appendix C (pages 343–96) of a typescript draft of Frank Joslyn Baum and Russell P. MacFall's biography of L. Frank Baum, *To Please a Child,* but it was not included in the published book. In their introduction to the script, Baum and MacFall noted that it had never been published and that the original was probably the only copy in existence. Interestingly, Baum's treatment of the tale is closer in many respects to dramatizations done after his death than to the one that was finally staged in his lifetime.

The draft of *To Please a Child* can be found in the L. Frank Baum Papers, Department of Special Collections, Syracuse University Library, Syracuse, N.Y. This collection also contains notes, photographs, correspondence, ephemera, and other materials gathered by Baum's son Frank and Russell P. MacFall for their book.

10. L. Frank Baum, "Wonderful Wizard of Oz," 372–73.

11. Ibid., 352.

12. "Life of a Stage Scarecrow and Its Queer Features," n.s., 13 July 1902.

13. "The Annual Summer Production at This Theatre Will Be 'The Wizard of Oz,'" flier, Grand Opera House, Chicago, 1902, Billy Rose Theatre Collection.

14. Ernest L. Hancock, "Julian Mitchell, Stage Director-Sharp, Declares That Women Are More Apt Pupils Than Men," n. s., n.d.

15. L. Frank Baum, Paul Tietjens, and W. W. Denslow (parties of the first part) and Fred R. Hamlin (party of the second part), "Memorandum of Agreement," with a rider including Julian Mitchell, 17 January 1902, courtesy of Michael Patrick Hearn; Baum and MacFall, *To Please a Child,* 12. A formal public announcement of these proceedings must not have been made for a few weeks, for on 6 February 1902 the *Chicago Record Herald* ran an article ("Baum's Wizard of Oz") reporting that "yesterday an important contract was signed by Hamlin and L. Frank Baum" to produce an extravaganza founded on *The Wonderful Wizard of Oz.*

16. Tietjens, diary, dated 22–23 September 1901 but referring to early 1902.

17. Fred R. Hamlin to Townsend Walsh, [spring 1902], Townsend Walsh Papers, Manuscript and Special Collections Division, New York Public Library;

The Wizard of Oz, Majestic Theatre, New York, 20 January 1903, program, Billy Rose Theatre Collection.

18. Tietjens, diary, dated 23 September 1901 but referring to April–May 1902.

19. Ibid.

20. Although promotional literature often boasted that the show had a cast of a hundred, programs for the musical list only sixty-eight performers. It is possible that uncredited extras were employed in some of the more elaborate scenes.

21. Hamlin to Walsh, n.d., Walsh Papers.

22. *Chicago Tribune*, 6 June 1902.

CHAPTER 2 *What Pleases the People*

1. Program and newspaper reviews for the premiere of *The Wizard of Oz*, Billy Rose Theatre Collection, New York Public Library for the Performing Arts; L. Frank Baum, "The Wizard of Oz: A Dramatic Composition in Three Acts," 1903, unpublished script, Rare Books and Special Collections Division, Library of Congress.

2. Glen MacDonough (words) and A. Baldwin Sloane (music), "Nicolo's [*sic*] Piccolo," manuscript music, Gaylord Music Library, Washington University, St. Louis.

3. Glen MacDonough (words) and A. Baldwin Sloane (music), "In Michigan," quoted in "Songs in New Extravaganza," *Chicago Inter Ocean*, 22 June 1902.

4. Glen MacDonough (words) and A. Baldwin Sloane (music), "Carrie Barry," quoted in "Songs in New Extravaganza."

5. "Alas for the Man without Brains," published as L. Frank Baum (words) and Paul Tietjens (music), "Scarecrow" (New York: M. Witmark & Sons, 1902), supplement of the *New York American and Journal*, 1 February 1903.

6. L. Frank Baum (words) and Paul Tietjens (music), "Love Is Love" (New York: M. Witmark & Sons, 1902).

7. L. Frank Baum (words) and Paul Tietjens (music), "When You Love, Love, Love!" (New York: M. Witmark & Sons, 1902).

8. "Poppy Chorus," published as L. Frank Baum (words) and Paul Tietjens (music), "The Poppy Song" (New York: M. Witmark & Sons, 1902).

9. L. Frank Baum (words) and Paul Tietjens (music), "The Guardian of the Gate" (New York: M. Witmark & Sons, 1902). The word *degree* appears as *decree* in the published sheet music; this must have been a typographical error.

10. L. Frank Baum (words) and Paul Tietjens (music), "When We Get What's A'Comin' to Us" (New York: M. Witmark & Sons, 1902).

11. William Jerome (words) and Jean Schwartz (music), "Mr. Dooley" (New York: Shapiro, Bernstein, 1902).

12. Louis Weslyn (words) and Charles Albert (music), "The Witch behind the Moon" (New York: M. Witmark & Sons, 1902).

13. L. Frank Baum (words) and Nathaniel D. Mann (music), "Different Ways of Making Love" (New York: M. Witmark and Sons, 1902).

14. James O'Dea (words) and Edward Hutchison (music), "Sammy" (New York: Sol Bloom, 1902).

15. L. Frank Baum (words) and Paul Tietjens (music), "Finale. Act II," manuscript music, Gaylord Music Library.

16. Frank Leo, "That's Where She Sits All Day" (New York: T. B. Harms, 1900). The program for opening night indicates that at this point in the show the Scarecrow and the Tin Woodman sang A. Fawcett's "Burlesque—'Cockney Negro Song.'" Reviews of the performance, however, reveal that the pair instead sang Leo's "That's Where She Sits All Day," another song of the same genre. It seems, then, that either an error was made in the program or there was a last-minute substitution.

17. L. Frank Baum (words) and Paul Tietjens (music), "The Traveller and the Pie" (New York: M. Witmark & Sons, 1902).

18. Barrett Eastman, "Wizard a Big Success," *Chicago Journal*, 17 June 1902. Ophelia's speech begins: "There's rosemary, that's for remembrance. Pray you, love, remember. And there is pansies, that's for thoughts."

19. L. Frank Baum, "The Wonderful Wizard of Oz," 1901, unpublished script, in Frank Joslyn Baum and Russell P. MacFall, "To Please a Child: A Biography of L. Frank Baum, Royal Historian of Oz," 353, 356, typescript draft, L. Frank Baum Papers, Department of Special Collections, Syracuse University Library, Syracuse, N.Y.

20. "Putting It into Shape," *Chicago Tribune*, 27 May 1902.

21. Unidentified clipping.

22. Tietjens, diary, 30 May and 22 September 1901, Newberry Library, Chicago.

23. L. Frank Baum, *Chicago Tribune*, 26 June 1904, quoted in Frank Joslyn Baum and Russell P. MacFall, *To Please a Child: A Biography of L. Frank Baum, Royal Historian of Oz* (Chicago: Reilly & Lee, 1961), 13–14.

CHAPTER 3 *"A Flare of Color"*

1. "Baum's Wizard of Oz," *Chicago Record Herald*, 6 February 1902.

2. "The Grand's Summer Play," n.s., n.d.

3. Unidentified clipping.

4. Unidentified clipping.

5. *Chicago Record Herald*, 11 April 1902.

6. See, e.g., "Grand's Summer Play."

7. "Hamlin's Big Production," n.s., n.d.

8. "Music and the Drama," [*Chicago Evening Post*], n.d.

9. "The Wizard of Oz," Grand Opera House, Chicago, [1902], booklet, Billy Rose Theatre Collection, New York Public Library for the Performing Arts.

10. "Putting It into Shape," *Chicago Tribune*, 27 May 1902.

11. Unidentified clipping.

12. "Gossip of the Green Room," n.s., n.d.; "Day in Scenery-Shop," *Chicago Evening Post*, 19 April 1902.

13. *Chicago Daily News*, 16 June 1902.

14. "The Wizard of Oz," n.s., [10 June 1902].

15. "The Wizard Postponed Again," n.s., n.d.

16. Olga Dammert to Russell P. MacFall, 17 November [1956?], L. Frank Baum Papers, Department of Special Collections, Syracuse University Library, Syracuse, N.Y.

17. Ibid.

18. Frank Joslyn Baum's recollections of opening night are preserved in a letter to Russell P. MacFall, 2 October 1956, Baum Papers.

19. L. Frank Baum, speech, 16 June 1902, quoted in Frank Joslyn Baum and Russell P. MacFall, *To Please A Child: A Biography of L. Frank Baum, Royal Historian of Oz* (Chicago: Reilly & Lee, 1961), 1–2.

20. "Topics of the Theater: Hard Task in Trimming 'The Wizard of Oz,'" n.s., n.d.; Barrett Eastman, "Wizard a Big Success," *Chicago Journal*, 17 June 1902; *New York Dramatic Mirror*, [5 July 1902].

21. "Grand Opera House: Sixth Week of the Fanciful Summer Humor, 'The Wizard of Oz,'" n.s., n.d.

22. "'The Wizard' Goes Merrily On," n.s., n.d.; *The Wizard of Oz* (advertisement), n.s., 3 November [1902].

23. Programs for the initial Chicago run of *The Wizard of Oz* can be found in the collection of the Chicago Historical Society, as well as the Billy Rose Theatre Collection. Manuscript music for select scenes is held by the Gaylord Music Library, Washington University, St. Louis.

24. Amy Leslie, "The Wizard of Oz," [*Chicago Daily News*], n.d.

25. Leone Langdon-Key, "'The Wizard of Oz' Is a Flare of Color," n.s., [17 June 1902].

26. Edward Freiberger, "The Players," *Chicago Evening Herald*, 21 June 1902.

27. "New Summer Show a Hit," n. s., n.d.

28. "Coming of the Cyclone Scene from 'The Wizard of Oz,'" *Chicago Record Herald*, 6 July 1902.

29. "Plays and Players," *Theatre Magazine*, August 1902, 4.

30. *Chicago Chronicle*, 29 June 1902.

31. L. Frank Baum, *The Wonderful Wizard of Oz* (New York: George M. Hill, 1900), 109, 116.

32. "Stories and Incidents Concerning People of the Stage," *Chicago Inter Ocean*, 22 June 1902.

33. According to the opening-night program, "The

Road through the Forest" was painted by Merrifield and Daniels, but this was apparently a mistake, for subsequent programs credited Gibson. Similarly, the opening-night program stated that "The Gates of the Emerald City" was painted by Gibson, but later programs credited the Daniels Scenic Company.

34. "New Summer Show a Hit."

35. Barrett Eastman, "The Wizard of Oz," n.s., n.d.; "Why Not Be in Season?" n.s., n.d.; Langdon-Key, "'The Wizard of Oz' Is a Flare of Color"; Max Maier to Russell P. MacFall, 27 October 1956, Baum Papers.

36. Unidentified clipping. Fred Stone's own account of this scene as it transpired on opening night is amusing:

They carried me on the stage too soon, and I hung motionless, my weight balanced on the side of one ankle, for eighteen minutes. As nobody, apparently, ever reads a program, the audience took it for granted that I was just a stuffed dummy and I dared not make the slightest gesture. I was hung on a stile by two nails, one in one sleeve of my costume and one in the elbow, with my whole body thrown off balance.

Why it is I don't know, but if you can't move you feel as though you can't keep still. My muscles were so strained by the uncomfortable position that I did not think I could possibly hold it. First one arm, then a foot went to sleep. It seemed to me I simply had to move; but I held on like grim death, with the sweat pouring down my face and into my eyes.

The part of the little Kansas girl, Dorothy, was played by Anna Laughlin, who had a good number just before she was to release me, and that night there was one encore after another. When she finally came up for me, I was so numb I just hung on to her for support. Fortunately, the audience, taken by surprise at having me come to life, burst into prolonged applause, which gave me a chance to limber up before I had to dance.

Fred Stone, *Rolling Stone* (New York: McGraw-Hill, Whittlesey House, 1945), 133.

37. "The Wizard of Oz," n.s., 14 September 1902.

A valuable backstage account of the Poppy scenes appears in "Transforming a Scene in the Wizard of Oz," *St. Paul Globe,* [29 September 1902]. This piece was written in reference to the St. Paul, Minnesota, production of *The Wizard of Oz* mounted soon after the show closed in Chicago. All evidence indicates that the Poppy scenes were not altered when the show was taken on the road.

38. "New Productions," n.s., 28 June 1902.

39. Unidentified clipping.

40. Photographs by Windeatt and other photographers of the 1902 Chicago stage production of *The Wizard of Oz,* Billy Rose Theatre Collection.

41. "Stories and Incidents Concerning People of the Stage."

42. "Plays and Players," 4; "Bobby Gaylor's Wizard," n.s., n.d.

43. Leslie, "The Wizard of Oz."

44. John Raftery, "Scarecrow and Tin Woodman behind the Scenes," *Chicago Record Herald,* 7 September 1902.

45. Ibid.; "Scarecrow and Tin Woodman New Figures in Comedy," *Chicago Chronicle Illustrated Weekly,* n.d.; "Life of a Stage Scarecrow and Its Queer Features," n.s., 13 July 1902.

46. Unidentified clipping.

47. "Stories and Incidents Concerning People of the Stage."

48. For the Munchkins, see "Plays and Players," 4, and Langdon-Key, "'The Wizard of Oz' Is a Flare of Color"; for the Ladies and Gentlemen of the Court, see "Chorus Girl Rivalry," n.s., n.d.

49. "Music and the Drama: Art of Imitation," [*Chicago Evening Post*], n.d.

50. "Actors Who Play Animals," *Chicago Tribune,* 28 June 1902; "Plays and Players," 5.

51. Leslie, "The Wizard of Oz."

52. Burns Mantle, "Ballyhoo and Judy Garland Lure Crowds to *Wizard of Oz;* Movie Recalls 1902 Version in Chicago Theatre," *Chicago Tribune,* 27 August 1939, reprinted in *Baum Bugle* 33 (autumn 1989): 16–17.

53. "Life of a Stage Scarecrow and Its Queer Features"; Stone, *Rolling Stone,* 129–32.

54. Leslie, "The Wizard of Oz."

55. *Chicago Tribune*, n.d., quoted in "Plays and Players," 5.

56. "Music and the Drama," *Chicago Evening Post*, 24 June 1902.

57. Leslie, "The Wizard of Oz."

58. Freiberger, "The Players"; "About the Theatres," [*Chicago Inter Ocean*], 20 July 1902.

59. Delancey M. Halbert, "Music and the Drama," [*Chicago Evening Post*], 17 June 1902.

60. Leslie, "The Wizard of Oz."

61. Langdon-Key, "'The Wizard of Oz' Is a Flare of Color."

62. Unidentified clipping.

63. Freiberger, "The Players."

64. Leslie, "The Wizard of Oz."

65. Percy Hammond, "Players in Triumph," *Chicago Evening Post*, n.d.

66. "Music and the Drama," [*Chicago Evening Post*], n.d.

67. "Bobby Gaylor's Wizard."

68. Unidentified clipping.

69. "Music and the Drama," [*Chicago Evening Post*], n.d.

70. Raftery, "Scarecrow and Tin Woodman behind the Scenes."

71. "Music and the Drama," [*Chicago Evening Post*], n.d.

72. Unidentified clippings.

73. "Hamlin's Big Production."

74. "Music and the Drama," [*Chicago Evening Post*], n.d.

75. "News of the Theaters," *Chicago Tribune*, 17 June 1902.

76. "Love Is Love" was never listed by title in the programs; rather, it was indicated by the generic name "Ballad Romanza," an indication that it could easily be replaced by any number of similar sentiment.

77. "New Summer Show a Hit."

78. "Music and the Drama," *Chicago Evening Post*, 24 June 1902.

79. "New Summer Show a Hit."

80. Unidentified clipping.

81. "'Sammy' Box in the Grand," n.s., n.d.

82. Freiberger, "The Players."

83. Ethan Mordden, "The Last Vaudeville: Baum's 'Wizard' on Broadway," *Baum Bugle* 28 (winter 1984): 8.

84. As previously mentioned, during an intermission on the show's opening night Baum reportedly recommended to Hamlin that he engage Montgomery and Stone for five years. In his autobiography, Fred Stone claimed that Hamlin summoned him and Montgomery into his office at the conclusion of the opening-night performance and signed them then and there to the five-year contract (Stone, *Rolling Stone*, 132). But while a contract may have been discussed then, and perhaps even agreed to, newspaper accounts suggest that the contract itself was actually signed on 28 June 1902 ("Grand Opera House," n.s., [1 July 1902]).

85. Lyman B. Glover, [*Chicago Record Herald*], n.d.; "Grand Opera House: Thirtieth Week of the Great and Wonderful Wizard of Oz," n.s., n.d.; "Departure of 'The Wizard,'" n.s., n.d.

86. Glover; Chicago, Milwaukee and St. Paul Railway Co., "Movement of 'Wizard of Oz,'" 10 October 1902, route form, Townsend Walsh Papers, Manuscript and Special Collections Division, New York Public Library.

87. "Amusements," *Sioux City Daily Tribune*, n.d.

88. "'The Wizard of Oz'—Auditorium," n.s., 4 November 1902.

89. "Amusements," *Omaha World Herald*, 10 October 1902; *Omaha Daily Bee*, 10 October 1902; unidentified clipping from Milwaukee; "'The Wizard of Oz': Magnificent Production at the Economic Theatre," n.s., n.d.

90. "'The Wizard of Oz': Magnificent Production at the Economic Theatre."

91. "The Wizard of Oz," *St. Paul Dispatch*, 23 September 1902.

92. "'The Wizard of Oz': Magnificent Production at the Economic Theatre."

93. "Amusements," *Memphis Commercial Appeal*, 25 November 1902.

94. Unidentified clipping from Milwaukee; "The Wizard of Oz at Greene's," *Cedar Rapids Republic*, n.d.

95. *The Wizard of Oz*, Grand Opera House, Chicago, 28 December 1902, program, Billy Rose Theatre Collection.

96. Amy Leslie, "Men of Tin and Straw," [*Chicago Daily News*, 29 December 1902].

97. Vincent Bryan (words) and Theodore F. Morse (music), "Hurrah for Baffin's Bay!" (New York: Howley, Haviland & Dresser, 1903).

98. Baum to MacFall, 2 October 1956.

CHAPTER 4 *"Something New under the Sun"*

1. Fred R. Hamlin to Townsend Walsh, 12 December 1902, Townsend Walsh Papers, Manuscript and Special Collections Division, New York Public Library.

2. Ibid., 15 December 1902.

3. Ibid., 24 December 1902.

4. Ibid., 29 December 1902.

5. Ibid., 2 January 1903.

6. Ibid., 7 January 1903.

7. *There Is Something New under the Sun* (New York: [1903]), pamphlet, Billy Rose Theatre Collection, New York Public Library for the Performing Arts.

8. Hamlin to Walsh, 2 January 1903, and Julian Mitchell to Walsh, 3 January 1903, Walsh Papers.

9. Mitchell to Walsh, 3 January 1903.

10. Unidentified clipping.

11. "The Wizard of Oz," *New York Times*, [21 January 1903].

12. Acton Davies, "News of the Theatres," *New York Evening Sun*, 21 January 1903.

13. "Wizard of Oz."

14. "Majestic—The Wizard of Oz," *New York Dramatic Mirror*, 31 January 1903.

15. Davies, "News of the Theatres."

16. Alan Dale, "The New Majestic Theatre Is a Model of Beauty and Comfort," n.s., n.d.

17. Kate Carew, "Wizard of Oz Comes to Town," n. s., n.d.

18. The Playgoer, "Town Topics: 'The Wizard of Oz' at the Majestic Theatre," n.s., n.d.

19. Unidentified clippings.

20. "All Records Broken by the Greatest Hit in Years!" Majestic Theatre, New York, 1903, broadside, Billy Rose Theatre Collection.

21. Unidentified clipping.

22. Useful in reconstructing *The Wizard of Oz* as it was presented on its opening night in New York are the program and reviews in the Billy Rose Theatre Collection. Also helpful is L. Frank Baum, "The Wizard of Oz: A Dramatic Composition in Three Acts," 1903, unpublished script, Rare Books and Special Collections Division, Library of Congress. This script, however, represents the show as it was staged later in the New York run and incorporates some minor changes in the action. It was submitted to the Library of Congress for copyright on 17 September.

23. *The Wizard of Oz*, Majestic Theatre, 20 January–3 October 1903, programs, Billy Rose Theatre Collection.

24. "Montgomery's Business Abroad," n.s., 18 July 1903.

25. Hamlin to Walsh, 15 December 1902; "Majestic—The Wizard of Oz."

26. Photographs by Byron of the 1903 New York stage production of *The Wizard of Oz*, Billy Rose Theatre Collection.

27. "A Lighting Invention," *New York Dramatic Mirror*, 18 April 1903.

28. Katherine Singer Kovács, "Georges Méliès and the *Féerie*," *Cinema Journal* 16 (fall 1976): 5.

29. Ethan Mordden, "The Last Vaudeville: Baum's 'Wizard' on Broadway," *Baum Bugle* 28 (winter 1984): 12.

30. Caroline Siedle, costume designs, *The Wizard of Oz*, [late 1902 or early 1903], Shubert Archive, New York; photographs by Byron of the 1903 New York stage production of *The Wizard of Oz*, Billy Rose Theatre Collection.

31. "Miss Faust Succeeds Miss Kimball As Trixie [*sic*] in the Wizard of Oz," *New York Morning Telegraph*, 30 January 1903.

32. David L. Greene and Dick Martin, *The Oz Scrapbook* (New York: Random House, 1967), 123.

33. R.W., in *New York Morning Telegraph*, 21 Jan-

uary 1903; Dale, "The New Majestic Theatre Is a Model of Beauty and Comfort."

34. "New Theatre Opens at Park Circle," *New York World,* [21 January 1903].

35. Carew, "Wizard of Oz Comes to Town."

36. James Montague, "The Majestic Opened, with a New Musical Piece That Smacks of Chicago," *New York Sun,* 21 January 1903.

37. "Death of Lotta Faust," *New York Dramatic Mirror,* 5 February 1910.

38. "Miss Faust Succeeds Miss Kimball As Trixie"; unidentified clipping.

39. Fred Stone, *Rolling Stone* (New York: McGraw-Hill, Whittlesey House, 1945), 136–37.

40. "A New Wizard of Oz," n.s., n.d.

41. Unidentified clipping.

42. Unidentified clipping.

43. "New Majestic Theatre Has a 'Sammy Box,'" n.s., n.d.; "Chorus Starts Poppy Hat Fad," *New York Evening Journal,* 18 May 1903.

44. "Permit Us, Ladies and Gentlemen—The Scarecrow, the Heifer, the Lion, and the Tin Woodman in 'The Wizard of Oz,'" n.s., n.d.

45. Unidentified clipping.

46. The information on Poole is from Helen Ten Broeck, n.s., n.d.; on Barron, unidentified clipping; on Fulton, unidentified clippings; on Payne, "Two Very Lucky Actresses," n.s., n.d.; on Faust, unidentified clipping; and on Fitzhugh, "Poppy Queen a Drug Victim," n.s., n.d.

47. Unidentified clippings; "Montgomery's Business Abroad."

48. "Queer Signatures to 'The Wizard of Oz' Payroll," *Stage,* n.d.

49. *The Wizard of Oz* (advertisement), n.s., 3 August 1903.

50. *New York Clipper,* 27 June 1903.

51. "All Kissed Sir Thomas," n.s., 16 August 1903.

52. The souvenirs for the 100th and 200th performances are described in Swann Galleries, *The Distinguished Collection of L. Frank Baum and Related Oziana, Including W. W. Denslow, Formed by Justin G. Schiller* (New York, 1978), no. 89; information about

the souvenir for the 125th is from an unidentified clipping; and for the 225th, "Wizard to Give Cups," n.s., n.d.

53. L. Frank Baum, Paul Tietjens, and W. W. Denslow (parties of the first part) and Fred R. Hamlin (party of the second part), "Memorandum of Agreement," 17 December 1902, courtesy of Michael Patrick Hearn.

54. Hamlin to Walsh, 3 March 1903, Walsh Papers.

55. "Fred Hamlin Branching Out," n.s., n.d.

CHAPTER 5 *The Wizard Deluxe and Redux*

1. The primary source for the itinerary of the two companies of *The Wizard of Oz* is the *New York Clipper,* which published their schedule weekly. Other sources include programs and newspaper reviews.

2. *The Wizard of Oz,* Empire Theatre, Albany, 21 September [1903], program, Billy Rose Theatre Collection, New York Public Library for the Performing Arts.

3. "Montauk Has the Real Scarecrow and Tin-Man," n.s., [8 September 1903].

4. *Brooklyn Standard Union,* [8 September 1903].

5. "Montauk Has the Real Scarecrow and Tin-Man."

6. Unidentified clipping.

7. "Week's Theatrical Bills," n.s., [22 September 1903].

8. Fred R. Hamlin to Townsend Walsh, 24 September 1903, Townsend Walsh Papers, Manuscript and Special Collections Division, New York Public Library.

9. Charles Mitchell to Walsh, 29 September 1903, ibid.

10. Fred Meek to Walsh, 20 February 1904, ibid.

11. Hamlin to Walsh, 26 February 1904, ibid.

12. Paul Tietjens, diary, 4, 8, 18, and 21 January 1904, Newberry Library, Chicago.

13. A route list for the two companies of *The Wizard of Oz* during 1904, compiled from the *New York Clipper,* can be found in the L. Frank Baum Papers, Department of Special Collections, Syracuse University Library, Syracuse, N.Y.

14. John R. Flaherty to Walsh, 26 February 1904, Walsh Papers.

15. "News of the Theatres: Fred Stone Receives an Ovation at the Majestic," n.s., 22 March 1904.

16. Ibid.

17. *The Wizard of Oz,* Majestic Theatre, New York, 4 April 1904, program, Billy Rose Theatre Collection.

18. Vincent Bryan (words) and J. B. Mullen (music), "'Twas Enough to Make a Perfect Lady Mad" (New York: Shapiro, Remick, 1904).

19. "Good-bye, Fedora" was published as Harry H. Williams (words) and Robert J. Adams (music), "Gooda Bye Fedora" (New York: Shapiro, Remick, 1904). It is not clear why the programs cite the song's lyricist as O'Dea but the sheet music credits Williams. Either one of the two sources was in error or else the words of the song were rewritten by a new lyricist at some point.

20. Will D. Cobb (words) and Gus Edwards (music), "Johnny I'll Take You" (New York: Shapiro, Remick, 1904).

21. *The Wizard of Oz,* Grand Opera House, Chicago, 13 June 1904, program, Billy Rose Theatre Collection.

22. J.O'D.B., "Music and the Drama," *Chicago Record Herald,* 25 May 1904.

23. *Chicago Journal,* 24 May 1904.

24. Percy Hammond to Walsh, n.d., Walsh Papers.

25. "Many New Shows Last Evening," *San Francisco Chronicle,* 20 September 1904; "The Playhouses," *Los Angeles Times,* 7 October 1904.

26. "Montgomery and Stone," n.s., n.d.

27. *The Wizard of Oz,* Academy of Music, New York, 7 November and 12 December 1904, programs, Billy Rose Theatre Collection.

28. "Doubleday, Page and Co.'s Theatre Party," *Publisher's Weekly,* 31 December 1904.

29. *New York Clipper,* 3 December 1904.

30. Ibid., 18 March 1905.

31. Programs for *The Wizard of Oz*'s 1905–6 season are held by the Chicago Historical Society and by the Billy Rose Theatre Collection.

32. Publicity release for *The Wizard of Oz,* 10 October 1905, Billy Rose Theatre Collection.

33. Unidentified clipping.

34. Vincent Bryan (words) and Charles Zimmerman (music), "Football" (New York: Vincent Bryan Music, 1905).

35. "Garrick—'The Wizard of Oz,'" n.s., [15 October 1905].

36. *New York Clipper,* 23 September 1905.

37. "'The Wizard of Oz.' Academy of Music," n.s., [31 October 1905].

38. Unidentified clipping.

39. Fred A. Stone, "Fred A. Stone As the Scarecrow," [*Milwaukee Sentinel*], n.d.

40. William M. Gray to Walsh, 18 December 1905, Walsh Papers.

41. "Gray and Mitchell After Injunction," n.s., n.d.

42. On 17 January 1907 Sam S. and Lee Shubert, Inc., purchased the scenery, properties, and effects of the second company of *The Wizard of Oz* (Julian Mitchell and William M. Gray, contract transferring *The Wizard of Oz* to Sam S. and Lee Shubert, Inc., 17 January 1907, Contract Series I, Shubert Archive, New York). The Shuberts never mounted this show, but they probably incorporated bits and pieces of sets and costumes into other productions.

43. *New York Daily Mirror,* 10 February 1936.

44. Bert Whitney to Klaw and Erlanger, quoted in Klaw and Erlanger to William M. Gray, 16 July 1906, Klaw and Erlanger Papers, Shubert Archive.

45. Sherman Brown to Klaw and Erlanger, 22 August 1906, Klaw and Erlanger Papers.

46. Brown to A. L. Erlanger, 23 August 1906, ibid.

47. Brown to Erlanger, 28 August 1906, ibid.

48. Gray to Klaw and Erlanger, 1 September 1906, ibid.

49. Klaw and Erlanger to Brown, 21 September 1906, ibid.

50. "What's in a Name?" n.s., 5 September 1906.

51. "Entertainments," *Minneapolis Tribune,* 29 October 1906.

52. Klaw and Erlanger to Brown, n.d., Klaw and

Erlanger Papers; "'The Wizard of Oz' to Be Sold To-day," n.s., 17 November 1906.

53. "World of Players," *New York Clipper*, 8 December 1906.

54. "On the Road," ibid., 24 November 1906.

55. *The Wizard of Oz*, Great Northern Theatre, Chicago, 19 May 1907, program, Chicago Public Library.

56. *The Wizard of Oz*, Majestic Theatre, Brooklyn, 8 March 1909, program, Theatre Collection, Museum of the City of New York.

57. David H. Wallace, "John Craig, a Producing Manager," *New York Dramatic Mirror*, 20 August 1913.

58. "Our Holiday Play," *Castle-Square Program Magazine*, 27 November 1911, Harvard Theatre Collection, Harvard University.

59. *Castle-Square Program Magazine*, 25 December 1911, Billy Rose Theatre Collection.

60. "Castle Sq. Theatre," n.s., n.d. The Harvard Theatre Collection is the source for the clippings cited here dealing with the Castle Square Theatre production.

61. K.M., "The Wizard of Oz," n.s., n.d.

62. "Wizard of Oz at Castle Square: Miss Young Makes an Ideal Dorothy Gale," n.s., n.d.

63. Wallace, "John Craig."

64. "Holiday Bill at Castle-Sq.," n.s., n.d.

65. "The Wizard of Oz," *Castle-Square Program Magazine*, 1 January 1912, Harvard Theatre Collection.

66. Caryl B. Storrs, "At the Playhouses," *Minneapolis Morning Tribune*, 21 July 1912.

67. *The Wizard of Oz*, Poli's Theatre, Washington, D.C., 1 April 1918, program, courtesy of Michael Patrick Hearn.

68. For *The Woggle-Bug*, see David L. Greene and Dick Martin, *Oz Scrapbook* (New York: Random House, 1967), 128–31, and Michael Patrick Hearn, "How Did the Woggle-Bug Do?" *Baum Bugle* 18 (Christmas 1974): 16–23.

69. Frederic Chapin to A. Erlanger, 5 November 1905, Klaw and Erlanger Papers.

70. Greene and Martin, *Oz Scrapbook*, 139–41.

CHAPTER 6 *"A Novel Entertainment"*

1. Major sources on *Fairylogue and Radio-Plays* include L. Frank Baum, *Fairylogue and Radio-Plays*, 1908, season program, L. Frank Baum Papers, Department of Special Collections, Syracuse University Library, Syracuse, N.Y.; "L. Frank Baum's Fairylogue, to Accompany His Radio-Plays of 'The Land of Oz' and 'John Dough and the Cherub,'" 1908, unpublished script (the operator's copy), courtesy of Michael Patrick Hearn; Frank Joslyn Baum and Russell P. MacFall, *To Please a Child: A Biography of L. Frank Baum, Royal Historian of Oz* (Chicago: Reilly & Lee, 1961), 246–49; Russell P. MacFall, "L. Frank Baum and the Radio-Plays," *Baum Bugle* 6 (August 1962): 3–4; David L. Greene and Dick Martin, *The Oz Scrapbook* (New York: Random House, 1967), 131–39; and Richard Mills, "The *Fairylogue and Radio Plays* of L. Frank Baum," *Baum Bugle* 14 (Christmas 1970): 4–7.

2. In an interview, Baum said that he coined the term *radio-play* because his films utilized a special coloring process devised by Michel Radio of Paris (MacFall, "L. Frank Baum and the Radio-Plays," 3). However, Radio's name does not appear in the show's program, while Duval Frères are credited for the hand-coloring process. Furthermore, research has not confirmed Radio's existence. Although there is no evidence for it, Baum may have been referring to the minor French film company Radios, established by Georges Maurice and Jules Dumien, but that firm was not named for a specific person (Richard Abel, *The Ciné Goes to Town: French Cinema, 1896–1914* [Berkeley: University of California Press, 1994], 37).

3. The prints of the radio-play films, long held by Baum's family, were discarded in the 1960s because they had decomposed (Michael Patrick Hearn, "Silent Oz," *Baum Bugle* 37 [winter 1993]: 4). For Baum's narration, see the script "L. Frank Baum's Fairylogue."

4. The slides used in *Fairylogue and Radio-Plays*, as well as a copy of the show's script, were sold at auction in 1978 to an unidentified buyer (Swann Galleries, *The Distinguished Collection of L. Frank Baum and*

Related Oziana, Including W. W. Denslow, Formed by Justin G. Schiller [New York, 1978], no. 181).

5. According to the itinerary appearing in MacFall, "L. Frank Baum and the Radio-Plays," 3, Baum ended his New York engagement on 16 December. According to advertisements appearing in the *New York Times,* however, he played that city through the end of the month.

6. L. Frank Baum, *Fairylogue and Radio-Plays,* Wieting Opera House, Syracuse, N.Y., 2–3 December 1908, typescript copy of program, Baum Papers.

7. L. Frank Baum to Mrs. Remus, 22 October [1908], Baum Papers; William Griffin, "First to See the Wizard," n.s., n.d. The Griffin article, as well as other clippings pertaining to *Fairylogue and Radio-Plays,* can be found in the Baum Papers.

8. Amy Leslie, "L. Frank Baum's Ideas," *Chicago Daily News,* 2 October 1908.

9. *Fairylogue and Radio-Plays* (advertisement), *Publisher's Weekly,* 19 September 1908, 591.

10. Selig and his film company are discussed in "Selig Polyscope Co.," *Billboard,* 27 June 1908, 25; Mills, "The *Fairylogue and Radio Plays* of L. Frank Baum," 6; and Kalton C. Lahue, ed., *Motion Picture Pioneer: The Selig Polyscope Company* (New York: A. S. Barnes, 1973).

11. John Fricke, "Romola," *Baum Bugle* 31 (autumn 1987): 13.

12. Ibid. Dorothy's appearance in the slides for the Wizard of Oz section of *Fairylogue and Radio-Plays* was also based on Neill's drawings, even though the slides were otherwise generally patterned after Denslow's drawings.

13. Leslie, "L. Frank Baum's Ideas."

14. Griffin, "First to See the Wizard."

15. Leslie, "L. Frank Baum's Ideas."

16. *Chicago Record Herald,* 2 October 1908.

17. "In the Fairy Land of Motion Pictures," *New York Herald,* 26 September 1909.

18. Burns Mantle, "L. Frank Baum in Fairylogue," *Chicago Tribune,* 3 October 1908.

19. *Chicago Record Herald,* 2 October 1908.

20. Mantle, "L. Frank Baum in Fairylogue."

21. *Chicago Record Herald,* 2 October 1908.

22. Baum, *Fairylogue,* Wieting Opera House.

23. O. L. Hall, "Fairy Tales Are Pictured," *Chicago Journal,* 2 October 1908.

24. *Chicago Record Herald,* 2 October 1908.

25. Louise Brand, *Milwaukee Sentinel,* and *St. Paul Pioneer Press,* quoted on the stationery of Henry J. Ormsbee, manager of *Fairylogue and Radio-Plays,* [1908], courtesy of Michael Patrick Hearn.

26. *Chicago Record Herald,* 2 October 1908.

27. "Bankruptcy Cases in the District Court of the United States, Southern District of California, Southern Division," file no. 779, 3 June 1911, Baum Papers.

CHAPTER 7 *A One-Reel Spectacle*

1. *Selig Polyscope News,* 15 March 1910.

2. "Moving Picture Notes," *Billboard,* 1 January 1910, 13. Michael Patrick Hearn, "Silent Oz," *Baum Bugle* 37 (winter 1993): 4–7, 28, provides a good introduction to Selig's *The Wonderful Wizard of Oz.*

3. For the history of the Selig studio in California, see Kalton C. Lahue, ed., *Motion Picture Pioneer: The Selig Polyscope Company* (New York: A. S. Barnes, 1973), 13–15.

4. Einar Lauritzen and Gunnar Lundquist, *American Film-Index, 1908–1915* (Stockholm, Sweden: Film-Index, 1976), 692.

5. Cedric Belfrage, "Mark My Words: That's What Hobart Bosworth Said in 1909 When He Brought the Movies to Hollywood," *Motion Picture Magazine,* April 1928, 34.

6. "Deaths," *New York Dramatic Mirror,* 13 April 1918, 532.

7. Selig Polyscope Company, "The Wizard of Oz," n.d., scenario, William Nicholas Selig Papers, Margaret Herrick Library, Academy of Motion Picture Arts and Sciences, Academy Foundation, Beverly Hills, courtesy of Michael Patrick Hearn.

8. The International Museum of Photography and Film at George Eastman House, Rochester, N.Y., now holds the film, which was acquired from Robert Dugan, a private collector (Jan-Christopher Horak, "The

Discovery of the Selig *Wizard of Oz*," *Baum Bugle* 37 [winter 1993]: 7). Before the discovery of this print, it was believed that Selig had created the film by re-editing his earlier *Fairylogue* footage and perhaps supplementing it with new material or with segments that had been cut from the 1908 version. It is now clear, however, that the motion picture was an entirely new production.

9. "Selig's Handsome Folder-Bulletin," *Film Index,* 2 April 1910, 4.

10. "Reviews of Licensed Films," *New York Dramatic Mirror,* 2 April 1910, 17.

11. Dorothy encountering the Scarecrow, photograph by Byron of the 1903 New York stage production of *The Wizard of Oz,* Billy Rose Theatre Collection, New York Public Library for the Performing Arts.

12. L. Frank Baum, *The Wonderful Wizard of Oz* (New York: George M. Hill, 1900), 217.

13. Ibid., 109.

14. Ibid., 140.

15. Ibid., 122, 207.

16. Maude S. Cheatham, "Bebe, the Oriental," *Motion Picture Magazine,* November 1919, 32–33, 123; De Witt Bodeen, "Bebe Daniels: Her Stardom in Silent Movies Was Topped by Her Work in Wartime London," *Films in Review* 15 (August–September 1964): 413–30.

17. Barbara Beach, "The Pioneer of the Shadowed Drama," *Motion Picture Magazine,* February 1922, 42, 88; Lahue, *Motion Picture Pioneer,* 14.

18. Evelyn Mack Truitt, *Who Was Who on Screen,* 3d ed. (New York: R. R. Bowker, 1983), 431.

19. F. N. Shorey, "Making a Selig Film," *Film Index,* 30 January 1909, quoted in Lahue, *Motion Picture Pioneer,* 49.

20. "Reviews of Licensed Films."

21. Ibid.

22. "Comments on the Films," *Moving Picture World,* 9 April 1910, 553.

23. Selig Polyscope Company, "Dorothy and the Scarecrow in Oz," n.d., scenario, Selig Papers, courtesy of Michael Patrick Hearn.

24. "Bankruptcy Cases in the District Court of the United States, Southern District of California, Southern Division," file no. 779, 3 June 1911, L. Frank Baum Papers, Department of Special Collections, Syracuse University Library, Syracuse, N.Y.

25. For the history of the Oz Film Manufacturing Company, see Frank Joslyn Baum, "The Oz Film Co. Was Unable to Turn the Wonderful Oz Books into Profitable Movies," *Films in Review* 8 (August–September 1956): 329–33; Frank Joslyn Baum and Russell P. MacFall, *To Please a Child: A Biography of L. Frank Baum, Royal Historian of Oz* (Chicago: Reilly & Lee, 1961), 257–63; David L. Greene and Dick Martin, *The Oz Scrapbook* (New York: Random House, 1967), 142–54; Richard Mills, "The Oz Film Manufacturing Company," pt. 1, *Baum Bugle* 16 (Christmas 1972): 5–11; Richard Mills and David L. Greene, "The Oz Film Manufacturing Company," pts. 2, 3, ibid., 17 (spring 1973): 5–10, (autumn 1973): 6–13; and David L. Greene, "L. Frank Baum on His Films," ibid., 17 (autumn 1973): 14–15.

26. "Doings at Los Angeles," *Moving Picture World,* 18 April 1914, 348.

27. Oz Film Manufacturing Company, "Oz Films" (Los Angeles, [1914]), circular, in *Baum Bugle* 17 (spring 1973).

28. Oz Film Manufacturing Company, "We Are Now Releasing Territorial Rights on Our Five-Reel Feature, Adapted from L. Frank Baum's Famous Musical Comedy 'The Wizard of Oz'" (n.p., n.d.), circular, in Greene and Martin, *Oz Scrapbook,* 157.

CHAPTER 8 *Hollywood High Jinks*

1. John Fricke, Jay Scarfone, and William Stillman, *"The Wizard of Oz": The Official 50th Anniversary Pictorial History* (New York: Warner Books, 1989), 5, 15; Michael Patrick Hearn, introduction to *The Wizard of Oz: The Screenplay,* by Noel Langley, Florence Ryerson, and Edgar Allan Woolf (New York: Dell, Delta, 1989), 3.

2. Hearn, introduction to *Wizard of Oz: The Screenplay,* 4.

3. Benjamin B. Hampton, *A History of the Movies*

(New York: Covici, Friede, 1931), reprinted as *History of the American Film Industry from Its Beginnings to 1931* (New York: Dover, 1970), 252–80, 304–25, traces the rise of the large film companies during the twenties.

4. "President Chadwick Voices Dangers Facing Independents," *Exhibitors Trade Review*, 15 November 1924, 26.

5. Kenneth Macgowan, *Behind the Screen: The History and Techniques of the Motion Picture* (New York: Dell, Delta, 1965), 258.

6. "I. E. Chadwick Product Proving Successful," *Motion Picture News*, 13 September 1924, 1389.

7. For biographical information on Semon, see "$1,200,000 a Year Is All Cartoonist Who Couldn't Make Good Is Getting Now," *New York Telegram*, 28 November 1919; Anthony Slide, *The Big V: A History of the Vitagraph Company* (Metuchen, N.J.: Scarecrow Press, 1976), 89–93; and George Katchmer, "Remembering the Great Silents," parts 1, 2, *Classic Images*, no. 165 (March 1989): center 20–24; no. 166 (April 1989): 57–59.

8. "Semon and Chadwick," *Variety*, 8 October 1924, 30.

9. "Semon Feature Comedy for July Release," *Motion Picture News*, 12 July 1924, 160. For reviews of the film, see "Girl in the Limousine," *Variety*, 8 October 1924, 30; and "Critical Paragraphs about New Productions," *Motion Picture Magazine*, November 1924, 78.

10. "Interest in Picture, Semon Gift to Fiancee," *Motion Picture News*, 20 September 1924, 1498.

11. "Larry Semon Arrives in New York," *Exhibitors Trade Review*, 10 January 1925, 38.

12. "Semon's 'Wizard of Oz' Ready for Release," *Motion Picture News*, 20 December 1924, 3182, refers to Chadwick's *The Wizard of Oz* as "an adaptation of the book and play by L. Frank Baum."

13. In the film's credits, Frank J. Baum is listed as L. Frank Baum Jr., to underline the connection with his father. Although uncredited, Charles Saxton assisted Lee with producing the intertitles ("Saxton Now Associated with Chadwick Pictures," *Motion Picture News*, 12 September 1925, 1246).

14. "Semon Starts 'Wizard' for Chadwick," *Exhibitors Trade Review*, 4 October 1924, 26; "Screen Notables Assembled for Wizard of Oz Cast," *Motion Picture News*, 11 October 1924, 1837; "Larry Semon As the 'Wiz,'" *Exhibitors Trade Review*, 18 October 1924, 34.

15. "Larry Semon As the 'Wiz.'"

16. "Studio Briefs," *Motion Picture News*, 22 November 1924, 2654. That the sets for Semon's film were said to be the largest ever erected on the lot is not surprising since the Film Booking Office specialized in small-set westerns.

17. "Elaborate Cast for 'Wizard of Oz,'" *Exhibitors Trade Review*, 18 October 1924, 27.

18. "Larry Semon As the 'Wiz.'"

19. "Selling Campaign for 'The Wizard of Oz,'" *Exhibitors Trade Review*, 1 November 1924, 34.

20. "I. E. Chadwick Back from Coast Trip," ibid., 20 December 1924, 28.

21. "Wizard of Oz Stills Reach New York," ibid., 13 December 1924, 28.

22. "Semon's 'Wizard of Oz' Ready for Release."

23. Katchmer, "Remembering the Great Silents," pt. 2, 57.

24. "Larry Semon Arrives in New York." For a review of Semon's vaudeville performance, see Sime [Silverman], "Larry Semon: Talks and Songs," *Variety*, 21 January 1925, 12.

25. "Interest in Picture, Semon Gift to Fiancee"; "Larry Semon Marrying," *Variety*, 21 January 1925, 1; Cal York, "Studio News and Gossip, East and West," *Photoplay*, April 1925, 46–47.

26. "'Wizard of Oz' May Go Out As Road Show," *Variety*, 14 January 1925, 21; "Chadwick Will Roadshow 'The Wizard of Oz,'" *Exhibitors Trade Review*, 24 January 1925, 18; "Special Runs for 'Wizard of Oz,'" *Motion Picture News*, 24 January 1925, 336.

27. "Chadwick Will Roadshow 'The Wizard.'"

28. *The Wizard of Oz* (advertisement), *Variety*, 14 January 1925, 31.

29. "Bitter Court Fight Pending over 'Wizard of Oz' Rights," ibid., 4 February 1925, 28.

30. "$5 Opening for Neighborhood House," *Variety*, 21 May 1924, 20; "Los Angeles Forum Tries Fi-

nance Scheme," ibid., 25 June 1924, 18; "Forum Wants New Film," ibid., 9 July 1924, 19; "Take Charge of Neighborhood Forum," ibid., 23 July 1924, 21.

31. "$50 Separates L.A. Leaders; 'Devils's Cargo' at $26,550 Tops," ibid., 18 February 1925, 26; "Inside Stuff on Pictures," ibid., 30; "Los Angeles Gets 'Wizard of Oz' First," *Exhibitors Trade Review*, 21 February 1925, 40.

32. *Los Angeles Times*, 6 February 1925, pt. 2, p. 9, and 8 February 1925, pt. 3, p. 20.

33. "$50 Separates L.A. Leaders"; "L.A. Falls Below Normal; Met's $23,500 Leads Town," *Variety*, 25 February 1925, 26; "Met, $28,000; 'Iron Horse,' $26,400; Los Angeles House Jump," ibid., 4 March 1925, 30.

34. "Met, $28,000."

35. Chadwick Pictures Corporation, *The Wizard of Oz*, Forum Theatre, Los Angeles, week of 7 February 1925, program, Special Collections, University Library, University of California, Los Angeles.

36. Special music cue sheets designed by Moses J. Mintz were supplied with Chadwick films. Whereas typical cue sheets merely listed the titles of the compositions to be played, the Mintz sheets also furnished sample strains from the pieces (Moses J. Mintz, U.S. Patent No. 1,463,288, "Music Cue Sheet for Motion Pictures," filed 30 March 1922, issued 31 July 1923; "Thematic Music Cue Sheet" [advertisement], *Exhibitors Trade Review*, 10 January 1925, 38).

37. *Los Angeles Times*, 11 March 1925; "First Runs for 'Wizard of Oz,'" *Moving Picture World*, 28 March 1925, 382.

38. "Colony's Terms Guarantee $25,000 for Run," *Variety*, 7 January 1925, 27; "B. S. Moss Colony Theatre," *Exhibitors Trade Review*, 28 February 1925, 49–51; "'Wizard of Oz,' April 12," *Variety*, 25 March 1925, 31.

39. *New York Daily News*, 12 April 1925, sec. F, p. 7.

40. "Broadway Picked Up Last Week with Rivoli Giving Kick," *Variety*, 22 April 1925, 31.

41. "'Wizard of Oz' in London," *Moving Picture World*, 16 May 1925, 351.

42. *New York Daily News*, 19 April 1925, sec. F, p. 9.

43. "'Sans Gene' Gives Rivoli Top Record; $41,300 with Extra Show Daily," *Variety*, 29 April 1925, 27.

44. "Intensive Exploitation on 'The Wizard of Oz,'" *Motion Picture News*, 1 August 1925, 608.

45. "Took a Full Page in New York Paper," *Moving Picture World*, 16 May 1925, 292.

46. *New York Daily News*, 21 April 1925.

47. For the Oz Doll and Toy Manufacturing Company, see Jay Scarfone and William Stillman, *The Wizard of Oz Collector's Treasury* (West Chester, Pa.: Schiffer, 1992), 20, 95.

48. *Motion Picture News*, 2 May 1925, 1950.

49. Sally Joy Brown, "200 Children See 'The Wizard of Oz' As Guests Today," *New York Daily News*, 18 April 1925.

50. The prizes included a Sleeper Monotrol radio receiver, a Columbia bicycle, Bonzo dolls, Yankeeboy playsuits, Dr. Posner's shoes and stockings, Flex-o-Tones (musical saws), photoplay editions of the book *The Wizard of Oz*, Hohner harmonicas, Wizard of Oz character dolls, and free film tickets ("Wizard Test Opens," *New York Daily Mirror*, 11 April 1925; "Last Chance!" ibid., 25 April 1925).

51. Chadwick Pictures Corporation, *The Wizard of Oz*, B. S. Moss's Colony Theatre, New York, [week of 12 April 1925], program, Billy Rose Theatre Collection, New York Public Library for the Performing Arts; Fred., "Colony," "A Musical Impression," and "Pastelle Ballet," *Variety*, 15 April 1925, 33; "Big First Run Presentations," *Moving Picture World*, 25 April 1925, 793.

52. Chadwick, *Wizard of Oz*, Colony Theatre.

53. Fred., "Colony."

54. *New York Daily News*, 19 April 1925, sec. F, p. 9; "Big First Run Presentations," *Moving Picture World*, 2 May 1925, 36–37.

55. In 1987 Video Yesteryear, of Sandy Hook, Connecticut, issued Chadwick Picture Corporation's *The Wizard of Oz* on videocassette.

CHAPTER 9 *A Slapstick Scarecrow*

1. See, e.g., "Chadwick Will Roadshow 'The Wizard of Oz,'" *Exhibitors Trade Review*, 24 January 1925, 18.

2. Charles S. Sewell, "The Wizard of Oz," *Moving Picture World,* 25 April 1925, 796.

3. "Larry Semon in His Latest Comedy at the Colony," *New York Evening Post,* 13 April 1925.

4. "Interest in Picture, Semon Gift to Fiancee," *Motion Picture News,* 20 September 1924, 1498; David Ragan, *Who's Who in Hollywood, 1900–1976* (New Rochelle, N.Y.: Arlington House, 1976), 783.

5. Fred., "The Wizard of Oz," *Variety,* 22 April 1925, 35.

6. Ibid.

7. "Production Highlights," *Exhibitors Trade Review,* 22 November 1924, 43.

8. Alice Tildesley, "The Roll-Call of the Old Guard," *Motion Picture Magazine,* June 1926, 31–32.

9. Richard Bishop, "Reputations," ibid., July 1922, 108.

10. Lynn Fairfield, "He Knows His Tank Towns," ibid., February 1928, 117–18; George Katchmer, "Remembering the Great Silents," pt. 2, *Classic Images,* no. 166 (April 1989): 58.

11. Perhaps Ko Vert was the female impersonator Frank Hayes, who had appeared in Semon's Vitagraph films (Anthony Slide, *The Big V: A History of the Vitagraph Company* [Metuchen, N.J.: Scarecrow Press, 1976], 92).

12. "The Wizard of Oz," *Exhibitors Trade Review,* 9 May 1925, 68.

13. An excellent analysis of the special effects in the Chadwick film is provided by Nick Barbaro, "*The Wizard of Oz* (1925)," *CinemaTexas Program Notes* 11 (8 November 1976).

14. Mildred Spain, "'Wizard of Oz' Semonly Funny; Children Will Grow Fat on It," *New York Daily News,* 17 April 1925.

15. Mordaunt Hall, "The Screen," *New York Times,* 14 April 1925.

16. George Gerhard, *New York Evening World,* quoted in "Metropolitan Critics Boost Chadwick's 'Wizard of Oz,'" *Moving Picture World,* 16 May 1925, 361.

17. Dorothy Herzog, "Wizard of Oz," *New York Daily Mirror,* 13 April 1925.

18. Spain, "'Wizard of Oz' Semonly Funny."

19. "Larry Semon in His Latest Comedy at the Colony."

20. Fred., "The Wizard of Oz"; Laurence Reid, "The Wizard of Oz," *Motion Picture News,* 25 April 1925, 1867.

21. "Larry Semon in His Latest Comedy at the Colony."

22. Reid, "The Wizard of Oz."

23. Fred., "The Wizard of Oz."

24. *The Wizard of Oz* (advertisement), *Motion Picture News,* 2 May 1925.

25. Sewell, "The Wizard of Oz."

26. Reid, "The Wizard of Oz."

27. Fred., "The Wizard of Oz."

28. "The Wizard of Oz," *Exhibitors Trade Review,* 9 May 1925, 68.

29. "First Runs for 'Wizard of Oz,'" *Moving Picture World,* 28 March 1925, 382; "'Wizard of Oz' on Broadway," ibid., 11 April 1925, 588.

30. In early April 1925 London's New Oxford Theatre had a special private preview of the film ("The Film World," *London Times,* 7 April 1925). For the picture's engagement at the Rialto, see "'Wizard of Oz' in London," *Moving Picture World,* 16 May 1925, 351.

31. "Independents Report Big Deals," *Motion Picture News,* 18 April 1925, 1738, 1740.

32. "Independents List New Sales," ibid., 18 July 1925, 298.

33. "Exhibitors Box-Office Reports," ibid., 26 September 1925, 1488; A. Van Buren Powell, ed., "Straight from the Shoulder Reports," *Moving Picture World,* 10 October 1925, 506.

34. "What the Picture Did for Me," *Exhibitors Herald,* 10 October 1925, 65.

35. "Box Office Record," ibid., 10 April 1926, sec. 2, p. 59.

36. "Herald Lists Money Makers of 1925," ibid., 25 December 1925, 55–61; "'Herald' Lists Money Makers of 1926," ibid., 25 December 1926, 37–43. Neither article states how many exhibitors were polled. However, both provide a partial list of respondents. The list for 1925 includes about 653 names, and that for 1926, 638 names.

37. "'Wizard of Oz' Deal Concluded by First National," *Motion Picture News,* 14 February 1925, 676; "The Film World."

38. George Katchmer, "Remembering the Great Silents," pt. 1, *Classic Images,* no. 165 (March 1989): center 20.

39. "Larry Semon," *Mon Ciné,* June-July 1925, in Jay Scarfone and William Stillman, *The Wizard of Oz Collector's Treasury* (West Chester, Pa.: Schiffer, 1992), 151.

40. "Series of Semon Feature-Length Comedies Added to Pathe List," *Moving Picture World,* 22 August 1925, 845.

41. "Film Comedian Larry Semon Dies," *New York Times,* 9 October 1928.

42. Chadwick resumed production during the early sound period, but the talking films that the studio issued generally were not as interesting as its silents had been.

43. DeForest Radio Company, "Television Topics," week of 8 June 1931, press release, DeForest Television Scrapbook, American Museum of the Moving Image, New York.

44. "'The Wizard of Oz' with the Wizardry Left Out," n.s., n.d., Harvard Theatre Collection, Harvard University.

45. Marc Lewis, "Oz on Film," *Baum Bugle* 27 (winter 1983): 8, 9.

46. Michael Patrick Hearn, introduction to *The Wizard of Oz: The Screenplay,* by Noel Langley, Florence Ryerson, and Edgar Allan Woolf (New York: Dell, Delta, 1989), 4; Marc Lewis, "Oz Films Revisited," *Baum Bugle* 37 (winter 1993): 11.

EPILOGUE

1. The production, distribution, reception, and history of MGM's *The Wizard of Oz* are thoroughly treated in Aljean Harmetz, *The Making of "The Wizard of Oz"* (1977; special reprint ed., New York: Dell, Delta, 1989); and John Fricke, Jay Scarfone, and William Stillman, *"The Wizard of Oz": The Official 50th Anniversary Pictorial History* (New York: Warner

Books, 1989). Michael Patrick Hearn, introduction to *The Wizard of Oz: The Screenplay,* by Noel Langley, Florence Ryerson, and Edgar Allan Woolf (New York: Dell, Delta, 1989), also provides a useful overview of the making of the film, particularly the drafting of its script.

2. Louella Parsons, quoted in Fricke, Scarfone, and Stillman, *"The Wizard of Oz,"* 39, 41.

3. Cannon suggested that the Scarecrow be a human so lacking in intelligence that all he could do for a living was stand in a cornfield and act like a scarecrow and that the Tin Woodman be an aggressive person sentenced to wear a tin suit because of his heartlessness.

4. In the final MGM film, Dorothy is emotionally closer to the Scarecrow than to her other two traveling companions, the Tin Man and the Cowardly Lion. In fact, as she is about to return to Kansas, she tells the Scarecrow that she will miss him the most. This is probably a remnant of the romantic relationship between the two characters proposed in Langley's drafts.

5. A scene showing the Wizard doing ordinary tricks to impress Dorothy and her friends was actually filmed but then deleted from the MGM movie (Rob Roy MacVeigh, "Oz under the Microscope [Revisited]," *Baum Bugle* 33 [autumn 1989]: 14).

6. Even during the filming, director Fleming was constantly battling with performers to keep their portrayals from being too broadly comic. Frank Morgan supposedly resented always being told to play his part straight, while Bert Lahr reported that the director "cut out bits of comedy that were funny, but too much burlesque for fantasy. He wanted to keep a certain mood" (Bert Lahr, quoted in Fricke, Scarfone, and Stillman, *"The Wizard of Oz,"* 104).

7. In one of Langley's drafts, in fact, the Good Witch calls upon Jack Frost to bring the snow, just as she summons the King of the Frost in the 1902 musical.

8. *Behind the Scenes at the Making of "The Wizard of Oz": The Complete NBC 'Maxwell House Good News' Radio Broadcast of June 29, 1939* (New York: Jass Records, 1988), record album.

9. Ray Bolger, quoted in Harmetz, *Making of "The Wizard of Oz,"* 114.

10. Arthur Freed, quoted in Hearn, introduction to *Wizard of Oz: The Screenplay,* 12.

11. Jay Scarfone and William Stillman, *The Wizard of Oz Collector's Treasury* (West Chester, Pa.: Schiffer, 1992), 23–25.

12. Maud Baum, quoted in Hearn, introduction to *Wizard of Oz: The Screenplay,* 6.

13. Jack Haley, quoted in Harmetz, *Making of "The Wizard of Oz,"* 292.

14. Ibid.

15. Colvin McPherson, "'The Wizard of Oz' Has Some Surprises," *St. Louis Post-Dispatch,* 11 August 1942; *The Wizard of Oz,* Municipal Opera, St. Louis, 10–16 August 1942, program, St. Louis Public Library.

16. Richard J. Anobile, *The Wiz Scrapbook* (New York: Berkley Windhover, 1978).

Works Cited

Books

Abel, Richard. *The Ciné Goes to Town: French Cinema, 1896–1914.* Berkeley: University of California Press, 1994.

Anobile, Richard J. *The Wiz Scrapbook.* New York: Berkley Windhover, 1978.

Baum, Frank Joslyn, and Russell P. MacFall. *To Please a Child: A Biography of L. Frank Baum, Royal Historian of Oz.* Chicago: Reilly & Lee, 1961.

Baum, L. Frank. *The Annotated Wizard of Oz: "The Wonderful Wizard of Oz" by L. Frank Baum.* New York: Clarkson N. Potter, 1973.

———. *The Art of Decorating Dry Goods Windows and Interiors.* Chicago: Show Window, 1900.

———. *The Wonderful Wizard of Oz.* Chicago: George M. Hill, 1900.

Bousky, Samuel. *The Wizard of Oz Revealed.* Weed, Calif.: Writers Consortium, 1995.

Carpenter, Angelica Shirley, and Jean Shirley. *L. Frank Baum: Royal Historian of Oz.* Minneapolis: Lerner, 1992.

Earle, Neil. *"The Wonderful Wizard of Oz" in American Popular Culture: Uneasy in Eden.* Lewiston, N.Y.: Edwin Mellen Press, 1993.

Eyles, Allen. *The World of Oz.* Tuscon: HP Books, 1985.

Fricke, John, Jay Scarfone, and William Stillman. *"The Wizard of Oz": The Official 50th Anniversary Pictorial History.* New York: Warner Books, 1989.

Goodspeed, Elizabeth Fuller. *The Wizard of Oz: A Play in Three Acts Dramatized by Elizabeth Fuller Goodspeed from the Story by L. Frank Baum.* New York: Samuel French, 1928.

Greene, David L., and Dick Martin. *The Oz Scrapbook.* New York: Random House, 1967.

Greene, Douglas G., and Michael Patrick Hearn. *W. W. Denslow.* Mt. Pleasant: Clarke Historical Library, Central Michigan University, 1976.

Griswold, Jerry. *Audacious Kids: Coming of Age in America's Classic Children's Books.* New York: Oxford University Press, 1992.

Hampton, Benjamin B. *A History of the Movies.* New York: Covici, Friede, 1931. Reprinted as *History of the American Film Industry from Its Beginnings to 1931.* New York: Dover, 1970.

Harmetz, Aljean. *The Making of "The Wizard of Oz."* 1977. Special reprint ed. New York: Dell, Delta, 1989.

Hearn, Michael Patrick. Introduction, notes, and bibliography to *The Annotated Wizard of Oz: "The Wonderful Wizard of Oz" by L. Frank Baum.* New York: Clarkson N. Potter, 1973.

———. Introduction to *The Wizard of Oz: The Screenplay,* by Noel Langley, Florence Ryerson, and Edgar Allan Woolf. New York: Dell, Delta, 1989.

———, ed. *"The Wizard of Oz" by L. Frank Baum.* New York: Schocken Books, 1983.

Kolbenschlag, Madonna. *Lost in the Land of Oz: The Search for Identity and Community in American Life.* San Francisco: Harper & Row, 1988.

Lahue, Kalton C., ed. *Motion Picture Pioneer: The Selig Polyscope Company.* New York: A. S. Barnes, 1973.

Lauritzen, Einar, and Gunnar Lundquist. *American Film-Index, 1908–1915.* Stockholm: Film-Index, 1976.

Leach, William R. *"The Wonderful Wizard of Oz" by L. Frank Baum.* Belmont, Calif.: Wadsworth, 1991.

Macgowan, Kenneth. *Behind the Screen: The History and Techniques of the Motion Picture.* New York: Dell, Delta, 1965.

McClelland, Doug. *Down the Yellow Brick Road: The Making of "The Wizard of Oz."* New York: Pyramid, 1976.

McNamara, Brooks. *Step Right Up.* Garden City, N.Y.: Doubleday, 1976.

Nathanson, Paul. *Over the Rainbow: "The Wizard of Oz" As a Secular Myth of America.* Albany: State University of New York Press, 1991.

Pearson, Carol, and Katherine Pope. *The Female Hero in American and British Literature.* New York: R. R. Bowker, 1981.

Ragan, David. *Who's Who in Hollywood, 1900–1976.* New Rochelle, N.Y.: Arlington House, 1976.

Scarfone, Jay, and William Stillman. *The Wizard of Oz Collector's Treasury.* West Chester, Pa.: Schiffer, 1992.

Slide, Anthony. *The Big V: A History of the Vitagraph Company.* Metuchen, N.J.: Scarecrow Press, 1976.

Stone, Fred. *Rolling Stone.* New York: McGraw-Hill, Whittlesey House, 1945.

Swann Galleries. *The Distinguished Collection of L. Frank Baum and Related Oziana, Including W. W. Denslow, Formed by Justin G. Schiller.* New York, 1978.

Truitt, Evelyn Mack. *Who Was Who on Screen.* 3d ed. New York: R. R. Bowker, 1983.

The Wizard of Oz. With a foreword by John Russell Taylor. Limpsfield, Great Britain: Dragon's World, 1989; New York: Crescent Books, 1991.

Articles

Algeo, John. "The Wizard of Oz: The Perilous Journey." *American Theosophist* 74 (fall 1986): 291–97.

Baker, B. A. "Royal Shakespeare Company Presents *The Wizard of Oz.*" *Baum Bugle* 32 (spring 1988): 19.

Barbaro, Nick. "*The Wizard of Oz* (1925)." *Cinema Texas Program Notes* 11 (8 November 1976).

Baughman, Roland. "L. Frank Baum and the 'Oz Books.'" *Columbia Library Columns* 4 (May 1955): 15–35.

Baum, Frank Joslyn. "The Oz Film Co. Was Unable to Turn the Wonderful Oz Books into Profitable Movies." *Films in Review* 8 (August–September 1956): 329–33.

Baum, Robert Stanton. "The Autobiography of Robert Stanton Baum." *Baum Bugle* 15 (spring 1971): 5–6.

Bauska, Barry. "The Land of Oz and the American Dream." *Markham Review* 5 (winter 1976): 21–24.

Billman, Carol. "'I've Seen the Movie': Oz Revisited." *Literature Film Quarterly* 9 (1981): 241–50.

Bodeen, De Witt. "Bebe Daniels: Her Stardom in Silent Movies Was Topped by Her Work in Wartime London." *Films in Review* 15 (August–September 1964): 413–30.

Culver, Stuart. "What Manikins Want: *The Wonderful Wizard of Oz* and *The Art of Decorating Dry Goods Windows.*" *Representations* 21 (winter 1978): 97–116.

"Doubleday, Page and Co.'s Theatre Party." *Publisher's Weekly,* 31 December 1904.

Fairylogue and Radio-Plays (advertisement). *Publisher's Weekly,* 19 September 1908, 591.

Fricke, John. "Believe It or Not: Maud Gage Baum." *Baum Bugle* 32 (spring 1988): 12–14.

———. "Romola." *Baum Bugle* 31 (autumn 1987): 12–13.

———, comp. "The Real Reel Critics." *Baum Bugle* 33 (autumn 1989): 4–9.

Greene, David L. "L. Frank Baum on His Films." *Baum Bugle* 17 (autumn 1973): 14–15.

Greene, Douglas G. "W. W. Denslow, Illustrator." *Journal of Popular Culture* 7 (summer 1973): 87–97.

Griswold, Jerry. "There's No Place but Home: *The Wizard of Oz.*" *Antioch Review* 45 (1987): 462–75.

Hearn, Michael Patrick. "How Did the Woggle-Bug Do?" *Baum Bugle* 18 (Christmas 1974): 16–23.

———. "L. Frank Baum." In *American Writers for Children, 1900–1960*, ed. John Cech, vol. 22 of *Dictionary of Literary Biography*, 13–36. Detroit: Gale Research, 1983.

———. "Silent Oz." *Baum Bugle* 37 (winter 1993): 4–7, 28.

Horak, Jan-Christopher. "The Discovery of the Selig *Wizard of Oz.*" *Baum Bugle* 37 (winter 1993): 7.

Hudlin, Edward W. "The Mythology of Oz: An Interpretation." *Papers on Language and Literature* 25 (fall 1989): 443–62.

Katchmer, George. "Remembering the Great Silents." Parts 1, 2. *Classic Images*, no. 165 (March 1989): center 20–24; no. 166 (April 1989): 57–59.

Kopp, Sheldon. "The Wizard behind the Couch." *Psychology Today*, March 1970, 70–73, 84.

Kovács, Katherine Singer. "Georges Méliès and the *Féerie.*" *Cinema Journal* 16 (fall 1976): 1–13.

Lewis, Marc. "Oz Films Revisited." *Baum Bugle* 37 (winter 1993): 10–14.

———. "Oz on Film." *Baum Bugle* 27 (winter 1983): 7–10.

MacFall, Russell P. "L. Frank Baum and the Radio-Plays." *Baum Bugle* 6 (August 1962): 3–4.

MacVeigh, Rob Roy. "Oz under the Microscope (Revisited)." *Baum Bugle* 33 (autumn 1989): 10–15.

Mills, Richard. "The *Fairylogue and Radio Plays* of L. Frank Baum." *Baum Bugle* 14 (Christmas 1970): 4–7.

———. "The Oz Film Manufacturing Company." Part 1. *Baum Bugle* 16 (Christmas 1972): 5–11.

Mills, Richard, and David L. Greene. "The Oz Film Manufacturing Company." Parts 2, 3. *Baum Bugle* 17 (spring 1973): 5–10, (autumn 1973): 6–13.

Mordden, Ethan. "The Last Vaudeville: Baum's 'Wizard' on Broadway." *Baum Bugle* 28 (winter 1984): 8–13.

Ritter, Gretchen. "Silver Slippers and a Golden Cap: L. Frank Baum's *The Wonderful Wizard of Oz* and Historical Memory in American Politics." *Journal of American Studies* 31 (1997): 171–202.

Schuman, Samuel. "Out of the Fryeing Pan and into the Pyre: Comedy, Myth and *The Wizard of Oz.*" *Journal of Popular Culture* 7 (fall 1973): 302–4.

Standard and Vanity Fair, 6 January 1905, 1–20.

St. John, Tom. "Lyman Frank Baum: Looking Back to the Promised Land." *Western Humanities Review* 36 (winter 1982): 349–60.

Local Newspapers

Brooklyn Standard Union, [8 September 1903].

Chicago Chronicle, 29 June 1902.

Chicago Daily News, 16 June 1902, [29 December 1902], 2 October 1908.

Chicago Evening Herald, 21 June 1902.

Chicago Evening Post, 19 April, 17, 24 June 1902.

Chicago Inter Ocean, 22 June, 20 July 1902.

Chicago Journal, 17 June 1902, 24 May 1904, 2 October 1908.

Chicago Record Herald, 6 February, 11 April, 6 July, 7 September 1902, 25 May 1904, 18 June 1905, 2 October 1908.

Chicago Tribune, 27 May, 6, 17, 28 June 1902, 3 October 1908, 27 August 1939.

London Times, 7 April 1925.

Los Angeles Times, 7 October 1904, 6, 8 February, 11 March 1925.

Memphis Commercial Appeal, 25 November 1902.

Minneapolis Morning Tribune, 21 July 1912.

Minneapolis Tribune, 29 October 1906.

New York Daily Mirror, 11, 13, 25 April 1925, 10 February 1936.

New York Daily News, 12, 17, 18, 19, 21 April 1925, 15 August 1989.

New York Evening Journal, 18 May 1903.

New York Evening Post, 13 April 1925.

New York Herald, 26 September 1909.

New York Morning Telegraph, 21, 30 January 1903.

New York Sun, 21 January 1903.

New York Telegram, 28 November 1919.

New York Times, [21 January 1903], 16–31 December 1908, 14 April 1925, 9 October 1928.

New York World, [21 January 1903].

Omaha Daily Bee, 10 October 1902.

Omaha World Herald, 10 October 1902.

San Francisco Chronicle, 20 September 1904.

St. Louis Post-Dispatch, 11 August 1942.

St. Paul Dispatch, 23 September 1902.

St. Paul Globe, [29 September 1902].

Trade and Fan Periodicals

Billboard, 27 June 1908, 1 January 1910.

Exhibitors Herald, 10 October, 25 December 1925, 10 April, 25 December 1926.

Exhibitors Trade Review, 4, 18 October, 1, 15, 22 November, 13, 20 December 1924, 10, 24 January, 21, 28 February, 9 May 1925.

Film Index, 2 April 1910.

Motion Picture Magazine, November 1919, February, July 1922, November 1924, June 1926, February, April 1928.

Motion Picture News, 6 February 1915, 12 July, 13, 20 September, 11 October, 22 November, 20 December 1924, 24 January, 14 February, 18, 25 April, 2 May, 18 July, 1 August, 12, 26 September 1925.

Moving Picture World, 9 April 1910, 18 April 1914, 28 March, 11, 18, 25 April, 2, 16 May, 22 August, 10 October 1925.

New York Clipper, 27 June 1903, 3 December 1904, 18 March, 23 September 1905, 24 November, 8 December 1906; route lists, 1903–9.

New York Dramatic Mirror, [5 July 1902], 31 January, 18 April 1903, 5 February, 2 April 1910, 20 August 1913, 13 April 1918.

Photoplay, April 1925.

Pictures and Picturegoer, May 1925.

Selig Polyscope News, 15 March 1910.

Theatre Magazine, July, August 1902, March 1903, July 1906.

Variety, 14, 21 May, 25 June, 9, 23 July, 8 October 1924, 7, 14, 21 January, 4, 18, 25 February, 4, 25 March, 15, 22, 29 April 1925.

Sheet Music

Baum, L. Frank (words), and Nathaniel D. Mann (music). "Different Ways of Making Love." New York: M. Witmark & Sons, 1902.

Baum, L. Frank (words), and Paul Tietjens (music). "The Guardian of the Gate." New York: M. Witmark & Sons, 1902.

———. "Love Is Love." New York: M. Witmark & Sons, 1902.

———. "The Poppy Song." New York: M. Witmark & Sons, 1902.

———. "Scarecrow." New York: M. Witmark & Sons, 1902. Published as a supplement of the *New York American and Journal,* 1 February 1903.

———. "The Traveller and the Pie." New York: M. Witmark & Sons, 1902.

———. "When We Get What's A'Comin' to Us." New York: M. Witmark & Sons, 1902.

———. "When You Love, Love, Love!" New York: M. Witmark & Sons, 1902.

Bryan, Vincent (words), and Theodore F. Morse (music). "Hurrah for Baffin's Bay!" New York: Howley, Haviland & Dresser, 1903.

Bryan, Vincent (words), and J. B. Mullen (music). "'Twas Enough to Make a Perfect Lady Mad." New York: Shapiro, Remick, 1904.

Bryan, Vincent (words), and Charles Zimmerman (music). "Football." New York: Vincent Bryan Music, 1905.

Cobb, Will D. (words), and Gus Edwards (music). "Johnny I'll Take You." New York: Shapiro, Remick, 1904.

Jerome, William (words), and Jean Schwartz (music). "Mr. Dooley." New York: Shapiro, Bernstein, 1902.

Leo, Frank. "That's Where She Sits All Day." New York: T. B. Harms, 1900.

O'Dea, James (words), and Edward Hutchison (music). "Sammy." New York: Sol Bloom, 1902.

Weslyn, Louis (words), and Charles Albert (music). "The Witch behind the Moon." New York: M. Witmark & Sons, 1902.

Williams, Harry H. (words), and Robert J. Adams

(music). "Gooda Bye Fedora." New York: Shapiro, Remick, 1904.

Audiovisuals

Behind the Scenes at the Making of "The Wizard of Oz": The Complete NBC 'Maxwell House Good News' Radio Broadcast of June 29, 1939. New York: Jass Records, 1988. Record album.

The Wizard of Oz (1925). Produced by Chadwick Pictures Corp. Directed by Larry Semon. Sandy Hook, Conn.: Video Yesteryear, 1987. Videocassette.

Ephemera, Manuscripts, and Special Collections

Academy of Motion Picture Arts and Sciences, Academy Foundation, Margaret Herrick Library, Beverly Hills. Scenarios (*The Wonderful Wizard of Oz* and *Dorothy and the Scarecrow in Oz,* both 1910), William Nicholas Selig Papers; and stills (*The Wizard of Oz,* 1925).

American Museum of the Moving Image, New York. DeForest Television Scrapbook. Press release (*The Wizard of Oz,* 1931 television broadcast).

Chicago Historical Society. Programs (*The Wizard of Oz,* 1902).

Chicago Public Library. Flier (*The Wizard of Oz,* 1905) and program (*The Wizard of Oz,* 1907).

Harvard University, Harvard Theatre Collection. Clippings (*The Wizard of Oz,* 1903–12 and 1925) and programs (*The Wizard of Oz,* 1903–12).

Library of Congress, Rare Books and Special Collections Division. Script (*The Wizard of Oz,* 1903).

Missouri Historical Society, St. Louis. Photograph (*The Wizard of Oz,* 1942).

Museum of the City of New York, Theatre Collection.

Clippings, photographs, and programs (*The Wizard of Oz,* 1903–9).

Newberry Library, Chicago. Clippings (Paul Tietjens; *The Wizard of Oz,* 1902) and diary (Paul Tietjens, 1901–4).

New York Public Library, Manuscript and Special Collections Division. Townsend Walsh Papers. Correspondence and route forms (*The Wizard of Oz,* 1902–5).

New York Public Library for the Performing Arts, Billy Rose Theatre Collection. Broadsides, clippings, fliers, pamphlets, photographs, posters, programs, publicity releases, and scrapbooks (various productions and personalities).

St. Louis Public Library. Program (*The Wizard of Oz,* 1942).

Shubert Archive, New York. Contract (*The Wizard of Oz,* 1907); correspondence (*The Wizard of Oz,* 1906), Klaw and Erlanger Papers; and costume designs (*The Wizard of Oz,* [late 1902 or early 1903]).

Syracuse University Library, Department of Special Collections, Syracuse, N. Y. L. Frank Baum Papers. Legal documents pertaining to the bankruptcy (L. Frank Baum, 1911), clippings (*Fairylogue and Radio-Plays,* 1908), correspondence (*The Wizard of Oz,* 1902, and *Fairylogue and Radio-Plays,* 1908), preliminary script (*The Wizard of Oz,* 1901), programs (*Fairylogue and Radio-Plays,* 1908), and route list (*The Wizard of Oz,* 1904).

University of California, Los Angeles, University Library, Special Collections. Program (*The Wizard of Oz,* 1925).

University of Wisconsin, Madison, Wisconsin Center for Film, Television, and Theatre Research. Stills (*The Wizard of Oz,* 1925).

Washington University, Gaylord Music Library, St. Louis. Manuscript music (*The Wizard of Oz,* 1902).

Index

Page numbers in italics refer to illustrations and photographs; page numbers preceded by *c* refer to pages in the color plates section.

CREDITS

Illustrations on pages 168, 174, and 176, courtesy Academy of Motion Picture Arts and Sciences; on page 6, courtesy American Literature Collection, Beineke Rare Book and Manuscript Library, Yale University; on page 203, courtesy Special Collections, University of California, Los Angeles, University Library; on page 257, photograph by Jerry Dalia; on pages 178 (*top and bottom*), 180 (*top and bottom*), and 182 (*top and bottom*), courtesy International Museum of Photography and Film at George Eastman House, Rochester, N. Y.; on page 207, courtesy Lilly Library, Indiana University, Bloomington; on pages 195 and 208, courtesy Museum of Modern Art, New York, N. Y.; on pages 210–11, 213, 214, 217, 229, and 233, courtesy Museum of Modern Art Film Stills Archive, New York, N. Y.; on page 256, photograph by Ruth Cunliff Russell, courtesy Missouri Historical Society, St. Louis; on pages 31, 62, 64, 70, 74, 75, 76, 80, 81, 82, 85, 86, 89, 95, 100, 105, 106, 109, 112, 113, 114, 116–17, 118, 120, 122, 123, 124, 126, 129, 130, 134, 147 (*top and bottom*), 151, and 153, courtesy Billy Rose Theatre Collection, New York Public Library for the Performing Arts, Astor, Lenox and Tilden Foundations; on pages 68–69 and 78, courtesy the Shubert Archive; on page 166 (*bottom*), Swann Galleries, *Distinguished Collection of L. Frank Baum*; on pages 8, 28, 163, and 193, courtesy L. Frank Baum Papers, Department of Special Collections, Syracuse University Library; on pages 216 and 218, courtesy Wisconsin Center for Film, Television, and Theater Research, Madison; on pages 4 and 139, courtesy Joe Yranski.

Illustrations for color insert: pages 1 (*bottom*), 2 (*top*), 3, 5 (*left*), and 6 (*top*), courtesy the Billy Rose Theatre Collection, New York Public Library for the Performing Arts, Astor, Lenox and Tilden Foundations; page 2 (*bottom*), courtesy Barbara Koelle; the four illustrations on page 4, courtesy the Shubert Archive; page 6 (*bottom*), from Swann Galleries, *Distinguished Collection of L. Frank Baum*; page 7 (*top*), from the collection of Scott Carmody; page 8, courtesy Joe Yranski.